SHOP STEWARDS

Dr J. F. B. Goodman is Senior Lecturer in Industrial Relations at the University of Manchester. After taking a first class honours BSc (Econ) and a post-graduate Diploma in Personnel Management at the London School of Economics he spent two years as an industrial relations officer in the motor industry. His present appointment was preceded by a period on the staff of the University of Nottingham and as an industrial relations adviser at the National Board for Prices and Incomes. He has published a number of articles on industrial relations topics in academic journals.

T. G. Whittingham took a BA degree in History at the University of Nottingham, and a Diploma in Personnel Management at the London School of Economics. Joint editor of the *Industrial Relations Journal* since its inception in 1970, he published many articles in learned journals both in Britain and overseas. He contributed to a number of other books, including *Bargaining for Change* (Allen & Unwin, 1973).

It is with deep regret that we must record the death of Mr Whittingham on December 20th, 1972, while the page proofs of this book were being corrected.

Management Series

SHOP STEWARDS

A revised and expanded edition of
Shop Stewards in British Industry

J. F. B. GOODMAN
*Senior Lecturer in Industrial Relations
University of Manchester*

T. G. WHITTINGHAM
*Staff Tutor in Industrial Relations
Department of Adult Education
University of Nottingham*

PAN BOOKS LTD : LONDON

First published 1969 as *Shop Stewards in
British Industry* by McGraw-Hill Publishing Co Ltd
This revised and expanded edition published 1973
by Pan Books Ltd, 33 Tothill Street, London SW1

ISBN 0 330 23571 0

*Made and Printed in Great Britain by
Cox & Wyman Ltd, London, Reading and Fakenham*

Contents

relations with other actors in workplace bargaining and with their members; shop steward training; shop stewards and strikes; stewards' influence over members; desire for promotion; shop stewards and their unions; stewards' desire for the job; importance of stewards to unions and members; factor analysis of stewards' responses; the East Midlands Survey; conclusions from the surveys; references.

Abbreviations Used in the Text

AEF	Amalgamated Engineering and Foundry Workers Union (formerly the AEU and now the AUEW)
ASE	Amalgamated Society of Engineers
ASLEF	Amalgamated Society of Locomotive Engineers and Firemen
ASPD	Amalgamated Society of Painters and Decorators
ASSET	Association of Supervisory Staffs, Executives and Technicians, now . . .
ASTMS	Association of Scientific, Technical and Managerial Staffs
AScW	Association of Scientific Workers
ASMM	Amalgamated Society of Metal Mechanics
ASW	Amalgamated Society of Woodworkers
AUBTW	Amalgamated Union of Building Trades Workers
AUEW	Amalgamated Union of Engineering Workers
AUFW	Amalgamated Union of Foundry Workers
BEA	British European Airways
BEC	British Employers Confederation
BISAKTA	British Iron, Steel and Kindred Trades Association
BMC	British Motor Corporation (now BLMC)
BOAC	British Overseas Airways Corporation
CAWU	Clerical and Administrative Workers' Union (now APEX)
CEU	Constructional Engineering Union
CIR	Commission on Industrial Relations
CM	Corresponding Members
CSEU	Confederation of Shipbuilding and Engineering Unions
CWU	Chemical Workers Union
DATA	Draughtsmen's and Allied Technicians' Association (now TASS)

EEF	Engineering Employers Federation
ETU	Electrical Trades Union (now EETU/PTU)
FOC	Father of the Chapel
HDEU	Heating and Domestic Engineers Union
ICI	Imperial Chemical Industries
IPM	Institute of Personnel Management
JCC	Joint Consultative Committee
JPC	Joint Production Committee
JSSC	Joint Shop Stewards Committee
JWC	Joint Works Committee
LDC	Local Departmental Committee (on the railways)
NACODS	National Association of Colliery Overmen, Deputies and Shotfirers
NASDS	National Amalgamated Stevedores' and Dockers' Society
NATSOPA	National Society of Operative Printers and Assistants
NBPI	National Board for Prices and Incomes
NCLC	National Council of Labour Colleges
NFBTO	National Federation of Building Trades Operatives
NGA	National Graphical Association
NIRC	National Industrial Relations Court
NJIC	National Joint Industrial Council
NJNC	National Joint Negotiating Committee
NSMM	National Society of Metal Mechanics
NUBSO	National Union of Boot and Shoe Operatives
NUFTO	National Union of Furniture Trades Operatives (now NUFLAT)
NUGMW	National Union of General and Municipal Workers
NUPBPW	National Union of Printing, Bookbinding and Paperworkers
NUPE	National Union of Public Employees
NUR	National Union of Railwaymen
NUS	National Union of Seamen

NUSMW & C	National Union of Sheet Metal Workers and Coppersmiths
NUVB	National Union of Vehicle Builders
PIB	National Board for Prices and Incomes
PKTF	Printing and Kindred Trades Federation
POEU	Post Office Engineering Union
PTU	Plumbing Trades Union
SOGAT	Society of Graphical and Allied Trades
T & GWU	Transport and General Workers Union
TUC	Trades Union Congress
TWU	Tobacco Workers' Union
UPOW	Union of Post Office Workers
USDAW	Union of Shop, Distributive and Allied Workers
WEA	Workers' Educational Association

Note: In several instances, unions have changed their titles consequent on amalgamation. We refer to the old titles in the text where these are appropriate to the time of our research, to union policies, or to union publications. The term trade union is used in the old sense and not as redefined by the Industrial Relations Act, 1971.

Preface

This second edition presents an opportunity to take account of the many developments which have occurred since the publication of the first edition early in 1969. Accidents of timing made it possible to include the Report of the Royal Commission on Trade Unions and Employers' Associations (Donovan Commission) and the Commission's Survey of Workplace Industrial Relations only as postscripts to that edition. In addition, the Industrial Relations Act of 1971 and its associated Code of Industrial Relations Practice have now been incorporated into the fabric of industrial relations in Britain, the Commission on Industrial Relations has been established and has published a number of reports dealing with the reform of collective bargaining and with procedural change directly affecting shop stewards. The CIR has published a report on the facilities afforded to shop stewards whilst the TUC has also outlined what it regards as desirable in this area, and has issued new statements on training and rulebook provisions. The period has also seen a number of prominent union officials emphasize the importance of decentralization of bargaining and of 'grass-roots' democracy.

In many ways the position of shop stewards is now better understood than at the time of preparing the first edition, and it is less necessary to emphasize their importance. In part this arises out of the publicity given to the Donovan Report's diagnosis of the emergence of an 'informal' system of industrial relations at workplace level in many major manufacturing industries, a development which had earlier been categorized by Professor Flanders as the 'challenge from below'. The Donovan Report concluded that the 'central defect of our industrial relations system is the disorder in factory and workshop relations and pay structures . . .' (para 162) thus emphasizing shortcomings at the level at which shop stewards operate, and it recommended radical changes in the nature of bargaining at this level. Thus shop stewards are of central importance not only to the operation of the present system but also to its reform.

It is proposed to underline the position of the shop steward as a focal point of many related trends in industrial relations, and in so doing to break down the fragmentation of study in this field. Consequently we shall outline and interpret the forces operating on, and in part generated by, the British system of industrial relations. Most of the problems of current concern involve the roles and interests of both management and unions, for both must influence shop steward behaviour and guide their future development. Management and union policies will be influential in determining, for example, the functions of workplace representatives and how they are formally accepted; and the strength of the link between unions and stewards in relation to unofficial strikes and less newsworthy industrial action; the extent, form, and direction of workplace bargaining; and the limitation of cost-push inflation at plant level, etc. Some of these topics illustrate the problems which arise from conflict of interest between stewards and management (and possibly their unions) in the regulation of employment relationships, though other difficulties arise from a shared preference between stewards and managers for the internalization of their dealings. Encouragement of shop stewards by management is an important but often overlooked element in workplace bargaining. At the same time, the reluctance of management to take the initiative in labour relations has been highlighted by strong workplace organization among its employees, and thus now represents an area of considerable opportunity for contemporary managements.

Essentially, our objective is to examine the nature, causes, and manifestations of what Flanders calls the 'challenge from below' and the Donovan Commission's 'informal system', and to assess the problems facing unions and management, and the institutions they have established jointly, as a result of the increased decentralization of industrial relations activity.

More precisely our aims are:

1. To study the factors responsible for the increased importance of shop stewards, and for variations in it.
2. To describe their present roles and the pressures and constraints which influence them.
3. To draw together information and hypotheses from specialist fields in the social sciences generally and industrial relations in particular, and to relate this specifically to workplace representatives.
4. To analyse the effects of the changed role status, and functions of shop stewards on trade unions, management, and collective-bargaining arrangements in relation to current needs in the labour-relations field.

We have endeavoured to collect findings from published material directly concerned with shop stewards, and other work of more indirect bearing on their position. Much is available only in academic journals or in publications dealing only incidentally with shop stewards. In addition, we undertook a number of research projects to illuminate certain topics but, due to the limitations of our samples and of the case-study approach, they have no claim to being definitive. We have, however, incorporated the large-scale survey evidence provided by the Government Social Survey's inquiry into Workplace Industrial Relations, which gives more authoritative data.

The study is informed by our experience in industry, including time spent on the shop floor in the motor industry, and as management representatives dealing with stewards. More generally, we have discussed the role, functions, and behaviour patterns of stewards with managers, personnel officers, full-time union officials, foremen, stewards, and rank-and-file union members – though these discussions took place over a long period and in a way not easily reported statistically. Finally, we have had experience of teaching on broadly educational and specifically constructed training courses for stewards, which give some insight into the problems from the stewards' point of view.

Our subject is large, diverse, and full of temptations to generalize. However, in our experience, variations exist between *and* within different plants of the same company, different industries, unions and between all these at various points in time. The problems raised by shop stewards therefore vary enormously in situation and time, and we anticipate that future research may reveal differences of which we are unaware. Like all issues of a human and economic nature, this is a dynamic one.

It is our contention that the importance of stewards in regulating industrial relationships is not widely understood. Shop stewards attract emotional and often extreme opinion, and seem more prone to examination in stereotype than others in the field of employment relations. Moreover, it appears that the role of stewards is likely to develop, as they become increasingly significant to unions, managers, and the country at large. They appeared initially as minor workplace supplements to the organizing and administrative hierarchy of the unions, as recruiters and reporters rather than as principals with representational functions. Since the Second World War, they have emerged as a force independent of existing institutions. Pragmatically, they have built up practices and organizations which have eroded old established arrangements. Yet 'independent' is perhaps too strong. Stewards are not independent of their unions. This would appear to be even more the case after the recent House of Lords' decision that the Transport and General Workers' Union was responsible for the actions of its shop stewards in the docks (this will be discussed later). Nor are they independent of management, whose behaviour can be important in determining *their* behaviour and attitudes. Yet, together with their constituents, they represent a relatively new and quickly developing interest group on the industrial relations scene for which the traditional external mechanisms have not adequately catered.

Like other institutions, employers' associations and trade unions tend to acquire their own institutional life and interests, tending, in time, to gain a justification separate from the original purposes. This process is also apparent in the joint institutions and old-established procedures through which they conduct their relationships. Additionally, if the institutions cling rigidly to existing patterns, their relevance diminishes and they are bypassed. Thus, individual managements and groups of union members (with their workplace leaders) have grown away from external institutions, though carefully preserving access to them where and when this is felt appropriate. The 'parent' bodies, employers' associations and trade unions, have become progressively less able (and often unwilling, due to the risk of further alienation) to regulate the behaviour of their members, though both occasionally issue threats or force resignations. Consequently, the validity of their claims to constitute the single voice of their members has been undermined, and their value to members often reduced.

Despite the more unified ideas of trade unions in comparison with employers' associations and their more centralized authority, the trend of *actual* power and initiative has been downward. Indeed, it would not be false to describe the relation of workplace organizations and the body of the unions in federal terms, with members paying low taxes, receiving poor services from and having only infrequent contact with the centre, and admitting only a few major decisions by the federal authority. Traditional concepts of union structure, of the functions of employers' associations, and of collective-bargaining arrangements, appear less and less tenable. The institutions and their procedures are no longer comprehensive, nor perhaps appropriate. Managements are widely subject to 'domestic' claims, and have their actions, performance, and values scrutinized by stewards. Many managements have fostered this process, preferring to build up their own pattern of labour relations. Union officials seem little perturbed by the drift of events, and many district officials rely on stewards to relieve them of their duties – especially in 'reasonable' firms with 'reasonable' managements. In practice, many accept decentralization, and liberally consider that the union exists for its members, or even that 'the members are the union'. If to this view we attach the widely held opinion (and fact!) that to many members 'the steward is the union', then the significance of members and stewards in relation to union hierarchies is apparent.

Whether the Industrial Relations Act, with its more hierarchial view of trade unions and (since the House of Lords' decision on the T & GWU's responsibility for its shop stewards) of worker's organizations also, will change this situation remains to be seen.

In spite of the Act, however, the trend still appears to be towards decentralization: from union executives, full-time officials, and branches, to stewards, and sometimes beyond stewards to other, informal, workplace leaders; and from employers' associations to company managements, plant and departmental managers, and labour specialists.

Needless to say, these processes have not been of equal incidence in the diverse arrangements which constitute the so-called industrial relations system. Moreover, the provisions of the Industrial Relations Act 1971 may act to check or reverse some of these trends, not least by encouraging more formal agreements and the closer definition of the role of shop stewards in procedure agreements and the rulebooks of registered trade unions. The possible impact of the new legislation is dealt with in Chapter 10.

We would like to express our gratitude to the numerous trade-union officers, shop stewards, managers, and supervisors who have answered our questions and referred both candidly and at length to their own experience. Several companies and unions gave us full facilities to conduct our investigations on their own premises, and we are greatly indebted to them.

J. F. B. Goodman
T. G. Whittingham

Chapter One

Shop Stewards:
An Introductory Survey

Definitions

The diversity of trade-union structure, rulebooks, and practice makes it difficult to establish a definition of a shop steward inclusive of the men and women it is sought to define, without becoming so loosely phrased as to be indefinite. Many collective agreements introduce the term 'shop steward' to describe 'representatives appointed from the members of the unions employed in the establishment to act on their behalf . . .'[1] This description is perhaps most common, that the shop steward is the representative of union members in the workplace, being acknowledged as such by the management and by his trade union, but who is neither a full-time officer nor a branch official whose workplace representational function derives solely from that office. This acknowledgement is usually shown by the workplace representative's function in the early stages of in-plant negotiations, which is frequently included in the procedural sections of collective agreements.

One problem arising from the definition of a shop steward as the representative of union members employed in the establishment where he himself works is that it is confusing in some industries. Here, this function is performed by a person like the workplace representative, but who does not, strictly, come within the definition. For example, in coal mining, the basic administrative unit of the National Union of Mineworkers is the branch, based on N U M membership at a *colliery*, rather than on the colliery village. This identification of the basic unit of the trade union with the workplace is the exception rather than the rule, but where it exists it implies difficulty in determining the duties a branch secretary may have as a result of his tenure of this office and which are the result of his, occasional, election as workplace representative in the above sense. This complicated picture is illustrated by the definitional problems posed by the hardworking trade unionist in one motor-vehicle plant who was simultaneously a shop steward for a section of workers, the convenor of shop stewards in the plant, and branch secretary of his union's newly established local (workplace-based) branch. Management, in this case, recognized him in the first two positions, but gave him no facilities from holding the branch secretaryship. This example indicates the reduced significance of branch positions in the settlement of industrial relations problems, though this decline is not of equal incidence in all industries and unions. Generally speaking, the functions of branch officials tend to coalesce with those of the workplace representative only where there are workplace-based branches, or where unions are, or aspire to be, industrial unions.

This book is concerned with shop stewards, using a working definition of the shop steward as:

(*a*) A representative of trade-union members at the place of work where he himself is employed.

(*b*) Someone who is tacitly or explicitly accepted as such by management and his trade union.

(*c*) Someone who has responsibility for the conduct of the initial stages of negotiations in the workplace. (This must not be interpreted as all-embracing. There are occasions, in practice, when local full-time officials initiate discussion on topics affecting the plant. Similarly, many procedure agreements emphasize that any employee who has a complaint must, initially,

refer to his foreman before approaching his shop
steward.)

(*d*) Someone, however, who is not a recognized full-time
official of his trade union and whose recognition is not
the result of his, possibly, holding branch office.

However, not all workplace representatives who fulfil these
conditions are called shop stewards. This is explained by lack
of standardized trade-union terminology for their workplace
representatives. Most widely known is 'father of the chapel'
in the printing unions, a title which indicates both the old-
established nature of this position and the importance of
tradition. Other titles used include those of 'corresponding
member' in DATA, 'staff representative' in the CAWU,
'local department committee representative' on the railways,
and in the Civil Service 'members of the Staff Sides of Local
Whitley Committees'.

A further point is the position of convenors of shop stewards. A convenor is usually the senior shop steward in a
plant, or of a union in it, and he is normally elected by his
fellow stewards. A convenor's responsibilities vary but he is
often acknowledged by management to have considerable
influence over other shop stewards, and is frequently able to
advise stewards within the plant on factory-wide practices
and possibly policy. Often, the title convenor is given to the
secretary of a shop stewards' committee formed by stewards
of one union, and works convenor to the occupant of the
equivalent position on the joint (ie, inter-union) shop
stewards' committee for the whole factory. The convenor
in a large factory may be influential in the progression of
disputes. He may join a steward in negotiations at a certain
stage or may raise points of a plant-wide nature *ab initio*. He
will usually become quickly involved if an issue is urgent.
The convenor may retain his duties as a shop steward to a
section of union members, and then it is easy to include him
in our definition of a shop steward. However, when a
convenor gives up his duties in favour of this higher position,
his inclusion becomes more problematical, though we feel

justified in allowing it – for the change is one of degree rather than kind. It is generally an extension of his representational function in the workplace rather than exclusion from it, though again it is necessary to emphasize variations.

We have sought to define the shop steward in terms which can be applied to any employment situation rather than by a catalogue of duties or functions. The only function regarded as essential to our definition is that of responsibility for the initial stages of in-plant negotiations, necessary to avoid confusion over the position of 'collecting' stewards. The collection of union dues and the checking of membership cards was one of the earliest duties of the workplace representative. The increased role and activities of shop stewards in some industries have involved a division of labour, and some unions, eg, NUGMW, appoint collecting stewards additionally, to be responsible for the collection of union dues. Where this is the limit of the collecting stewards' activities, we will not be concerned with him. Only where he has progressed to a representational role would he come within our definition.

Shop stewards, or perhaps more usually convenors, have occasionally found that their representative duties have so developed that they become occupied with plant industrial relations for much of their working week. It is important to distinguish between representatives engaged for the whole working week on industrial relations problems in the workplace and the full-time officials of the trade unions.

Shop stewards, or convenors, usually rank as lay officials of their trade union, but generally receive little or no remuneration for their services. In the two largest general unions, stewards who collect dues are paid a commission, $7\frac{1}{2}$ per cent in the T & GWU and 10 per cent in the NUGMW. The basis of payment for the shop steward or convenor whose representational activities, initially subsidiary to his employment, have in time virtually come to replace his nominal occupation with the firm, varies between companies. Management may formally recognize the position and pay the convenor for his duties, but probably will leave the position undefined and pay the convenor as if still engaged in his nominal occupation. Alternatively, where a firm refuses to pay a steward for time spent away from his 'normal' job, a steward's members may well contribute to make up his wages. The full-time trade-union official, on the other hand, is a paid employee of the union, his salary deriving from central funds, he being answerable in the normal way to his superiors.

Within the framework of our definition, it might be possible to refer to *the* shop steward, implying a basic uniformity of all shop stewards. Obviously, any definition describes characteristics shared by all included within it, but with shop stewards the common denominator is fixed at a fairly low level. There is great diversity in different industries, and even between different plants of one firm in one industry. Managerial company-wide policies, and similarly guiding lines postulated by a union for its stewards, become subject to local pressures, traditions, and interpretation by individuals. Such factors, *and* many others, determine whether the steward can extend his activities within and possibly beyond our basic definition.

The difficulties in deriving an inclusive but specific definition of a shop steward are indicative of a major contemporary problem. Practice varies, but generally trade-union rulebooks are vague in defining a shop steward; many evade the issue either by introducing the term without definition, or by wholly omitting to mention stewards or their equivalent. A close definition of stewards, of their actual duties and functions, is a first step towards the clarification of problems which their existence presents in industry.

The role and functions of shop stewards

Role has been defined as 'the actions performed by a person to validate his occupation of a position. The role is linked to the position and not to the person who is temporarily occupying it.' (See *Handbook of Social Psychology*, ed G. Lindzey,

Addison-Wesley, 1954, Chapter VIII.) This definition may be applicable for a closely defined role, but that of shop steward is not usually precisely defined. Elliot Jacques (in *The Changing Culture of a Factory*) observes that rigid adherence to the role required by each situation becomes possible only when the role itself has been precisely defined. This is clearly not true of shop stewards, for the nearest approach to role definition may often be found in the shop stewards' handbook (in those cases where they exist) and, with one exception, these are certainly not meant to be definitive. Role is therefore defined in this study as the actions performed by a person to justify his occupation of a position (which is usually imprecisely defined). The role is linked to a collection of variables rather than to the position itself.

The role of a shop steward varies between workplaces and unions, and within both. Its content also depends on which of the interested parties is describing the stewards' role.

Traditionally, unions have tended to regard stewards chiefly as union administrators, as voluntary assistants within often large-scale organizations. Historically, they have been the chief recruiting agents, and so influence the numerical and organizational strength of the unions. They must maintain membership, and frequently collect weekly dues and check cards. They are also sources of information about shop practices and changes, and are expected to pass on information to their branch officials. Conversely, they disseminate information about the union, explaining policy to the rank and file. Moreover, they should ensure that union rules and the terms of collective agreements are observed, and report irregularities. They are involved in the event of accidents, and advise members of benefits and services available through the union to meet such eventualities.

If incentive payment schemes are in operation they should defend members' interests, discussing grievances with management. If a member cannot resolve a grievance, or if the problem is collective, the steward should assist in representations to management. In the event of continued dispute, the steward will be relied on to brief the full-time official.

Management, similarly, may prefer to regard the shop steward's role largely as a communications link, passing information in both directions between his constituents and management. He will be expected to state grievances arising from the shop floor and, having reached an agreement with management, will be expected to carry his members with him. As such, management may have a vested interest in his strength, regarding him as both representative and advocate. Additionally, he will be expected to lead, as well as reflect, shop-floor opinion. The steward's representational role may be further emphasized by participation in joint consultative committees, about which he should also disseminate information. Finally, the steward will normally be acknowledged to assist with complaints between workers and management. Management may however endeavour to minimize this role, attempting to restrict the influence of the steward by stressing its own receptiveness to an individual's complaints and by pursuing policies which attempt to identify the interests of the firm and its employees.

Such, then, are the historical stereotypes of the steward's functions. They see the steward predominantly as a neutral agent, carrying information between union and management hierarchies. He is regarded as a recruiter and servicer of union members, a guardian of national agreements, and a useful aide in solving minor problems between management and members in the workplace, thus relieving busy, full-time officers. His role in communications is assumed to be of an almost catalytic nature. However, these stereotypes do not accord with practice in many industries. The steward, while a lay official of the union, acknowledged by management as an accredited representative, is elected by union members in his shop, and usually feels primarily responsible to them. Though non-branch-attending members may look to the steward for information about the union, their prime concern is with his ability to protect and advance their interests. As such it is their expectations, rather than union rulebooks and management conventions, which influence his behaviour, though other influences are numerous.

With full employment and buoyant product markets, workgroups have enhanced their influence, largely through the agency of shop stewards. Management styles have, by design or necessity, come to be more consultative than the old autocratic methods. Labour scarcity, expensive training, rapid technical change, and the teachings of human-relations doctrines have emphasized the desirability of this style. In the last resort, the added impact of sanctions available to employees has induced management to lead rather than to drive, the consent of organized employees being necessary to continued operations. In large plants, obtaining consent demands a representational system, and thus places the occupants of this representative role in a strategic position. With the support of their members, shop stewards can determine the terms and conditions of consent. These developments have enabled shop stewards to emerge as a semi-independent force in the industrial relations system, with tenuous ties with the old-established machinery. They have achieved bargaining functions on a multitude of directly and indirectly pecuniary topics, and on issues concerned with workers' status and rights which, cumulatively, have a powerful influence on the total working environment. This change, unevenly consolidated within British industry, partly reflects and is partly a cause of the changed power structure within and beyond the workplace.

The employment relationship is basically (though not exclusively) one of economic expediency, and within the workplace groups come together to further their own interests. These interests may not coincide with those of other groups, nor will they be identical with management's interests or those of their trade union, though all are to varying degrees interdependent. Thus, just as management needs the acquiescence of its labour force, so union full-time officers need the support of their members. In practice, they rely on the advice of shop stewards, as well as on their own position and direct contact with members. Stewards are generally better acquainted with their workmates' views, can assess likely reaction to a given proposal, and it is they who supervise the day-to-day working of any agreement from the union side. Indeed, this fact has often brought stewards into negotiations with management on topics previously the exclusive province of district officials. Stewards have been largely responsible for extending the area which is subject to joint (ie, union/management) regulation, and thus have developed negotiating or consultative rights on topics on which management would not previously accept the legitimacy of union officials' representations, let alone those of stewards. Their importance in some cases has meant that stewards negotiate at length with senior management, as they are beyond the competence of lower levels of the management hierarchy. Thus, the steward has engendered two separate but related changes – first, in extending the range of topics on which his constituents can legitimately express their views and exert influence on management's decisions and, secondly, in dealing with increasingly senior levels of management. The effect of both is to enlarge the competence of stewards and to enhance the status of the steward.

Continuous and detailed promotion of members' interests in day-to-day employment relations is not possible from outside the plant, and so close attention is inevitably left to workplace representatives. As noted, the parochial and short-term interests of members do not necessarily coincide with those of the union. When in disagreement, work groups have felt and been free to pursue their objectives independently. This has meant that occasionally workplace leaders ignore the union, or act against the advice of its officials. The unions, for their part, have seldom exercised sanctions against non-conformist behaviour by a body of their members, considering that coercion would alienate those members and risk the unions' future influence over their membership.

Thus, the emergence of powerful shop stewards places the unions in a dilemma. If they take action to restrict stewards' functions they will, in effect, reduce union influence over the working conditions of their members, and forfeit opportunities for gaining improvements. The advance of stewards has been inextricably bound up with the achievement of the unions' central purpose, ie, to advance their members' interests, for inevitably, in obtaining benefits for members, stewards increase their status in the eyes of the membership. Full-time officials are overworked, their access to factories is frequently restricted, some problems are urgent, others are extremely time-consuming. The increased volume of 'business' has meant, in practice, the devolution of wider functions to shop stewards. This was rarely the result of positive decisions of union policy, of explicit delegation, but rather has been a consequence of institutional rigidity in the changed post-war environment.

The sources of shop stewards' power

(*1*) *Trade-union structure*
British trade-union structure has followed no preconceived pattern of development; British trade unions have developed to cater for different needs, in differing circumstances, and at different times. The result is a complicated structure reflecting little method and a multiplicity of organizational bases. Most prominent is horizontal organization, of either a certain occupation in different industries, or of categories of workers irrespective of industry or occupation, although a few incipient 'industrial unions' have tried to organize vertically. The implications of the occupational/general form of organization and its piecemeal development are that several different unions will have members in a factory, and a union's membership will cover many, possibly unrelated, industries. While the union may try to follow uniform policies for all members and all stewards, the variety of their workplaces will exert different influences, making standardization of other than minimal conditions and functions impossible.

The presence of members of many unions with different interests makes it difficult for outside full-time officials to develop common policies and apply close supervision to one plant. Rivalries may inhibit their cooperation locally. Also, if plant-wide topics arise, it is difficult to ensure the simultaneous availability of the officials of several unions, thus making it expedient for management to deal with stewards. While some inter-union conflicts, eg, over membership and demarcation, may affect or be generated by stewards, they frequently form joint stewards' committees to overcome the deficiencies of the union structure. The bond of common employment, experience of the employer, and the presence of bargaining opportunities within the plant stimulates joint organization, which thus facilitates concerted approaches to the employer. The committees' multi-union composition means that no single union can supervise its activities, and it *may* follow policies contrary to those of some unions or in defiance of all.

(2) Branch organization

In contrast with the generally haphazard development of trade unions, their internal administration, especially at local level, is not dissimilar. Rank-and-file members belong to a branch, and are able to participate in its policies by attending meetings, joining in discussions, and voting on resolutions and for officials. In practice, union branch meetings, like evening activities of many voluntary associations, are poorly attended. Professor Roberts states that, in large unions, branch attendances range from 3 per cent to 15 per cent, with a concentration between 4 per cent and 7 per cent in most cases.[2] A more recent sample survey of AEU and NUGMW branches revealed that average attendance at branch meetings was 9 per cent and 5 per cent, respectively.[3] The functions of the branch have been eroded over the years, being now predominantly administrative. Union members, it seems, dislike administration, and the democratic participation and control outlined in the rulebooks are not fully exercised.

For reasons of history, tactics, and economy, union branches are typically based on the place of residence rather than the place of work. Workmates in the same factory seldom belong to one branch unless they live in the same area and, even if these two coincide, the branch will normally be concerned with issues at other factories also. So, without a deep interest in union affairs, or an urgent problem at their factory, attending the branch is not an attractive proposition. Their steward will normally attend, and let them know what has transpired. Thus, direct contact between the union hierarchy and members is cut.

Secondly, stewards are often held responsible to the branch and its officers. However, unless membership is based on employment at one workplace, in which case branch officials may themselves be stewards, contact, let alone coordination and control, is usually minimal. Stewards' reports are records of past events. So, the low level of attendance, the preponderantly residential basis of branch membership, and increasingly close affinity of union members with fellow employees rather than fellow unionists elsewhere all emphasize the workplace as the centre of their attention, and the steward as the focus of union-type activities. The declining significance of the 'standard union wage rate', the sterility of branch activities, and the unity inspired by a common employer have contributed to this trend, revealing an institutional gap in trade-union organization which the steward has come to occupy.

(3) Collective bargaining institutions

Typically, though not universally, collective bargaining is based on industry-wide institutions representing employers, formed into employers' associations, and the trade unions with members in these same undertakings. Bargaining is based on an industrial form of organization and is centralized, the terms of agreements being therefore generalized. As agreements cover many different employers, they cannot take account of the individual circumstances of each firm and offer opportunities for supplementary bargaining in the workplace. Although some employers' associations have continued to persuade their members not to exceed nationally negotiated basic wage rates, they have been unable to prevent other variations in workplaces. The industry-wide agreements provide the unions with guaranteed minimum conditions, which do not prevent employers providing more favourable conditions. Secondly, national agreements are not comprehensive, omitting many important topics, and providing only permissive guidance on others. Clearly, external machinery, generally, fails to provide more than the framework for the regulation of employment relationships. It leaves innumerable topics to be settled locally – or, more accurately, within the plant or company. The Donovan Commission saw the industry-wide agreements as the centrepiece of the old-established 'formal system', but felt they were no more than a façade which could no longer pretend to regulate relationships fully and effectively. The sketchy contents of most industry-wide agreements certainly ensure a role for workplace representatives, who will be able to exploit any peculiarities of their immediate situation and thus develop into bargainers.

(4) Union rulebooks

Union rulebooks vary in the provision they make for shop stewards, particularly in relation to their functions *vis-à-vis* management. All withhold authority to initiate industrial action, but most rulebooks, and the supplementary handbooks of the larger unions, leave to the steward's discretion which problems he passes to his branch or district officials, and when. Most imply that the steward should not negotiate agreements or reach 'understandings' prejudicial to national agreements, but leave him free to improve on them. Stewards are able to enlarge the vague 'job description' contained in union rulebooks as circumstances permit. Their scope varies, but, as in all human relationships, niceties distinguish apparently similar cases. Clearly, multi-industry trade unions find it difficult to prescribe the duties of their stewards *vis-à-vis* management strictly and comprehensively. While rulebooks *may* provide for the election, period of office, union administrative duties, and liaison with the branch and its officials, they largely fail to reflect the actual functions of stewards as *bargainers*. It is questionable how much influence a rulebook exerts on a steward, other than, for example, his attendance at union meetings. His role is much more likely to be affected by his relations with other stewards, including those of other unions, with full-time officials, by the nature of his constituency and constituents, and management itself.

(5) *Full-time officials*

The history and militant image of shop stewards' movements occasionally makes higher union officials apprehensive of the semi-autonomous position of shop stewards. The unions exercise a parental authority over them, almost invariably defending them from external attack, but are unable to make them conform always. The supervisory role of union officials is becoming increasingly difficult. Figures published during the 1960s show that the ratio of full-time officials to members has been fairly steady over the post-war decades, but the proportion of stewards to full-time officers and of stewards to members has been rising dramatically in some unions.[4] The frequency of contact and the quality of informal relationships are very influential in determining how stewards are integrated into their unions, yet district officials can often establish only a superficial acquaintanceship with their stewards. The problem is exacerbated when officials have stewards in many different and possibly small factories, and when turnover of stewards is high. Increased industrial relations activity in the workplace, and the overloading of full-time officials, necessarily allows stewards increased discretion, as well as inducing them to forgo assistance whenever possible. So, although stewards are lay officials of the union, they can continue, assuming stoppages are avoided, with very little supervision from full-time officers.

(6) Work groups

For the rank and file, the shop steward is often the only contact with the union. It is common for a member not only to think of the steward as the union, but to refer to him as such. The steward may have persuaded him to enrol, collects his dues, provides advice, spreads union news, advances complaints to management, sits on joint committees, etc. To other members, perhaps better versed in union affairs, his advice may not have the same predictability as that of the full-time official, nor its implications of delay engender the suspicion that he has other, more urgent, problems. Unlike the steward, the full-time official is not on the spot, and cannot apply himself fully to the problems of one department or one factory.

The crux of the power of any shop steward is his ability to carry his members with him in a course of action. Without the tacit support of the work groups he represents (which may be several and diversely composed), the steward is impotent, and from management's point of view he may be a hindrance to the development of a good representational system. A steward may be closely watched by his members and his performance of the job assessed, but the pressure exerted on him by his members will vary in frequency, direction, and intensity. They may apply direct pressure for specific objectives, or allow him to interpret their implicit expectations. In some shops, the position may be keenly sought, in others it may be difficult to find someone to do the job. However, if a steward is to lead, he must be responsive to the changing needs and expectations of his group, for failure to respond – in the absence of complete apathy – will lead to his effective replacement.

The traditions, behaviour, and atmosphere of a factory may induce a certain kind of steward to emerge, and to adopt a certain approach. However, the steward is not necessarily a mere reflection of his members and their views. He has his own personal qualities, he may be able to anticipate their requirements, and use his initiative to project them. A successful record will help him maintain his position, though his tactics may not always command unanimous support. His leadership is strengthened by his superior knowledge, his access to information, and his participation in negotiations with management. He may persuade members by quoting information and circumstances they cannot challenge. The information available to rank-and-file members is at best imperfect and at worst non-existent, a source of security and power to stewards, though occasionally it reacts against them. Stewards usually have few facilities to speak to their members collectively, and risk the distortion of messages circulating through the shop. Between mass meetings, which often have a large emotional content and activist tendencies, the steward may exercise his own discretion and members have little opportunity to form a consensus view. Information put out by management may be ridiculed simply because of its source, particularly when there is conflict. The shop steward's leadership is reinforced by the almost inbred solidarity of trade unionists and the social consequences of nonconformity. Confidence in a steward may derive from his previous performance, and the steward can therefore expect to be followed, at least initially.

Thus, the steward's strength stems from his leadership being accepted by the work groups he represents. He cannot retain his leadership if he fails to fulfil their implicit or explicit requirements. He may be closely scrutinized by some of his constituents, but even where this occurs – and it may not be widespread – his position allows him discretion to lead as well as to reflect. The extent of this discretion depends on his experience, record, and personality, but may be extended by apathy in the workplace and the imperfect facilities (Code of Industrial Relations Practice notwithstanding) for checking with, and being checked by, his constituents, especially in the short run.

(7) *Management*

Whether as a positive policy, or as the unconsidered concomitant of decisions on other topics, management may enhance the scope, power, and authority of shop stewards. Historically, many managements would have preferred unions to develop along lines internal rather than external to the workplace. Being on the payroll means that union representatives are subject to the sanctions of the firm and enables the management to exert some influence over them. However, the results of the recently developed internal system have been somewhat different from those previously anticipated, for the labour market has changed and stewards can appeal for external support if necessary. Managements often prefer to deal with shop stewards rather than full-time officials. Stewards are available, better informed of the history, facts, and implications of a shop-floor dispute, and may obtain the acceptance of an agreement by their members more reliably. They will be concerned with its implementation, which may be easier if they have participated in its negotiation, while their continuous presence enables management to build up informal as well as formal relationships with them. Nor are all factory issues raised by stewards. Management, too, may initiate discussions and negotiations over changes in production, working arrangements, etc, and may seek their acceptance by stewards before making a change. If problems are important and urgent, management may prefer to involve stewards rather than outside officials.

On the other hand, management is often placed in a dilemma over what facilities to give stewards, on which topics to allow stewards' representations, which to disallow, and which to confine to outside officials and their associations. The tendency has largely been to keep issues within the workplace. Similarly, management faced with implicit threats from stewards who 'can't hold their members much longer in the absence of concessions' has to decide where to draw the line, on which issues and at which times resistance is justified 'at any cost'. The balance of comparative costs is always a fine one, but continuous surrender to stewards, especially over issues on which the claims of full-time officials have been rejected, provokes little sympathy when management appeals to those officials to control their members. If a management is thought only to understand force, then a premium is placed on its use, and concessions to it make it a viable exercise. Such a management is adding to the power of militant stewards, and inducing its frequent demonstration.

Some management policies, and the absence of policy, add to the power of stewards. Decentralized supervision of payment schemes, procrastination in dealing with problems, inconsistencies of treatment by different managers, and arbitrary actions all facilitate the development of strong workplace representatives, all afford opportunities for militant activities. Management has quite widely fostered the growth of shop stewards and promoted their wider areas of responsibility. How this enhanced role is exploited is often dependent upon management's behaviour. Encouragement of stewards has often reached the level of active policy. In many instances, it is a realization of the influential position which labour scarcity and the institutional structure afford the stewards. However, many managements are reluctant to accept the division of authority and loyalty epitomized by stewards, and regard the representatives of this division as an intolerable challenge to their right to manage. Many resent the time consumed by acknowledging the existence of a pluralist system internally, regarding such time as non-productive and as a secondary part of the manager's job.

Any generalization about relations between stewards and managers is subject to qualification, but mostly they co-operate satisfactorily. Many managers go to great pains to achieve, and subsequently take pride in, cordial relations with their stewards. This relationship is often a personal one, in which both sides respect the individuals they are dealing with, rather than being achieved through the domination of one side by the other. However, their relationships involve conflict, for their objectives are dissimilar. Stewards will try to derive benefits from any situation, will seek to extend their own influence while limiting the freedom of management. They will strive for the most favourable interpretation of agreements and precedents, and in so doing enhance their own role. Thus, there is a nearly continuous struggle for power and influence, not only between stewards and management, but occasionally between stewards and their unions externally. Both have their own dynamic, and are at best settled only in a temporary sense, rather than being solved in a final sense.

The challenge of shop stewards and its problems

Behind the institutional and behavioural features which have facilitated the development of the steward's role is a background of labour scarcity, of buoyant product markets, and the attitude that cost increases can be passed on to the consumer. Thus, in as far as the activities of stewards involve cost increases they are of public concern, particularly in the export industries. The incidence of wage drift reflects the success of stewards' pressure, though such indexes do not indicate all the stewards' activities. Not all disputes are about wages, and many issues which arise have only indirect effects on costs. However, increased bargaining in the workplace has implications for the development of incomes policies which seek to influence the rate of increase in prices and wages and the distribution of rewards. In certain industries, wages systems and structures, and the organization of work facilitate workplace bargaining. Others afford fewer opportunities, thus ensuring that equality of central influence and of sacrifice will be difficult if not impossible to achieve. Under such policies unions, and particularly stewards, are in effect asked to restrain the exercise of their local bargaining strength.

Wage drift not only affects labour costs, it also reduces the significance of industry-wide collective agreements. Between new agreements, decisions determining major components of earnings are taken at plant level and so transfer both unions' and members' attention to this level.

The widening gap between earnings and wage rates demonstrates this tendency, and the failure to consolidate improvements gained at workplace level into national agreements perpetuates the failure in regulation by external negotiators. Industry-wide bargaining has become unrealistic on the earnings and hours equation. Collective bargaining remains the principal method used by trade unions to achieve their objectives, but its location is increasingly decentralized. In many industries, it is open to question whether industry-wide negotiations are not now subsidiary. Because shop stewards are partly the agents of wage drift[5] they can jeopardize incomes *and* prices planning in individual workplaces, as well as undermining traditional bargaining institutions. The stewards present a challenge to both.

Another feature of their challenge is increasing unofficial industrial action, notably strikes and overtime bans. Over the post-war period the power structure within trade unions has come to resemble an inverted pyramid, rather than the orthodox structure established in their formal organization. Power, as opposed to formal authority, rests with the rank and file who may entrust it to external officials or seek to exercise it themselves. Unofficial action demonstrates the autonomy of work groups and shop stewards, and its persistence illustrates the inadequacy of both union and management sanctions. It remains to be seen what use will be made, and what influence will be exerted, by the new liabilities facing those who can be shown to have induced breach of contract under the Industrial Relations Act. The Act provides new remedies for employers through legal actions against the leaders of such industrial action, and places new responsibilities on registered trade unions to take 'all such steps as are reasonably practicable' to ensure their members observe legally enforceable agreements. The Act thus gives those unions which register the opportunity to bolster their central authority, and on paper it increases the deterrents against precipitate industrial action.

Early cases under the Act indicate that it also has implications in this area for non-registered 'workers' organizations'. The House of Lords' judgement which held that the T & GWU was responsible for the actions of its shop stewards in the docks,[6] although it had specifically condemned these actions, suggests that where unions are held to have given implied authority to stewards to take certain actions then the unions are liable in law for their stewards' actions. The Law Lords ruled that such implied authority may derive from several sources – namely the rulebook, the stewards' handbook and authority delegated upwards either expressly or implicitly from the membership and from custom and practice.[7] Many actions taken by shop stewards in 'workers' organizations' will be covered by one or other of these sources and these organizations now appear to be responsible in law for unfair industrial practices committed by stewards unless they take disciplinary action against them, such as withdrawing their credentials, which is acceptable to the courts. This important decision was restricted to one particular case, but to the extent that it is regarded as a *general* interpretation of the law, it increases the pressures on the unions to exercise closer control over their stewards, since they will be liable at law for their actions. The implications of this situation will be examined in Chapter 10.

In many ways the increased application of workplace pressure and the increased frequency of unofficial actions have been an almost inevitable consequence of the devolution of bargaining activity from periodic negotiations at industry level. Bargaining has become more diffuse, and so has the incidence of strike activity. Bargaining assumes sanctions are available to both sides and workplace representatives can imply, subtly or otherwise, that the members they represent will take action to coerce management. Not all unofficial action is regarded unsympathetically by union officials, although some workplace leaders have persistently led strikes in defiance of union advice. Most unofficial strikes are contrary to agreed procedures and may, as the Devlin Committee felt, 'be best explained by the fact that (in the post-war period) men have felt freer to follow their own inclinations and to strike ... if they want to.'[8] The causes of such strikes are seldom susceptible of exhaustive analysis. They may be analysed as practical exercises of bargaining strength, or emotional outbursts of moral indignation, as a safety valve for accumulated frustrations, as aggressive actions in support of new claims, or as a responsive defence of rights in the face of management encroachment. Strikes stem from causes which differ not only in their ostensible explanation, but in their more fundamental purposes.

The identification of stewards with the leadership of unofficial strikes is an oversimplification. It is not unknown for a steward's advice to be ignored by his members, and if his advice is rejected the steward must accept the views of the majority if he is to retain his position and influence. The Donovan Report, based on extensive research, did much to rehabilitate the shop steward's 'image'. The Commission considered it was often inaccurate to describe shop stewards as 'trouble-makers', and concluded that the steward was more of a lubricant than an irritant. In particular, the Report noted, 'Shop floor decisions which generally precede unofficial strikes are often taken against the advice of shop stewards. Thus shop stewards are rarely agitators pushing workers towards unconstitutional action. In some instances they may be the mere mouthpieces of their work groups. But quite commonly they are supporters of order exercising a restraining influence on their members in conditions which promote disorder'.[9] Thus the part played by shop stewards in unofficial action, at least in initiating it, is somewhat obscure, despite the association which is frequently made in the Press and other news media. The economic damage caused by unofficial strikes cannot be measured easily, but such strikes clearly demonstrate the independence of work groups for close trade-union control. This freedom from trade-union control exists potentially in most workshops, but despite increasing unofficial strikes (especially outside the coal industry) it is comparatively seldom exploited to the point of stoppage. The available power of the unofficial strike does much to enhance the influence of workplace representatives, compensating for the uncertainties induced by the absence of detailed and realistic agreements over their roles.

A similar manifestation of a steward's only partial reliance on his union is the formation of inter-union committees of stewards for an establishment, company, or for different companies in the same industry. The first two types fulfil a real organizational need, while the last is the logical extension of them. Joint stewards' committees in the workplace commonly take on policy-making activities, either sometimes because they are ignorant of their union's position, or to fill gaps in the official policy, or in defiance of it. Such a committee cannot be held answerable to any single union, though the union federations in the engineering, shipbuilding, and building industries have tried to integrate them. The similarity with strike action is apparent. Individual stewards may call strikes independently of their union or may use this as a last resort, but the potential freedom of committees to ignore union advice is even greater than a steward's to defy his union. Joint shop-steward committees may pursue policies not sanctioned by the unions to which their members belong, and undermine union policy-making bodies. Certainly, there is little guarantee that their policies will be acceptable to all the unions. On the other hand, stewards' committees often act as a focus for union activity in the plant, enabling management to solve plant-wide problems, and senior stewards to influence less experienced colleagues. By the same token, some committees have exacerbated problems for political as well as 'selfish' motives. The present system permits, or rather risks, abuse. It is surprising, and heartening, with the failure of unions and bargaining institutions to accommodate these developments, that irresponsible behaviour is not more common.

Stewards are concerned with the intricacies of workplace relationships. The tardy reaction to their emergence has left them much initiative, which may be welcomed or resisted by the management concerned. They have discretionary power, though their own values, their constituents' expectations, and, more recently, the new legal framework prevent them from operating in a vacuum. Their accountability is divided; they may make themselves variously answerable to their electorate, to branch and union officials, or to the need to retain the respect of their fellow stewards.

In the past regulation has been exercised not by union rulebooks, nor legal prohibitions, but by the social constraints of human relationships. The Industrial Relations Act, the Code of Industrial Relations Practice and the activities of the CIR and of the unions themselves may modify the context in which stewards operate, but the habits, practices and values of several decades will not change overnight.

Society's expectations of the system of industrial relations are changing, and the recent changes in the law and in the forms of Government intervention reflect this. Industrial peace and the prevention of exploitation remain highly valued, but the freedom of the parties to pursue self-interest and reach 'private' agreements is no longer sacrosanct. Wages affect prices, one agreement affects another elsewhere, unofficial strikes cause widespread concern, and restrictive practices are widely condemned even if both sides are relatively content. All these workplace problems involve shop stewards, and any change which is sought necessarily affects them. Success will depend on an understanding of their position, and an appreciation of their difficulties as well as their faults. The challenge posed by shop stewards is not simply that of discouraging their less desirable activities: it is also to harness positively the forces their emergence reflects, and the opportunities it provides, to the benefit of both sides of industry, and of the community.

References

1. Handbook of Agreements in the Engineering, Shipbuilding and Ship Repairing Industries.
2. Roberts, B. C., *Trade Union Government and Administration in Great Britain*, G. Bell and Sons Ltd, 1957, p 95.

3. Royal Commission on Trade Unions and Employers' Associations, Research Papers, No 1. *The Role of Shop Stewards in British Industrial Relations* by W. E. J. McCarthy, HMSO, 1966, para 68.

4. Clegg, H. A., Killick, J., and Adams, Rex, *Trade Union Officers*, Basil Blackwell, 1961, p 40. See also Marsh, A. I., and Coker, E. E., 'Shop Steward Organization in the Engineering Industry', *British Journal of Industrial Relations*, June, 1963.

5. See Chapter 7 for a definition and discussion of wage drift.

6. The case was Heaton's Transport (St Helen's) Ltd v Transport and General Workers' Union; Craddock Bros v T & GWU; Panalpina Services Ltd v T & GWU and NASD.

7. For details of the case see Times Law Report for July 27th, *The Times*, July 28th, 1972.

8. Final Report of the Committee of Inquiry into Certain Matters concerning the Port Transport Industry, HMSO, Cmnd 2734, 1965, para 17.

9. *Report of the Royal Commission on Trade Unions and Employers' Associations* (Donovan Report), Cmnd 3623, HMSO, 1968, para 110.

Chapter Two

The Early Growth and Development of Shop Stewards

The British system of industrial relations, and its largely voluntary institutions, have evolved to meet immediate needs rather than being of planned or of revolutionary origin. The democratic political background to the emerging system ensured the rejection of revolutionary methods by most trade unionists, even when social conditions provoked deep discontent. Thus, for example, it was completely in character for the movement to turn to a new, democratically based political party when its very existence was threatened by the House of Lords' decision in the Taff Vale case in 1901. While their fellow trade unionists in France talked of revolution, British unionists sought constitutionally to achieve their aims.

Developments in industrial relations have been largely piecemeal, as unions and employers adopted expediency in dealing with problems as they arose, and settled them pragmatically. Consequently, *ad hoc* solutions to problems have created institutions and behaviour which quickly became entrenched, and, although much is of lasting value, trade unions' evolution and subsequent rigidity have raised problems. For example, some believe that the TUC (which originated to articulate the trade-union voice and to act as a pressure group) should be given powers of leadership which the trade-union movement in the late nineteenth century thought neither necessary nor desirable. So, too, with shop stewards, since their early duties consisted of checking the cards of newcomers, urging new staff to join the union, checking that existing members were paying their dues, keeping a watch generally on the observance of union rules and practices in the shop, and making a periodic report to the district officer and his committee.[1] Since this time stewards have enlarged their roles, but no parallel movement has brought their enlarged roles within the rules of our industrial relations system. The reasons for this lie not solely, however, in the British system, but also in the historical development of the steward's position.

Early developments

There has probably always been a spokesman for the unions inside an establishment once organization has started. Apart from those in the printing industry, however, these were not official. In printing, the unions have organized on the basis of chapels for a long time,[2] and the father of the chapel has always performed at least some of the functions of a modern shop steward, although not until the end of the last century did he engage in negotiations. In other industries, however, the history of shop stewards goes back to the period 1824–31. At this time, delegate meetings were held by the Foundry Workers' Union (then the Friendly Ironmoulders' Society) in districts in Scotland; each shop sent two delegates, one elected by the shop, one by the meeting itself. In addition, a financial delegate was elected in each shop to collect contributions, to give 'leaving lines' (ie, certificates of employment and union membership) to members leaving, and to see that new workers were union members.[3] At this time, also, the cotton unions exhibited at the local level some of the features of modern trade unions. 'There is the same federal superstructure – the shop stewards (head shop men or "box stewards") forming the local committee.'[4]

These stewards appeared, however, to be largely content with collecting contributions and inspecting the cards of

those starting work.[5] But, possibly unrecorded, their duties
might have come to be representational, although with no
extant records probably it was only on a minor scale. At the
end of the nineteenth century, a powerful shop-steward
movement was built up in the Amalgamated Society of
Engineers, which in 1878 gave its district committees power
to appoint stewards. Not until the nineties did these stewards appear in any great numbers.[6] Their growth seems to
have originated in the change in industrial techniques and
workplace management, especially the introduction of piece
rate, incentive systems, and high-speed machine tools. So, a
local representative with an intimate knowledge of the workshop was necessary to represent employees, since full-time
officials found it increasingly difficult to keep up with the
bewildering variety of developments. These workplace representatives, however, aroused some suspicion from full-
time officials, who feared that they would make independent
agreements with employers cutting across union policy,
and that they might be used by employers to reach agreements which the official union policy could not support.[7]
Probably, however, most stewards contented themselves
with checking the cards of newcomers, urging newcomers
to join the union and other day-to-day responsibilities
listed above.[8] In the Amalgamated Society of Engineers,
stewards were for many years unknown outside Scotland
and Belfast, and their functions were limited to ensuring
members were in benefit and that newcomers were Society
men.[9]

The administrative duties of stewards were not all,
however. H. A. Clegg[10] notes that, as early as 1872, the
Tees District of the Tyneside and National Labourers'
Union reported that 'the shop stewards have worked like
niggers and several disputes between the platers and platers'
helpers have been satisfactorily settled'. He notes that this
suggests that the stewards' functions were being extended
from recruiting members and collecting contributions to
taking part in negotiations. Professor Clegg states that,
within a few years, it was accepted practice for the official

delegate to take the steward into the office when he went to talk to the employers. Also, in the case of the Amalgamated Society of Engineers, evidence suggests that stewards were trying to enlarge their scope to include negotiating functions. The Glasgow and District Engineers' and Boilermakers' Association in a minute of 1896 referred to 'members of the newly formed Vigilance Committee of the ASE known as shop stewards' and complained of cases 'where individual men were quite satisfied with the pay and increases they had received but yet were practically driven out of the shop' by stewards.[11] This conflicting evidence suggests differences in the duties of stewards according to union, industry, job, locations, personality, etc, and probably the behaviour of management and the vicissitudes of the trade cycle.

In the coal mines, factors such as management attitudes, militancy of the union and the need for a check on work led to a local representative at an early date. Since 1845, when the Miners' Association of Great Britain was a vigorous force, miners had been demanding a representative to check the weight of their output, but were unsatisfied until 1860 when an Act of Parliament provided for a permanent official in each lodge to act as a checker of weights, or 'checkweighman'. This official became specially important in the miners' unions owing to a growing lack of communication between the membership of the district council and the groupings of workmen. As early as December, 1860, a miners' circular stated that such people negotiated, for it said: ' . . . having a man of our own in every pit would render free access to our employees at all times and on all occasions reason would do the work of strife and contention.'[12] The Mines Regulation Act of 1872 slightly strengthened the position of the checkweighman and, despite bitter struggles with some employers, the numbers employed in at least one part of the country, West Yorkshire, rapidly increased.[13] Contemporary writers spoke of some of the fathers of the chapel in printing receiving similar powers,[14] and here, with the branch based on the workplace, communications with full-time officials were better than where it had a residential basis. Indeed, the rule of geographical rather than workplace location of branches added to the difficulties of communication already created by local variations in technology and the increasing variety of industry.

The development of the shop steward was thus spasmodic and patchy, constituting a development in industrial relations which occurred piecemeal and pragmatically and which varied according to a variety of factors. As with other union developments, it became entrenched before the problems involved could be examined by the parties concerned and the public at large. Policy during the war, aimed to achieve other objectives, actually speeded up the movement towards workshop representation. At the same time, it provoked some activities which were long to colour the attitudes of the major interested parties towards stewards.

It was during the First World War that the fears of union officials, that shop stewards might disrupt and challenge the authority of the full-time officials, were realized through the growth of the Shop Stewards' Movement.

The Shop Stewards' Movement

Change through revolution is not readily acceptable in a democracy. Here, social institutions in the democratic framework affected by change should themselves broadly concur with a new direction being consciously adopted. This axiom is supreme in British industrial relations with its high regard for the voluntary principle. Consequently, advocates of revolutionary change are regarded with suspicion by the major parties in collective bargaining – the trade unions, management, and government. The Shop Stewards' Movement was so regarded, and it is pertinent to ask how such a revolutionary movement developed in a country so dedicated to constitutionalism, except for a small minority. G. D. H. Cole[15] traces two factors underlying the growth of the movement. He points to the disarmament of the official union movement in the face of the international situation, and the fact that the outbreak of the First World War led to the suspension of the ordinary sanctions behind trade-union bargaining. Secondly, he instances extensive industrial unrest, and its mobilization in organizations readily capable of workshop form. These dissatisfactions were later accentuated by the dilution of labour and the relaxation of some customary trade practices, following the Treasury Agreements of March, 1915.

The Shop Stewards' Movement was firmly rooted in the engineering industry, and usually the local workers' committee consisted of workshop representatives.[16] Its rapid expansion was brought about by dilution and other changes calling for effective workshop organization, by the weakening of the engineering unions following the Treasury Agreements, and by widespread industrial unrest during the war.

The Movement originated on the Clyde, its powerhouse being the Clyde Workers' Committee – the rump of the Central Withdrawal of Labour Committee – which remained in being after the Clyde strike of February, 1915.[17] Clydeside had been among the areas in which, before the war, union members had been most active in seeking to appoint shop stewards. Also, several unofficial and semi-official bodies based on steward and workshop organization had come into existence there before 1914. The Socialist Labour Party was influential, always stressing in its industrial propaganda the importance of workshop organization in obtaining control in industry. More generally, the pre-war neglect by the unions of the growth of workshop organizations,[18] especially on the Clyde with its dearth of full-time officials, also contributed. This neglect allowed local, unofficial movements to develop and encouraged attitudes more local than national. The background to this development was the increase in the number of stewards immediately before 1914. Many unofficial stewards were elected, in unskilled as well as skilled unions, though the former

remained inadequately represented in the wartime Shop
Stewards' Movement.

The war transformed the position of shop stewards since
many, especially those officially accepted by their unions,
became negotiators and representatives in dealing with the
foremen and management on many workshop problems.[19]
In effect, the Treasury Agreements and Munitions of War
Act of July 2nd, 1915, by introducing dilution of labour
and 'leaving certificates' (employees could not leave their
jobs without the consent of their employers) demanded
such representatives, since a union official was needed to
implement these concessions. They were also able to negotiate as technology advanced apace under the impetus of
war and as piece rates became more prevalent. Ironically,
therefore, it was the three main parties to wartime collective
bargaining, Government, management, and unions, who
speeded up the advent of shop stewards. Yet, certain
developments in fact caused the alienation of the three major
parties.

The spark which set the movement alight was the strike
called by the engineering shop stewards on the Clyde against
the Treasury Agreements. For a fortnight, under the leadership of the Central Withdrawal of Labour Committee (the
nucleus of the Shop Stewards' Movement) 8,000–10,000
engineers struck, demanding a wage increase to keep pace
with the increased cost of living. They attracted, however,
the wrath of the Press and of public opinion by disturbing
the supply of munitions and acting against the advice of
their full-time officials.[20] The Committee, however, won
most of its immediate aims, though remaining concerned
about abuses in the dilution of labour and in the system of
leaving certificates. This discontent was not allayed by the
Amending Act of January 1916, which stated that dilutees
(unskilled workers replacing the skilled) should receive
skilled men's pay and laid down safeguards in the use of
leaving certificates. The Committee struck unofficially early
in 1916 against the Government's policy, some receiving
prison sentences.[21] Undeterred, however, an unofficial

strike committee remained in being, linking with others to form a National Workers' Committee Movement to oppose compulsory arbitration and create industrial unionism and workers' control of industry.

From the beginning, the Movement spread. Workshop committees of local stewards sprang up around the country, usually covering a big city such as Sheffield, or a wider area such as Merseyside. Most were content to take their lead from the Clyde Workers' Committee, to accept its policies and constitution. The Movement was strengthened since most employers, wishing to operate dilution and leaving certificates schemes smoothly, were forced to grant *de facto* recognition to shop stewards and the workshop committees.[22] Stewards reported to their organizations on all introductions of dilutee labour, readjustment processes, reduced wages or threats to established union customs; but it was the steward in the workplace upon whom the ordinary member increasingly relied. The majority of shop stewards were not members of the Movement, however, contenting themselves with detailed workshop readjustments.

Many stewards in the Movement were not content merely to negotiate but were also fed on a diet of political ideas by numerous political movements. Thus, the Socialist Labour Party, a Marxist body, counted all leading members of the Clyde Workers' Committee as adherents except William Gallacher (then in the British Socialist Party) and David Kirkwood (who belonged to the Independent Labour Party). The Socialist Labour Party believed in revolution with an industrial take-over by the workers and the dissolution of Parliament instigated by Socialist members. It regarded existing trade unions as bulwarks of capitalism to be destroyed. Consequently, it wanted the Movement to form a new industrial union, and became very critical when its demands were not met.

The influence of the Guild Socialists was far less direct than that of the Socialist Labour Party. They advocated ownership of all means of production by self-governing committees, which would then hand them over to be administered by the workers organized in national guilds. These would, in turn, pay rent to the central coordinating organ of society. This last would be a Guild Congress, which would coordinate national economic development, settle disputes between guilds, and cooperate with bodies representing consumers. All these managing bodies from the workshop to the Guild Congress were to be democratically elected and subject to the control of their constituents. Their establishment was to be by 'encroaching control' accomplished by union pressure to be applied peacefully. These doctrines, depending on gradualism, alienated the Shop Stewards' and Workers' Committee Movement; consequently it, and the Guild Socialists, moved apart in the period 1918–19.

The Syndicalist influence was not strong, only being found in Amalgamation Committees, groups of stewards favouring a distinct revolutionary union movement and calling for violent industrial action. These were disintegrating by 1915.

The Clyde Workers' Committee itself sought control of engineering establishments by workers and management representing the state (not absolute control along Syndicalist lines). The main instrument was to be an all grades committee, composed of representatives of all grades of workers within an establishment. Its desires were revolutionary in involving the abolition of private ownership. The constitution of the committee put its objectives in the following order:

(a) To obtain increasing control over workshop conditions.

(b) To regulate the terms upon which the workers shall be employed.

(c) To organize the workers upon a class basis and to maintain the class struggle until the overthrow of the wages system, the freedom of the workers and the establishment of industrial democracy had been obtained.

'It was,' says Pribicevic, 'perhaps the first major workers' organization to put workers' control in the form of an immediate demand instead of an ultimate objective.'[23]

The Movement believed that emancipation of the workers was to be achieved by themselves, rejecting the state Socialist ideas of nationalization and progressive state action leading to industrial unions as instruments to overthrow capitalism. It left unargued the state's role and whether its industrial organization could administer industry, nor did it examine the mechanics of the struggle for power except to suppose it would be confined to, and decisive in, industry. They presumed that the state would disappear after the fundamental change.

After the 1917 Bolshevik revolution in Russia, the influence of Russian Communism over the Movement increased. Writing in the Movement's journal *Direct Action*, in December, 1919, Gallacher and Campbell stated that the social and industrial organizations would have to 'fight the capitalist state, not to take possession of it but to smash it', and the task of the workers was to develop repressive functions which would 'reduce the capitalist minority to political and social impotence'. These ideas were borrowed directly from Lenin who expounded them in *The State and the Revolution*. The Second Congress of the International enthused the shop steward delegates with the Communist ideal, and in *The Worker* of February 14th, 1920, joint control was repudiated, the National Conference officially declaring workers' control to be the objective. In 1921, the National Conference adopted a clause in the Constitution of the National Workers' Movement stating that 'the objects of the organization shall be the overthrow of capitalism and the setting up of workers' control and management of industry shall be developed'. Only the engineering section of the Committee, its administrative apex, queried the practicability of these ideas and proposed an interregnum of state-appointed managers.

During the war, the engineering and allied industries took the lead, but later the mining industry took over. In 1918, the Miners' Federation of Great Britain had defined its

fundamental demands as nationalization and the concession
of a partial control of the mines to the workers. Indeed, at
the beginning of 1919, a threatened national strike over these
and other demands was only averted by the establishment of
the Royal Commission on the Coal Industry. Among the
miners' demands to it were the establishment of a representative Mining Council, and of coalfield and pit committees,
to which management under public ownership should be
entrusted. Later developments led to the General Strike.[24]

The railways were also centres of militant organization,
and numerous national or local 'Vigilance Committees' or
line committees were formed to guard the interests of sections of workers and to ensure that their grievances received
quick attention from the union. These Vigilance Committees
were ready centres for the ideas of the Movement as they
were unofficial and not subject to union control; together
with the vehicle builders of the locomotive shops, they made
railwaymen active in the Movement. Thus, it was predominantly workers in engineering, railways, and the mines who
chiefly supported it.

Yet, by the early twenties, this revolutionary movement
had petered out. There was no realistic means of attaining
its ends, and the idea of one industrial union, based on the
workshop and workers' committees and envisaged as a
weapon to smash the state, was bound to fail. There were no
'industrial' unions in the country. Secondly, there was little
thought about the role of the state in the proposed general
strike, it being assumed that it would 'wither away' as
Marx predicted. Again, the unions would not have had
sufficient technical expertise to run industries and to fulfil
their functions of representation, protection, and education.
In an established democracy, they had to remain free and
voluntary, which was hardly possible if they were to run
industries. British unionists have been traditionally suspicious of becoming involved in management since they
dislike the idea of facing their own representatives directly or
indirectly in collective bargaining. In any case, since the
unions were at the basis of the politically democratic labour

movement, there was no hope of securing such control unconstitutionally. Indeed, the whole ethos of the Movement ran contrary to the traditional approach of the union movement and most parliamentarians to problems of social change. In a country where constitutionalism was so firmly embedded it was unrealistic to expect unions and workers to use their industrial power against the legal government on such an issue. Yet the authorities became concerned by the National Workers' Committee Movement, thinking it more typical of the feeling of the rank and file than it actually was. It was felt that the popular demand for 'workers' control' might be moderated if national, local, and workshop committees discussed not only wages and conditions of employment but also problems of efficiency and management.[25]

The very real problems of industrial relations of the pre-war years, accentuated by the Shop Stewards' Movement, served as a background to the setting up by the Government in 1916 of a committee, under the chairmanship of J. H. Whitley, to recommend permanent means of improvement in relations between employers and workers. The Reports of this committee are landmarks in the history of British industrial relations; of specific relevance here is that supporting the establishment of joint committees at the workplace. These works committees were to represent employers and workers, and to promote industrial harmony and efficiency. However, after spirited growth between 1917 and 1922, most collapsed, those surviving being more restricted in scope than as envisaged by the Whitley Committee. The composition and functions of this shortlived attempt at workplace consultation varied widely, and unfortunately there is no evidence of the role played by stewards, nor whether they modified more extreme demands for workers' control. However, a lasting hierarchy of Whitley Councils was set up in some sectors, notably in the Civil Service and the Post Office. Perhaps the most important long-term effect of the Shop Stewards' Movement was to tarnish the shop stewards' image as being revolutionary, and therefore made it extremely suspect. This image persisted through the inter-war period, and was exacerbated by events in the early part of the Second World War. After the First World War, the leaders of the Shop Stewards' Movement became even more extreme politically, many becoming connected with the Communist Party in Great Britain, formed in 1920, and directed their energies to its cause.

Partly because of these revolutionary tendencies, some unions brought stewards within the scope of their rulebooks in order to control them. This is true, for example, of the Amalgamated Society of Woodworkers and the Amalgamated Society of Engineers. Some employers also moved towards formal recognition. In engineering, stewards had no nationally recognized rights in workshop negotiations until the end of the First World War. The Engineering and National Employers' Federation and a number of engineering unions, including the Amalgamated Society of Engineers, concluded shop-steward and works-committee agreements in 1917 and 1919. These agreements, consolidated in the Procedure Agreement (in force until 1971 and applying to thirty unions), provided that, in federated establishments, any society party to the agreements might appoint stewards for shops, and that their names and their unions should, on election, be indicated officially to the management. These national agreements did not include recognition of 'grades' of steward or joint shop-steward organization in the workplace, with the exception of works committees, and still do not do so. The convenors of shop stewards authorized by the Amalgamated Engineering Union in 1920, and the Joint Shop Stewards' Works Committees and Confederation stewards sanctioned by the Confederation of Shipbuilding and Engineering Unions twenty-seven years later, do not enjoy formal recognition by federated engineering employers, though individual managements can negotiate with them. Yet the 1917–19 agreements represented 'a most important incentive for engineering stewards',[26] since they gave them the basis of formal status in the factory 'even though this was not as comprehensive as some of them may have desired'.

Even this process of constitutionalization could not, however, prevent the disappearance of many representatives *qua* representatives during the period 1920–35. 'Successive reports by the AEU's executive council suggest that the breakdown in domestic negotiations was widespread though not necessarily complete. The evidence shows, however, that many firms were no longer prepared to tolerate the activities of stewards.'[27] Given the stewards' image in general, it is not surprising that during the Depression of the twenties and thirties, firms ended negotiations with stewards, and that the Amalgamated Engineering Union's full-time officials failed to strengthen their stewards' position beyond the agreement of 1922.

In 1920–35, there appears to have been little shop-steward activity beyond 'minimum' union administration, and no evidence is available either from union histories or published works on the General Strike. Firstly, with the onset of recession in 1921, and the Depression, union organization in the workshop was badly hit. Largely, representatives either ceased to exist as such, or were reduced to being watchdogs, merely ensuring that employers complied with minimum terms and conditions of employment. With labour markets favouring employers, stewards could attempt little but to maintain the *status quo*, and were presumably often victimized. Even in those industries which traditionally had stewards, such as printing, the fathers of the chapel, although still existing, had few opportunities to be other than defensive in their dealings with management. Also, the radical characteristics of the Shop Stewards' Movement probably alienated many union leaders, who may have countenanced even the disappearance of some stewards rather than fight employers on the issue. This attitude might have been buttressed by the opinion that the way to economic recovery was by cutting wages to reduce prices, thus making goods more competitive. Such an atmosphere was hardly conducive to strong workshop representation. Finally, although important during the war, stewards had not long been accepted in industry, not being considered as essential as they are today. Their disappearance would not therefore have created much opposition.

The Second World War and after

With the improvement in the trade position in the later thirties came a revival in the numbers of stewards. Evidence from the A E U shows[28] that numbers increased since average payments to stewards in 1935–8 were nearly three times as great as for the preceding four years. However, it was not until the Second World War that this increase became really marked. It is widely, though not universally, accepted that, during the 1939–45 period, stewards channelled their energies into more constructive activities *within* the official framework than in the First World War.[29] Mrs Inman[30] notes that, during rearmament and early war years, an unofficial stewards' organization developed in the engineering and shipbuilding industries, and as early as 1936 there were signs of a movement in the aircraft industry. Workers in this industry were to be the vanguard as the unofficial movement developed during the war.

Early in April 1940, the first meeting of a national shop stewards' council took place in Birmingham and planned to develop nationally. Political aims were not mentioned, the council concentrating on wage grievances among munition workers, and particularly those in shipbuilding. Apparently, some of the rank and file wanted to follow such an organization, and the author notes feeling among them against the union officials who once again were drawn into official collaboration with the Government, which was considered by some members as tantamount to 'selling out to the bosses'. An aggravating fact was that educational work to explain government and trade-union policy to the rank and file had not been extensively developed by the union movement. Further, experienced trade-union officials at headquarters and in the districts had accepted jobs in expanded Government bodies, their successors lacking experience and being often less effective. This contributed to the growth of work-place bargaining, as stewards became more numerous and important in order to cope with dilution problems and quickening technological changes, as in the First World War. Indeed, this process was extended as the branch declined in importance due to difficulties of attendance at branch meetings.[31] Opportunities were therefore plentiful for stewards to act independently of the unions, as well as facilitating the growth of the unofficial organization.

Yet, in practice, the influence of the unofficial shop-steward movement over ordinary members was severely limited. This can be illustrated by the number of strikes, which increased after 1941 despite being condemned by the Communist Party, which had much influence through its members in the unofficial shop-steward movement. As Professor Turner has observed, these figures appear to convict the Communists of agitational incompetence.[32]

The strength of the movement was the aircraft industry in the Midlands and the engineering shops and shipyards on the Clyde. Twice, in the winter of 1940–1, shop stewards on the Clyde settled strikes through the intervention of men well known in public life, in each case bypassing the con-stitutional negotiating machinery. Inman notes that these disputes indicated that the movement drew strength from the tactless and highhanded actions of some foremen and managements, and from lack of cooperation between managements and men. Finally, in the engineering industry, stewards did not always pass grievances to the Confedera-tion Committees, not being represented on them, and many stewards took care to negotiate as much as possible them-selves.

The impact of the unofficial stewards' movement was marginal, for two principal reasons. Firstly, the Communist Party encouraged the war effort after the invasion of Russia in June, 1941. Secondly, to ensure better cooperation at plant level, joint production committees were organized under the auspices of the Government, after – but not necessarily as a consequence of – the Engineering Shop

Stewards' National Council meeting in London during October, 1941. These committees were supported by the Engineering and Allied Trades Shop Stewards' National Council largely through *The New Propeller*, the organ of the unofficial organization in the aircraft industry. The functions of these committees varied widely. Sometimes, they took the lead in discussions with management, even on questions normally reserved for the collective-bargaining procedure, such as wage rates, and the role of the stewards other than as committee members was small. Elsewhere, the committees' discussions concerned technical and production questions, others being left to the stewards. The committees varied in strength but the best were where trade-union organization was strong, where the stewards actively supported the committee with the aim of winning the war, where representatives were technically able, and where the stewards joined them to discuss problems and solutions.[33] Certainly, shop stewards did much constructive work during the war, and this had many byproducts. For example, Jefferys observed that 'the prodigious growth in membership and influence of the AEU was by no means an automatic process. It rested largely on the painstaking work and feats performed by the stewards up and down the country who gave up much of their limited spare time and evenings and frequently sacrificed their earnings to devote their attention to improving the condition of their workmates'.[34]

This attitude encouraged unions to appoint stewards more freely, and accounts for their increased numbers during the Second World War. More fundamentally, however, such factors as the change in the balance of power in the labour market resulting from reductions in the numbers unemployed, technological developments necessitating changes in jobs and job rates, the dilution of labour, the relaxation of trade-union custom and practice, and innumerable new regulations to be explained to members all brought an increase in steward numbers. Further, the increasing numbers of women in trade unions during the war demanded shop stewards to represent this special group, women stewards again swelling the total. Marsh and Coker noted that the AEU's survey of 1947 revealed that almost 5 per cent of stewards were women.[35] In addition, the Engineering Employers' Federation agreed with some unions, including the AEU, that steward approval had to be sought by federated employers before labour was diluted in any establishment.[36] This increased the importance of stewards.

The numbers of stewards have also increased since the war. After examining AEU records, Marsh and Coker[37] suggest that the increase was about 50 per cent between 1947 and 1961. They showed that the increase in federated engineering establishments was proportionately greater than overall, a possible explanation being that the 1919 Agreement made recognition of stewards obligatory on federated firms, firms outside having no such duty. However, as the AEU relies more on its stewards than some unions, its growth of shop steward numbers may be somewhat higher. Marsh and Coker indicate that the numbers of AEU shop stewards in federated establishments increased three times faster than that of manual workers in such establishments in 1947–61.[38]

The total number of shop stewards in the United Kingdom has been variously estimated, at different times, at 90,000, 100,000–120,000, 175,000 and 200,000. The first figure was suggested by Clegg, Killick and Adams in 1961 although they admit that it was 'little better than a guess'[39], and Marsh and Coker suggested the second in their article already referred to. The third, and most authoritative estimate appeared in 1968, being that of W. E. J. McCarthy and S. R. Parker. They suggest that ' . . . the total of stewards may be put at about 175,000. This represents an increase of about 14% over the last ten years.'[40] The fourth figure is taken from the TUC Annual Report of 1960. All are estimates and, given the fact that trade unions do not keep accurate records of shop steward numbers, it is not possible to be more specific.

Over the post-war decades, the ratio of full-time union officials to union members has improved little, against a dramatic increase in the number of shop stewards. This means that officials have to cope with increasingly large numbers of stewards, which clearly complicates the problems of union control of workplace activity. The supervision of full-time officials must often be minimal, and wide responsibilities are in practice now carried by stewards. In many cases, the continued functioning of unions rests on their voluntary efforts. This strengthens many shop stewards *vis-à-vis* their unions, and emphasizes the problem of controlling them. With imperfect and inadequate official union links with the workplace, the precise relationship between workplace representatives and the unions externally becomes important. A useful starting point is the instructions to stewards in union rulebooks, and the advice in handbooks published for their use, for these documents outline the formal relationship between stewards and their unions.

References

1. Phelps Brown, E. H., *The Growth of British Industrial Relations*, Macmillan, 1959, p 297.
2. The earliest mention of the chapel system is to be found in Joseph Moxton's *Mechanical Exercises*, 1682.
3. Fyrth, H. J. and Collins, Henry, *The Foundry Workers*, Amalgamated Union of Foundry Workers, 1960, p 26.
4. Turner, H. A., *Trade Union Growth, Structure and Policy*, George Allen and Unwin, 1962, p 85.
5. Fyrth and Collins, *op cit*, p 128.
6. Jefferys, James B., *The Story of the Engineers*, Lawrence and Wishart, 1945, p 137.
7. Roberts, B. C., *Trade Union Government and Administration*, G. Bell and Sons, 1957, p 58.
8. Phelps-Brown, *op cit*, p 287.
9. Jefferys, *op cit*, pp 165–6.
10. Clegg, H. A., *General Union in a Changing Society*, Blackwell, 1964, p 27–8.
11. Quoted in Clegg, H. A., Fox, Allan, and Thompson, A. F., *A History of British Trade Unions since 1889*, Vol 1, Oxford University Press, 1964, p 432.

12. Machin, Frank, *The Yorkshire Miners*, National Union of Mineworkers, 1958.
13. *Ibid*, p 248.
14. Webb, Sidney and Beatrice, *History of Trade Unionism*, Longmans, Green and Co., 1950 edition, p 299.
15. Cole, G. D. H., *Workshop Organization*, Oxford University Press, 1923.
16. See Pribicevic, B., *The Shop Steward Movement and Workers' Control*, Basil Blackwell, 1959.
17. Cole, G. D. H., *op cit*, pp 28–35.
18. *Ibid*, p 36.
19. *Ibid*, p 42.
20. Pelling, H., *A History of British Trade Unionism*, Penguin Books, 1963, p 151.
21. *Ibid*, pp 154–5.
22. Cole, G. D. H., *op cit*, p 66.
23. Pribicevic, B., *op cit*.
24. Cole, G. D. H., *op cit*, p 127.
25. See Pelling, H., *op cit*, p 160.
26. Marsh, A. I. and Coker, E. E., 'Shop Steward Organization in the Engineering Industry', *British Journal of Industrial Relations*, June 1963.
27. Marsh and Coker, *op cit*, p 175.
28. Jefferys, *op cit*, pp 241–2.
29. Marsh and Coker, *op cit*.
30. Inman, P., *Labour in the Munitions Industries*, HMSO and Longmans, Green and Co., 1957, p 401.
31. Inman, *op cit*, p 400.
32. Turner, H. A., *The Trend of Strikes*, Leeds University Press, 1963.
33. Inman, *op cit*, p 388.
34. Jefferys, *op cit*, p 201.
35. Marsh and Coker, *op cit*.
36. *Ibid*.
37. *Ibid*.
38. *Ibid*, p 40.
39. See *Trade Union Officers*, *op cit*, p 153.
40. See Research Paper 10 for the Royal Commission on Trade Unions and Employers' Associations, *Shop Stewards and Workshop Relations*, HMSO, London, 1968, p 15, para 56.

Chapter Three

Unions, Shop Stewards and Rulebooks

A problem which faces all shop stewards is that of reconciling his role as a representative of union *members* with that of representing the *union* in the workplace. The unions, as institutions, face a similar dilemma in regulating their stewards' activities without stifling initiative. This chapter examines the nature of the instructions and advice given to stewards by different unions' rulebooks and in some shop-steward handbooks. As will be seen, their provisions are sparsely and vaguely worded, though a primary source of reference for all union officers. The failure of some rulebooks to define realistically a steward's function and responsibilities may reflect the attitude of a union to workplace representatives. Some unions appear to want to play down their significance, others deliberately leave their role relatively undefined to allow enlargement as dictated by local circumstances. In other cases, such brevity may merely reflect the difficulties of making rules for the wide range of industries and workplaces involved. Further, there are variations between unions in the method and degree to which executive leadership is balanced by lay control. However, contact between a union's higher officials and its stewards can take many forms, and unions may well prefer informality. Nevertheless, few rulebooks have been amended to cover the new roles of stewards, or to build in additional facilities for them within the unions' administrative and policy forming (or informing) *machinery*.

We first outline in detail the provisions made for stewards in the rulebooks and handbooks of seven unions. The dates of the rulebooks are given where possible, and occasional reference is made to the procedural sections of some collective agreements.

The Transport and General Workers' Union (1962)

The union issues a handbook of some eighty pages to shop stewards, but its rulebook deals with them in a few lines. Rule 11 provides that 'shop stewards shall be elected wherever possible by the membership in organized factories, garages, depots, wharves and on building jobs', but it does not list their functions. Rather, it goes on to assure stewards of the union's 'fullest support and protection'. Emphasis is given by the provision that ' . . . immediate inquiry shall be undertaken by the appropriate trade group committee into every case of dismissal of a shop steward with a view to preventing victimization either open or concealed'. The same rule, alternatively, allows a branch to appoint collectors and/or shop stewards to gather members' contributions. Those who undertake these duties are remunerated in accordance with General Executive Council regulations – currently $7\frac{1}{2}$ per cent of contributions collected. The union formerly debarred members of the Communist or Fascist Parties from holding either lay or full-time office.

Shop stewards are supervised by their branch, defined in the members' handbook as 'the place to which the member takes his problems . . .' The subordinate role of stewards to branch officers is further emphasized in the Members' *Handbook*, viz.: 'Where collectors are appointed they operate under the supervision of the branch secretary. This also applies, in certain cases, to shop stewards, who have the responsibility for dealing with minor matters arising at their members' place of work.'

The shop stewards' handbook

The handbook offers advice to T & G W U representatives in
all industries, acknowledging that the steward *is* the union
as far as members are concerned, being thus responsible for
the image of the union. The need for unity and loyalty is
stressed, and stewards are asked to help members with
grievances and problems, either personally or via the union.
Stewards are reminded of their responsibilities to recruit
new members, maintain membership, and turn 'card holders
into trade unionists'. They are advised to know their agreements and the procedure, never to depart from the latter
and, if in doubt, to consult the district officer. Informal
agreements, custom and practice are stressed as no less
important.

In relations with managements, stewards are counselled
not to bypass the foreman, for tactical as well as courtesy
reasons. Skill and honesty rather than noise and sharp
practice are recommended in negotiations. Stewards should
build up the loyalty of their members by their handling of
grievances, to keep them informed, etc, to be confident of
support and room for manoeuvre in negotiations. Stewards
should pass on union news, circulate the union journal,
stimulate interest in branch activities, and encourage participation.

Looking after members' problems in the workshop is put
forward as the steward's main function, but close liaison
with the district officer is again firmly recommended, particularly at all stages of major developments. The handbook
stresses that he is normally necessary in important negotiations. A systematic plan for progressing grievances is recommended, emphasizing the need to obtain and check the facts,
to follow procedure and the manner in which to approach
management, reporting back to the member concerned,
other members, and the branch, etc.

The handbook then outlines the major features of the
Factories Act, and the steward's role in its enforcement. He
is advised to press for and support joint factory safety
committees, to report all accidents and, with management's

permission, to check the accident book. The pamphlet outlines the procedure for claiming, and the level of, state and union benefits.

Six pages are devoted to joint consultation and its uses, outlining the topics normally acknowledged as appropriate to it, and recommending it as a source of information as well as a body which may rectify some grievances. Some differences of function between negotiation and consultation, and the consequent need for different approaches, are explained. Stewards are advised to report to the branch officer anything arising on a JCC which appears to conflict with union policy or rights, and the union explains that for these reasons it likes to control the nominations for worker representatives.

The handbook tells stewards how to recruit new members, how to write letters, make reports, and claim union financial benefits. It then outlines the structure of the union, sources of information within it, educational facilities, and covers local Trades Councils and the TUC.

The National Union of General and Municipal Workers (1965)

The NUGMW makes provision for collecting stewards, under the direction of the Branch Secretary and the Branch Committee, and shop stewards, who fall under the District Committee. (Often one member holds both positions.) The collecting steward can sign membership cards, receiving 10 per cent as commission. In addition, 'he shall, in a legitimate manner, see that the workers at any place of work become members of the union', and 'shall notify the Branch Secretary of any infringement of the rules of the union coming to his notice'.

There are several methods of appointment or election of NUGMW shop stewards, depending 'whichever is the most suitable in a particular case'. This can be by majority vote on a show of hands, or by ballot, of the members at the workplace, or 'by a majority vote on a show of hands at a branch meeting', or 'by common consent among the members that the office shall be filled by a member appointed by the District Secretary'. Stewards must give the District Committee 'an undertaking to observe the rules of the union, and at all times act in conformity with the decisions and policy laid down by the governing authorities of the union'. District secretaries are to be informed of all appointments. With the permission of District Committees, branches may levy members to provide funds for negotiating stewards for loss of earnings not otherwise provided for.

The NUGMW is unique in that its rulebook states that shop stewards' duties shall be as defined in the shop stewards' handbook.

The shop stewards' handbook

This emphasizes the recently extended work of stewards, particularly in joint consultation. Their organization and protective function in the workshop is acknowledged. Stewards are expected to set a good example by observing union rules, attending branch meetings regularly, and keeping informed of union activities and policies. A thorough knowledge of agreements, of PAYE, National Insurance, and bonus calculations is desirable. The union's educational facilities are recommended. The handbook covers methods of election, recruitment, and collecting duties – stressing the aim of a 100 per cent membership.

Stewards must take an interest in members' welfare, from individual grievances to safety, and the Factories Act. Poor attendance at branch meetings is deprecated but acknowledged, and the consequent value of stewards as linking the union's machinery to the rank and file is stressed. They are asked to publicize the union's activities and services, particularly in passing on information during national negotiations. Conversely, they should 'report all matters of consequence on organization, members' requirements, grievances settled and practices of management that may affect working agreements' to the branch secretary.

On handling members' complaints involving negotiations with management, the handbook says that 'no hard and fast line can be drawn between cases that come within his power to deal with and those which should be referred to the Branch for action by District officials. In the absence of specific instructions from the District Secretary he should be guided by the custom and practice of the industry.' However, the handbook suggests that the following can usually be dealt with at shop level – breaches of agreements or established working conditions, piecework and rates subsidiary to agreements, overtime working, holidays, canteens, and general factory welfare, and personal matters affecting individual employees.

The handbook then emphasizes that 'any question implicating the terms of a signed agreement or which can be properly regarded as a subject for such an agreement must be reported without delay to the branch secretary who will refer it to the District office. This applies also to important questions of principle by which a number of members would be affected.' The steward is reminded that he has no power to sanction strikes, and that, should his members suddenly stop work, he should ascertain the cause, advising an immediate resumption. He should then start the procedure to discuss the grievance with management. Stewards are told always to approach management accompanied by the member concerned in any question, or by another shop steward. Moreover, before any approach, he should know that the member, or the majority of members, approve of the action he proposes.

The handbook refers to the inter-union workplace machinery of the CSEU, but where none exists, shop stewards 'should nevertheless consult and cooperate with stewards of other unions if joint action appears to be advisable'. They should attempt to reach agreement with other unions' stewards particularly on questions of demarcation, but any attempts by such stewards to persuade the unions' members to transfer must be reported immediately.

Joint consultative machinery is recommended to stewards,

whose potential contribution to its effectiveness is under-
lined. The importance of safety, and of recording all accidents is stressed. The handbook then briefly outlines the structure and organization of the union, concluding with copies
of the procedural sections of three collective agreements.

The Amalgamated Engineering Union (1960)

Like many other craft and ex-craft unions, the AEU is char-
acterized by considerable decentralized and lay authority,
this being embodied in the District Committee. AEU shop
stewards are authorized by the District Committee, and are
responsible to it.

Rule 13 provides that 'District Committees shall authorize
the appointment of shop stewards and shop committees in
Works and departments in their respective districts . . . and
committees (are) to be under the direction and control of the
District Committee'. Stewards elected by the members
cannot function without the District Committee's approval.
Moreover, 'the powers and duties of shop stewards and shop
committees shall be defined by the District Committees with
the approval of the Executive Council . . .' The union allows
that 'stewards or shop committees may appoint a convenor,
who must himself be a shop steward . . .', but again the
District Committee defines his powers and duties.

Shop stewards, as lay officials, are strongly represented on
the District Committee, thus helping to define their own
powers and duties and those of other stewards. Rule 13
states that 'shop stewards shall be directly represented on the
District Committee on the basis of one shop steward for
every 5,000 members or part thereof . . . elected at a meeting
of shop stewards called by the District Secretary in December'. The District Committee must convene the shop stewards and convenors at least once a quarter, paying 10*s* (50p)
to stewards and 12*s* 6*d* (62½p) to convenors attending.
Smaller fees are paid to those who only submit written
reports to the meeting.

Rule 13 lays down four minimum duties for AEU shop stewards, shop committees, and convenors:

(*a*) To examine and sign the contribution cards of all members at least once a quarter. Members refusing to show their cards to the shop steward are to be reported to the District Committee. This also applies to pay tickets.

(*b*) 'To use every endeavour to see that all men starting are duly qualified trade unionists.'

(*c*) To see that all persons are complying with the practice of the shop and district, and receiving approved rates.

(*d*) 'To report to the District Committee any case in which the position is not satisfactory and cannot be adjusted within the shop.'

Stewards are to 'interview' foremen or other management representatives on questions arising in the shop 'only when accompanied by another member ... provided that no question involving a principle, change of practice or stoppage of work shall be determined in any shop until it has been reported to and ratified by the District Committee, and that in all matters shop stewards, convenors and shop committees shall act within the rules and principles laid down by the District Committee and the Executive Council ... and in national or district agreements.'

Stewards must have twelve months' adult membership, with discretion for new shops. Rule 19 permits payment of dispute benefit for 'members discharged for acting on legitimate shop deputations, authorized, or afterwards sanctioned, by the Branch or District Committee ...'

The shop stewards' Manual

The manual aims to guide stewards in general principles, and emphasizes the trust placed in him by his members. The manual assumes that the steward will represent them for the next twelve months in matters connected with their employment. Stewards' representation on the District Committees and their quarterly meetings is used to illustrate special channels open to them in the union.

The A E U divides the steward's job into two, placing recruitment and maintenance of membership before the 'maintenance of the best possible wages and working conditions for our members', although the manual devotes more space to the latter. The aim suggested is that of 100 per cent membership via at least quarterly card inspections, but in recruiting stewards are told that a volunteer outweighs a 'conscript'. Stewards should keep members interested in the union's work, encourage branch attendance, and circulate the union's journal. Special sections detail the recruitment of juvenile and women workers. On promoting members' interests, stewards are advised to ensure that wages, etc, at least equal those provided for by collective agreements, if necessary by examining payslips, and if they fall below these to report to the convenor or district secretary. 'Justifiable grievances' are to go through normal procedures, and stewards are reminded that many of these involve members first approaching the foreman. Frequently raising trivial matters with the foreman is regarded as bad tactics, and stewards should be sure always to have a witness. Any settlement is to be reported immediately to the convenor or district secretary. Stewards' bargaining opportunities are described thus: 'Remember that you, at shop or factory level, have the best chance to settle any grievance. The higher the stage in procedure, the more difficult it becomes to reach mutual agreement. One of the employers' most familiar arguments at national level is "we cannot grant you this for the workers at this firm, because your members all over the country will want the same".'

The procedure for fixing piecework prices or times in 'federated' establishments is then covered; stewards in doubt should, again, consult the convenor or the district secretary. The role of the convenor is outlined, all correspondence to the district secretary going through him. Stewards should fill in quarterly report forms, and also inform the convenor and district secretary of developments concerning wages, conditions, or membership.

The function of a Joint Shop Stewards' Committee under the CSEU is mentioned, with the need for constant co-operation between various union workshop representatives. Joint production committees, and the steward's role in the event of accidents, are explained.

Finally, the manual advises stewards to be firm but flexible, to remember they do not function separately, and should never decide nor act in isolation. The steward is reminded of the supporting services available to him from the convenor and District Secretary to specialists in the head office, and his responsibility to keep them informed is impressed on him. The union recommends its own and external educational courses, and gives a reading list. The final section contains procedural and other agreements with the EEF and the AEU rules relating to shop stewards.

The Electrical Trades Union (1965)

The ETU rulebook places its stewards explicitly under the (elected) area full-time official, ordering them to obey the executive council (Rule 17). 'In each shop, yard and under-taking of any description a shop steward shall be elected at a meeting convened for that purpose . . .' An existing steward must call such a meeting annually for the elections. All voting is by show of hands, with a second vote between the two leading candidates, failing an absolute majority. In the event of a tie ' . . . the candidate to be elected shall be determined by lot'. Area secretaries are to be notified of the election of a steward.

The union provides for senior stewards 'in large under-takings where there are shop stewards in several depart-ments'. These *may* be appointed by the stewards themselves or 'if they consider it necessary then a meeting of all the members employed in the shop . . . shall be convened for the purpose'. The senior shop steward must already be a shop steward, and is annually re-elected.

The rank and file can call a meeting of all members in the shop. A shop steward may do this '. . . at such times as he thinks proper and whenever requested to do so by one quarter of the members so employed . . .' Members are to produce their cards for inspection or periodic collection by the steward on notification. Any member refusing, and failing to give good reason to a *meeting of members* on the job, is to be reported by the steward to his branch secretary.

Unusually, the ETU provides for the cooperation of their members 'on jobs where less than four members are employed and a shop steward of another trade has been appointed . . .' with another union's steward, in inspecting cards and maintaining of union conditions.

The ETU rulebook outlines a comparatively detailed list of duties. These include reporting to the area secretary on card inspections, or violation of rates, conditions, and customary privileges at the workplace, and all cases of over-time work. He is to interview the foreman or a manager on any question arising on the job 'provided that no question involving a principle, change of practice or stoppage of work shall be determined by the shop steward or other members on any job until the matter has been reported and the decision has had the approval of the appropriate Area official or . . . the Executive Council'. He is to ensure that union rules are observed in any strike or lockout. He can only accept conditions on a job where members have given prior approval, and if conditions comply with union rules, agreements, and policies. The ETU emphasizes inter-union cooperation in the workplace, in that the steward is to work in conjunction with other shop stewards and works commit-tees. However, he cannot commit his members to any joint decision without their consent, or contrary to the policies of the union. Finally, the steward is to perform any other duties required from time to time by the area official or executive council.

Rule 10 clarifies the role of the steward in relation to the individual member. The member is to report to his branch any matter of the conduct or business of the union, or the conduct of any of its officers or members, but any matter concerning his employment to his shop steward, or failing one, with his area official.

Stewards must have one year's membership and male stewards must be over twenty-one, but women qualify for appointment at eighteen. Members of the Communist Party cannot hold office (Rule 9). While the payment of contributions is the responsibility of each member, twelve or more employed together may appoint a money steward, with branch approval. He is paid 5 per cent of his collections.

The ETU has improved its communications machinery, and Rule 18 provides for national and area meetings of shop stewards (and others) on industrial lines. National Industrial Conferences are to be convened between each Biennial Delegate Conference of delegates from electrical contracting, electricity supply, shipbuilding and ship repair engineering, and other industries. Secondly, area secretaries are to convene annual Area Industrial Conferences of shop stewards from the same industries, to elect delegates and submit motions to the National Industrial Conferences. Further, area officials may call meetings of stewards in a given section of industry, to aid communication on issues as they arise. The executive council consider such meetings to be of benefit to the members concerned.

The National Graphical Association (1964)

The NGA makes the formation of at least one chapel and the appointment of a father of the chapel obligatory on members in all offices recognized by the union, if there are four or more members. The members are to draw up rules for administration, to be submitted to the appropriate branch for approval. Chapel collectors are to be appointed by the chapels, and the FOC must sign monthly subscription lists, indicating those in arrears, before dispatch to the branch.

Part-time union officers, whether branch secretaries or

presidents or fathers or clerks of chapels, are given special
compensation against victimization. They receive benefit at
the rate nationally agreed for their job, unless all members
are affected by a strike or lockout. Ordinary members receive
one-third or one-half the minimum grade rate of the
branch, depending on how many are involved.

The rulebook emphasizes the role of the branch, rather
than of the chapel and its officials, in rectifying breaches of
union rules, encroachments on the customs of the trade, the
regulation of apprenticeships, hours, wages, etc. Where
settlement is impossible, branches and regions must refer
to the executive council.

The British Iron, Steel and Kindred Trades Association

Works representatives in BISAKTA are branch officers,
elected at special meetings each December. The branch committee is to supervise ballots. 'Any member refusing without
reasonable cause to take office in a branch when nominated
shall be fined 2s 6d (12½p).' Rule 9 further provides that 'No
person ... who has been guilty of ... acting in any way
injuriously to the Association should be permitted to hold
any office whatsoever in the branch ... or hold any position
as an officer or representative of the Association'. The
executive council has wide discretion in interpretation here.

Works representatives are 'to interview employers when
instructed by the branch committee on matters arising in the
works affecting the terms or conditions of employment' of
branch members. However, if 'the matter is one of urgency
the works representative may, after consultation with the
branch secretary, arrange to interview the employer's representatives before receiving the instructions of the branch
committee, but the case must be reported to the branch committee without unnecessary delay. The works representative
should, as far as is practicable, be accompanied by the branch
secretary, together with a small deputation of ... members

concerned.' The Association explicitly withholds allowance
for loss of work from deputation members, except for works
representatives and branch secretaries, for whom allowance
is made only for unavoidable loss. Such claims go forward
to Central Office only after the approval of the branch
committee.

The procedural role of the works representative is given in
Rule 19, which states that should a dispute arise 'which in
any way might lead to a stoppage of work, arrangements
shall be made for the works representative accompanied by a
deputation to interview the employer or his representative.
. . . Failing a settlement by this means the branch secretary
shall without delay report the whole facts of the dispute to
the divisional officer . . . It shall not be permissible for any
member(s) to strike employment without the authority and
sanction of the Executive Council.'

When payment of contributions at branch meetings is
impracticable, the executive council may authorize other
arrangements through branch stewards, who are paid
quarterly on an incentive basis.

Rule 31 allows for the payment of 'victim benefit' to any
member dismissed for taking active part in the affairs of the
Association. No handbook for works representatives is
published.

The Draughtsmen's and Allied Technicians' Association (1965)

DATA provides for the annual election of an office committee of at least three members, the number of members
permitting. The committees are to ensure the observation of
all company, local, or national agreements and to report
difficulties to the branch secretary or divisional organizer.
In disputes, it is their first duty to report to the branch
secretary and divisional organizer to obtain advice on how
to conduct negotiations. The committee is thus responsible
for all negotiations between the office and management,

'unless it is considered advisable that such negotiations should be conducted through the branch or divisional council or through the executive committee'. The committee is to report the results of negotiations to members, and to the branch council on its exercise of its functions, ensuring that the corresponding member carries out his duties satisfactorily to members and the council. It is to form the nucleus to represent members on joint committees with other workers. The committee is to be 'linked up' with the Branch council, kept informed of Association affairs, and to meet fortnightly, although special meetings of the committee or office may be convened.

The corresponding member has to place all correspondence and information dealing with the Association before the committee. A corresponding member is to be elected annually in each office, retiring members being eligible for re-election. DATA lays down that, in large offices, there shall be at least one CM for approximately every thirty members.

A single CM is to act as secretary and treasurer of the office committee; otherwise, the committee selects one of the CMs to act in these capacities. The corresponding member is to collect members' subscriptions, circulate the union's journals, notices, leaflets, etc, and maintain records required by the Association. He is to advise the branch secretary and divisional organizer of any changes in office conditions, wages, etc, and must attend meetings of CMs convened by the branch council. Committee and corresponding members' expenses are paid by the branch secretary, after approval.

In offices with insufficient members to form an office committee, the members are to appoint a CM, being themselves responsible for the functions of a committee.

Appraisal

A glimpse at these union handbooks and at the response to our questionnaire shows that union rulebooks are not exhaustive in providing regulations for shop stewards. This is a common and accurate supposition among students of industrial relations, though this survey shows that union rulebooks display wide differences in approach and comprehensiveness. Some unions, such as USDAW and NUFTO, which have shop stewards, fail to mention them; others, notably the ETU, have made efforts to outline their position and duties and also to cater for their increased importance. Therefore, it may be useful to summarize the major provisions made for stewards, noting issues on which rulebooks are silent.

In addition to those outlined above, the rulebooks and, *where issued*, steward handbooks of another twenty-three unions have been studied,[1] being referred to below. Some of these unions have recently amalgamated, but their rulebooks nevertheless indicate the different approaches to, and provisions made for, workplace representatives.

(1) *The presence of shop stewards*

Although, in practice, most stewards are elected by the members they are to represent, this is not always made clear. Some rulebooks prescribe that stewards are to be elected, eg, T & GWU, CWU, AUFW, ETU, but few provide for suitable special meetings. Others simply state, unspecifically, that they 'be appointed'. Two, the NUGMW and the CEU, allow the district official or union executive to appoint stewards in certain circumstances. Unions vary in their requirements of when stewards are to be present. Some state that they 'shall' or must be appointed or elected, eg, the ETU, NUSMW & C, CEU, DATA, Bakers, CWU, etc; others lay down that there 'shall' be stewards 'wherever possible' (T & GWU) or 'wherever necessary' (NUGMW), and others that there 'may' be stewards, eg, HDEU. As noted, some unions make no provision at all. Perhaps the greatest emphasis on workplace representatives is among the printing unions, and those with a large proportion of members in the building industry. The NUPBPW and the NGA insist on the formation of a chapel and the appointment of an FOC when there are, respectively, two or four members employed. The ASW and the PTU oblige the first member on a site to act as steward, pending the employment of more and an election. In the latter union, the district secretary can convene a meeting for this purpose, issuing credentials immediately on the site. If there is no steward in a bakery, the 'senior man' is to organize an election; in the ETU and the ASW, the 'retiring' steward has this responsibility. Among the white-collar unions, DATA members must undertake the duties of corresponding member and office committee failing sufficient numbers for normal elections. The method of election and the electorate are rarely specified, though the ETU stipulates a show of hands, laying down procedure if there is no overall majority. The common practice appears to be a show of hands by the members of the union to be represented,[2] but in some cases, eg, BISAKTA, elections are at branch meetings.

Although, in practice, most stewards are eligible for repeated re-election, this is infrequently stated. Some unions do not state a period of office, eg, AEU, NUSMW & C, but many specify twelve months, eg, NUPBPW, ETU, PTU, and AUFW. Fathers of the chapel in NATSOPA are subject to quarterly re-election, and the NUFTO handbook recommends twice yearly elections.

The qualifications of those eligible to stand are rarely mentioned. Among others, the AEU, ETU, and rubber-workers make one year's union membership a condition (except in new factories), while the CEU recommends three years at the trade where practicable. The ETU is the only one to stipulate a minimum age, and the HDEU alone in explicitly debarring those holding supervisory positions. Members of the Communist Party or Fascist Parties are not eligible in the ETU and HDEU by rule, while members or supporters of 'prescribed bodies' are ineligible in the CAWU as are 'members acting injuriously to the Association' in BISAKTA.

The NUPBPW and the Bakers allow for deputies on different shifts, as does the CEU in other circumstances, but only the Bakers and DATA recommend specific maximum limits to constituency size, though the AUFW does this more generally.

Only one union, the Bakers, *explicitly* allows for stewards to be removed by shop meetings while in office, though the confidence of members and union executives is a *sine qua non* to most stewards. In several unions, the executive body can replace a steward 'in the interests of the union'. The emphasis on obeying rules implicitly makes any steward in breach of any rule liable to lose his credentials, though by whose authority is seldom specified.

(2) *Collectors*

Practically all the unions studied either permit the appointment of collectors or make this a function of the shop steward. In practice, many stewards hold both positions, and no union prohibited this. Generally, the procedure for collecting and paying dues is outlined in detail, often fairly severe penalties being provided for any breach. The commission paid to collectors varies widely, from $2\frac{1}{2}$ per cent in NUFTO to 10 per cent in the NUGMW and NUPE. Most ex-craft unions pay 5 per cent, while the Tailors and Garment Workers rewards collections from female members more highly and the BISAKTA operates an elaborate incentive scheme.

While stewards may benefit from being collectors, few rulebooks provide for specific payment to stewards for their other duties. NUBSO provides for loss of earnings to be covered by the branch, NUGMW branches can levy members to cover stewards' 'loss of earnings', the NUSMW & C allows 8*s* 6*d* ($42\frac{1}{2}$p) per hour for employment lost, the PTU allows a nominal sum for out-of-pocket expenses, the CWU payment of an honorarium by the branch, ASSET covers any loss of salary, and chapel funds in NATSOPA have to 'pay the FOC for his services'. The AEU pays stewards 10*s* (50p) and convenors 12*s* 6*d* ($62\frac{1}{2}$p) for attending quarterly meetings. Thus, rulebooks do not provide for stewards' remuneration other than to cover loss of earnings and expenses, though some do not explicitly cover this. BISAKTA emphasizes this financial constraint to works representatives and deputation members.

(3) *The answerability of stewards*

In few unions could a steward give a straightforward reply to a question on this topic. His reply would vary with the problem he faced and while, for example, he might normally report to his branch secretary, this might be only monthly. But the secretary himself would be subject to both the branch meeting and, between meetings, to the branch committee. The frequency of such meetings varies, and the branch is not always coterminous with the factory.

Though responsibility to the district committee is stressed, eg, by the AEU, NUGMW, PTU, and ASW, a distinction must be drawn between these predominantly lay committees and the full-time district officials.

Stewards often have a choice of contacting a part-time branch official or a full-time union officer in an emergency, while sometimes informing both. Some unions stress reporting to and being instructed by shop or factory committees, or shop meetings. In others, stewards, *ex officio*, carry the status of branch officials. Given the democratic checks and balances in most constitutions, it is often impossible to define answerability clearly, and informal arrangements are doubtless of much greater significance than rulebook provisions. The relations with the various officials 'above' the steward may determine the pattern of communication; so may the ratio of stewards and members to these officials.

In practice, the room for manoeuvre within the rules varies widely between unions. For instance, the AEU rules are vague about stewards' negotiating responsibilities, but the handbook specifically emphasizes their unique opportunity for improving members' conditions, encouraging them to bargain at this level. Moreover, stewards are responsible to the district committees, which have very strong steward representation. The ETU stewards are directly responsible to the area full-time officials, rather than to a committee consisting predominantly of lay members and, as the rule-book is more specific about stewards' duties, they may there-fore operate closer control. Bargaining activities at factory or site level are encouraged in the ASW handbook, stewards again being responsible to a largely lay management committee. In these and other unions, there are strong traditions of membership control over full-time officials. They are subject to periodic re-election, which further weakens their powers *vis-à-vis* the stewards, who can in-fluence support or opposition to officialdom.

In other unions, the position of stewards, on paper and in fact, is not so strong. For instance, the NUGMW par-ticularly emphasizes obedience to the rulebook, allowing district secretaries to define matters which may or may not be dealt with by stewards. In fact, district secretaries have a commanding position in relation to both stewards and dis-trict committees. The union has expelled stewards for un-constitutional action.[3] Prior to the policy change in the late 1960s, T & GWU full-time officials appeared to regulate the activities of most stewards fairly closely. Having in-vestigated ten (federated) engineering firms in Birmingham, Derber[4] showed that T & GWU officials were in frequent contact with members and stewards, often being asked for advice as well as negotiating. He concluded that T & GWU stewards were subject to much closer supervision by their district officials than were AEU stewards. Thus, while the traditions of the industry or the plant may exert pressure towards uniformity, union affiliation affects the degree of their autonomy in practice.

BISAKTA seeks to control its stewards closely, particu-larly insisting on the involvement of branch officials in their negotiating activities. Expulsions have occurred for disobedience of the rules. In the printing industry, the close liaison between FOCs and branches, and the orderly pattern of chapel rules, helps regulate the duties of FOCs.

(4) *Local officials*
Local full-time officials are extremely important to the shop

steward, often constituting his direct point of contact with the union. Furthermore, they are able to interpret union policy on local matters and deal with local problems. Their power and responsibility under union rules therefore closely affect that enjoyed by stewards. For instance, in the AEU, the district committee's powers limit those of the district secretary considerably, and here the official will often only enter into bargaining if the stewards cannot succeed. In addition, they are re-elected every three years, which inhibits 'unpopular' control over stewards or the district committee. Similarly, ETU area officials are periodically re-elected, their responsibilities being limited to 'such duties as the Executive Council, or branches in their area with the consent of the Executive Council, entrust to them'. (ETU Rulebook, Rule 12.) In other unions, eg, BISAKTA and NUGMW, district officials have much greater power; in the former, they are not even encumbered by elected district councils or committees, being directly under the jurisdiction of the executive council.

However, the formal constitution of a trade union is only the skeleton, and it is impossible to specify the exact position of a full-time official since the experience and personality of individuals influences their power. Without examining individual cases, it is therefore difficult to estimate the influence of local full-time officials, even within the same union. Moreover, the writers are acquainted with AEU officials who exercise considerable influence over their stewards and members, and T & GWU officials who have difficulty avoiding repudiation by their membership, despite their very different constitutional positions. In practice, many members regard full-time officials as mediators, between the stewards and management, and as legal claims experts rather than as their representatives.

Immediately, stewards consider themselves responsible to the members who elect them, but seldom do rulebooks prescribe regular meetings in the factory or on site to obtain mandates or authorization. The NUGMW (Handbook) and the ETU require stewards to have members' approval before taking action or accepting conditions of work. A few rule-books enjoin stewards to call shop (or equivalent) meetings when a proportion of the members so request: eg, ETU one quarter, PTU, unspecified, and NATSOPA, an agreed proportion. The NUFTO handbook recommends frequent and regular shop meetings, but generally provisions for democratic processes are scanty. The Bakers' Union hand-book constantly recommends extended communication with individuals, but only NUFTO is explicitly confident of employers regularly providing facilities for frequent in-structional meetings. Some unions compensate by emphasiz-ing the importance of shop committees, looking to them to supervise stewards' activities and to keep them in touch with the members, and with union rules and policy, eg, CWU, AUFW, Hosiery Workers, and the Office Committees of DATA.

(5) *Internal communications*

Many unions examined provide for special meetings of stewards. AEU stewards attend quarterly meetings of the district committee, having special representation on it. The PTU and NUSMW & C hold quarterly meetings of stewards in the different areas. These are provided for at unspecified intervals in the ASW and DATA, while the ETU area secretaries must now call annual area industrial conferences of stewards in several industries, and may convene stewards merely *ad hoc* to improve communications. Other unions, of course, also do this, but are seldom explicit in rulebooks. The ETU rules include national conferences of stewards from defined industries. Of the unions examined, only the ETU and the Tailors and Garment Workers' rules specify the organization of meetings between stewards at different plants of the same firm, though this is mentioned in the ASSET handbook.

The Chemical Workers' general secretary is to send copies of correspondence relating to their shops to stewards and branch secretaries. The executive council of the AUFW can explicitly communicate direct with stewards; all NATSOPA correspondence is to go through FOCs, and HDEU full-time officials visiting a factory must contact stewards before meeting management.

(6) *Convenors*

Only the AEU, ETU, PTU, and AUFW provide for the appointment of convenors or senior stewards, although both ASW and CAWU handbooks recommend it. Of these, only the PTU says that a convenor 'shall' be appointed but does not state how. In the AUFW, the shop committee 'decides', in the ETU the senior steward may be elected by and from the stewards, or from them by the membership, while the AEU allows stewards or shop committees to appoint one. A few unions, though not defining the position, allow for a system of seniority among members of shop, factory, or office committees; eg, Hosiery Workers and NUFTO handbook.

(7) *Duties and functions*

As shown, many rulebooks make stewards responsible for collecting union dues. Allied to this, many emphasize their duty of gaining new members and maintaining membership, particularly of the need to approach new employees. The maintenance of members is, in part, provided for by the holding of card inspections, which most craft and ex-craft unions stipulate. These may be monthly, as in the HDEU and ASW, or quarterly. Usually, members in arrears are to be reported to the branch or district officials, but the ETU and ASW provide for those in arrears to appear before meetings of members on the job.

Several unions, eg, the AUFW and the NUSMW & C, stress the duty of informing members of branch meetings, while the HDEU insists that stewards always attend. More generally, union rules often charge the steward with disseminating information from both branch and other sources to the membership. On the other hand, the steward's duty of passing information about workshop conditions, wages, hours, etc, is more often stated, and periodic reports in writing are usually to be supplemented by reports of all changes. Any violation of rates, customs, privileges, agreements, or union rules is often specified for immediate report to branches, branch, or district committees or full-time officials. Some stewards are required to check that all members receive union rates, and follow union or district practices. Others provide that stewards keep the relevant local body informed 'on all matters', or maintain close contact.

Some unions, notably the T & GWU and USDAW, do not list any functions for stewards in their rulebook, while those in printing provide for chapels to draw up rules and duties for the FOC, but give an outline in the rulebooks. A few, eg, the AEU, ETU, and DATA, allow for the performance of duties 'delegated' to stewards. Others, often individually, allocate additional duties specifically. Most common is to report accidents, but others include reporting overtime, NUSMW & C and ETU; keeping lists of piecework prices, AUFW; ensuring the observation of union rules during strikes, ETU; notifying job vacancies, Chemical Workers and the printing unions; handling legal claims, etc. At least two, the NUSMW & C and the AUFW, provide for a shop or pricing committee, rather than individual stewards, to handle piecework or incentive schemes.

The predominant impression is that most unions, though there are exceptions, do not issue a detailed job description in their rulebooks. The duties mentioned emphasize the steward as a recruiter of members, a contribution collector, a card checker and a custodian of agreements and practices; he is also given responsibility for communications, particularly in passing information out of the factory. The steward's representational and negotiating role is often unmentioned and, where mentioned, is constrained rather than promoted by the rules. But some, notably the white-collar unions and some with a craft tradition, are relatively open in allowing this function. Two manual unions, the Bakers' and NATSOPA, protect the steward by giving him an exclusive position in progressing members' complaints, grievances, and disputes, but many others provide members with alternative channels.

The most frequently encountered rule about the steward's negotiating role is that taking up grievances with management representatives is permissible provided no question of a *principle* or *change of practice* or *stoppage of work* shall be determined without prior external approval. Some ex-craft unions, eg, the CEU, leave the situation undefined and few prescribe which topics come within the steward's competence, or otherwise. Several unions, eg, AUFW and Chemical Workers, insist on stewards being closely superintended in negotiations by shop or office committees, while others, eg, the Hosiery Workers, ASSET, and DATA, allocate this function to committees rather than individuals. Others require stewards to be accompanied, or to inform the convenor and, in a few cases, stewards are to take up issues only under instruction from the membership or branch committees. The ETU and NUGMW handbook appear to require the consent of the members before any settlement is accepted.

Clearly, the rulebooks offer little from which to glean the steward's bargaining functions in day-to-day factory life. The less formal handbooks give more indication, though a few are at pains to play down this role in relation to recruitment. As they offer advice on conducting negotiations they now appear to accept that this is a major function of the steward. It is difficult to account for its scanty coverage in rulebooks. Certainly the unions know of the real dangers of stewards not taking opportunities, or making bad agreements, or breaking union rules, but some seem even more afraid of promoting, or acknowledging, a shift in the balance of power in the unions' central activity – that of bargaining.

(8) *Relations with other unions*

Only three unions studied provided for building up contact with the stewards of other unions. Of these, the ETU goes furthest in enjoining stewards to work with other stewards and to join in joint shop-steward committees. DATA's office committee members are to represent members on joint committees with other employees, though again there is vagueness. The CAWU allows its representatives and committees to cooperate with other unionists for common purposes, and the NUGMW handbook, which contains rules rather than advice, recommends inter-union cooperation at the workplace. Otherwise, this topic is unmentioned, though many unions approve of joint workplace committees. In view of the proliferation of joint shop-steward committees, this reticence again indicates the inadequacy of rulebooks in guiding stewards.

(9) *Shop-steward handbooks*

For many stewards, the union's rulebook and handbook are the only formal guidance received. Only one union, the NUGMW, makes its handbook binding on stewards, others being issued principally to offer advice about parts of the job, his responsibilities, his priorities, and how to function successfully. Often, the advice is very similar, eg, in how to prepare a case before negotiating with management and how to conduct such negotiations. However, several interesting points emerge from the composition of these handbooks. In some, eg, USDAW's, the recruiting function is very heavily stressed, in others, eg, the ASW's, the representational role. Unions place different explicit emphasis on loyalty to the union, and when and on what topics stewards are to refer to external union officials varies quite widely, eg, AEU and ASW stewards compared with those of USDAW and the CAWU. Some describe union constitutions fully; others outline financial benefits at the expense of guidance on other topics. Practically all emphasize the duty of consultation when in doubt, and a steward's duty to pass information to members, to 'turn card holders into active union members'.

There is very little evidence about internal communications between unions and their members. The Royal Commission research survey asked union members where they got information about what was happening in their unions.[5]

The sources mentioned were as follows: union journal (41%); the shop steward (40%); circulars (36%); notice boards at work (30%); branch meetings (20%); talk at work (14%); and meetings at work (8%). Of those who saw their union journal, 54% got it from their steward, and he is also likely to hand out circulars and post up notices.

This admittedly slight evidence implies that information and discussion is concentrated on the workplace, rather than on the often poorly attended branch, and the steward's duty in informing members' discussions appear enormous. While this, and consequent emphasis on the steward's communication function in handbooks is not surprising, it is perplexing that so few unions provide other methods of informing either stewards or members directly of the union's affairs. Similarly, while only three unions refer to inter-union cooperation at the workplace, a further six mention it encouragingly in their handbooks.

Some handbooks are clear and concise on stewards' duties, eg, NUFTO; others leave contentious problems open, but stress the need of external advice. Clearly, the assistance given by these handbooks is variable, but, without detailed study, their actual readership and impact cannot be estimated. At least, most are more attractively presented than the average rulebook.

The Industrial Relations Act and other recent developments

A number of pressures have been put on trade unions in recent years to revise their rulebooks, and particularly to increase and clarify the provisions they make for shop stewards. The Donovan Report recommended that trade-union rules should clearly and unambiguously as a statutory requirement of registration prescribe rules for the election of shop stewards, their term of office, and the authority charged with the issue and withdrawal of credentials. Further the Commission felt union rules should cover the filling of casual vacancies, the bounds of the shop steward's jurisdiction (eg, by defining the relationship between shop meetings and the branch), the relationship between shop stewards and other union officials and offices, they should clearly state the authority within the union to which the steward is finally responsible and which can suspend or dismiss him from office, and, finally, union rules should make explicit provision for multi-union workplace committees (para 698). The Donovan Commission felt that 'such rules will make it reasonable to expect stewards (and their members) to act constitutionally, since they will at last be able to perform their functions within the compass of the rules' (para 699).

In a circular to trade unions in December 1969 the TUC asked unions to clarify, in rules or handbooks, exactly how stewards were to fit into their organization. Specifically, the TUC took up many of the Donovan suggestions, although it acknowledged the difficulties of setting out a precise definition of shop stewards' duties, given the variety of situations in which stewards operated. It was felt that union publications should clarify how stewards are elected or appointed, to whom they are responsible, the limits of their authority, the role of workplace meetings of members *vis-à-vis* union policy and industrial agreements. Multi-union joint shop stewards' committees should be formally recognized and the role of convenors should be covered.

The CIR, in a report in May 1971, 'felt that whilst more could be done in industry-wide agreements to set out the main functions of shop stewards and broad principles relating to the provision of facilities, there was much greater scope to cover the activities of shop stewards in company or establishment agreements. Nevertheless, the CIR also thought that union rulebooks had a part to play, and recommended the following (para 215):

The initiative of the TUC should be continued in an effort to achieve a greater degree of standardization of union rulebooks. Rulebooks should cover in general terms the main areas of steward functions, particularly his role as a grievance handler, his responsibilities for consultation and communication with his members, his responsibilities to the union and the observance of agreements. Rulebooks should also cover the manner of election of stewards, the issue of union credentials, and the method of notification to management of appointments and resignations. All unions which at present do not do so should consider issuing a stewards' handbook or manual to serve as a guide in greater detail to the functions the steward should perform.

The impact which the crescendo of exhortation outlined above has had is difficult to assess, but it does not seem to have been very great so far. The amendment of union rulebooks involves elaborate constitutional procedures which don't help to accelerate progress. Secondly, as indicated at the beginning of this chapter, the unions may for tactical purposes prefer to leave the steward free to enlarge his role from a fairly minimal base in the rulebook. Thirdly, the whole question of the contents of trade-union rules is at the centre of the trade unions' opposition to registration under the Industrial Relations Act. Those unions (or legally speaking, organizations of workers) which are determined not to register have been too preoccupied with amending their rules to meet the new situation created by the Act to undertake radical revisions of the rules relating to shop stewards.

Compared with the detailed suggestions of the Donovan Commission and the CIR, the Act itself contains little of a specific nature on this topic, although the Code is more explicit and tends to follow the CIR's recommendations. The Act, in Schedule 4, stipulates that if a (registered) trade union has officials such as shop stewards or workplace representatives who are not officers of the organization the rules '. . . must make provision for their election or appointment and for the manner in which they can be removed from office'. Further, 'the rules must specify the powers and duties of . . . officials who are not officers of the organization'. As yet it is too early to judge how the Chief Registrar will interpret these requirements in relation to the shop stewards of unions seeking to register. Although the Code of Industrial Relations Conduct is not legally enforceable it may not be unreasonable to suppose that its provisions covering the definition of stewards' functions, rights and responsibilities will influence the Registrar. However, the Code simply repeats the requirement of Schedule 4 (6) of the Act outlined above, and adds that trade unions should give their stewards written credentials setting out their union rights and obligations, periods of office and the precise group of employees they represent. Otherwise, the section of the Code relating to shop stewards stresses the desirability of *joint agreements* between management and trade unions rather than union rulebooks as the appropriate vehicle for the definition of rights, facilities, etc.

Overall, there appears to be a fair degree of agreement that trade-union rulebooks and handbooks can and should do more to acknowledge the representational role of stewards and to build a more detailed framework which would allow stewards' activities to be incorporated within the formal rules of the industrial relations system. If rulebooks were to be brought closer to day-to-day reality they could become a more significant influence on stewards' behaviour than they have been in the past, thus enabling them to feel more closely integrated with their unions.

References

1. The other unions whose rulebooks and handbooks (where issued) have been studied are as follows: USDAW (1961); PTU; ASW; NUFTO (1964); ASSET (1964); CAWU (1964); AUFW (1964); NUPBPW (1960); NATSOPA (1960); HDEU (1963); NUSMW & C (1965); CEU (1963); NUBSO (1965); NUPE (1965); POEU; UPOW; AScW; ASLEF; NU of Hosiery Workers (1963); NU of Dyers, Bleachers and Textile Workers; NU of Tailors and Garment

Workers (1963); Chemical Workers Union (1961): United Rubber-workers (1963); AU of Operative Bakers; and the Amalgamated Weavers Association.

2. Constituencies are normally based on union membership. The practice at the Ford Motor Co Ltd, of basing constituencies for non-skilled workers on geographical workplace zones irrespective of union affiliation, is exceptional.

3. See Clegg, H. A., *General Union*, p 113 and pp 124–33.

4. Derber, Milton, *Labour Management Relations at the Plant Level under Industry Wide Bargaining*, University of Illinois, 1955.

5. *Workplace Industrial Relations*, HMSO, 1968, p 122.

6. Commission on Industrial Relations, Report No 17, *Facilities Afforded to Shop Stewards*, Cmnd 4668, HMSO, 1971.

Chapter Four

Shop Stewards and Work Groups

Union rulebooks and handbooks constitute *one* guide for stewards' behaviour, though their comprehensiveness varies between unions. So, too, does their influence over day-to-day activities. A more immediate influence is the relationship between stewards and members in the workplace.

Relationships between stewards and their constituents are complex and variable, ranging from constituents allowing a steward wide discretion to interpret their requirements to specific pressure for defined improvements. A steward's activities may, continuously, be a subject of interest to only a few members, and pressures on him may derive chiefly from individuals. For example, an aspirant to his position may seize every opportunity to press points he knows to be popular with constituents. Dissident members may repeatedly raise trivial or even imaginary problems, and strong personalities may criticize his failure to be sufficiently militant. Clearly, many issues a steward raises with management will be of a largely individual nature, others having broader implications and involving *all* members. Sociologists have repeatedly emphasized the primary work group as an important determinant of behaviour, suggesting that informal leadership is bestowed on those most close to the norms and values which bind the group. Thus, while day-to-day pressures on stewards may stem from individuals, in the longer term they are influenced by the need to avoid repudiation by or, more positively, to maintain the approval of, their members collectively. In our experience, stewards take this as axiomatic, regarding their constituents as their primary source of reference. Consequently, recent theories of social organization in the workplace are important in an understanding of the relationship between stewards and their members.

The group in industry

The importance of the primary work group in industry is now almost universally recognized. Perhaps the most positive recent recognition has come from Mr Allan Flanders, who has gone as far as to say 'under conditions of full employment trade unions may enter into agreements which neither they nor management have the power to enforce. They meet with resistance on the shop floor which cannot be crushed because neither party has sanctions strong enough to override the interests of the work group, enjoying as it does a life and authority of its own.'[1]

This recognition arose initially from the findings of the Hawthorne experiments, refined, but in many ways substantiated, by more recent research. Before the Hawthorne experiments, industrial psychology had been focused on the *individual* worker – by F. W. Taylor, Frank Gilbreth, and others, who studied the worker as an isolated unit of production, exaggerating the importance of the economic factor in work. From this, techniques of work measurement were developed, calculated to maximize the individual's efficiency, with similar attempts to optimize his environmental working conditions. They attached great importance to effective movements while working, sufficient rest periods, effective lighting, and suitable economic incentives to stimulate maximum effort. They concentrated attention on the worker primarily as an isolated production unit, regarding him as principally, if not exclusively, motivated by economic factors. It was supposed that he could be enticed to maximum productive effort simply by promises of reward or threats of punishment.

These simple theories were challenged by the work of some early sociologists and social psychologists, Elton Mayo being most important. He discovered that the primary work group was an essential element in work life, and argued that this group life could lead to contented workers prepared to cooperate in production for the good of the company. Mayo and his researchers created a new attitude to labour–management relations which stressed the great importance of group relations and led away from economic deterministic theories. This thought has been supported by many post-war writers.

Some developments in primary-group theories

More recent developments of industrial group theories have come from the United States. Significantly, L. R. Sayles postulated[2] that the primary work groups on the factory floor are not only important, but largely *determine* the quality of workplace relations. By far the most significant factor in determining the nature and composition of work groups is technology. For example, Sayles says, 'The technology of certain plants can predispose the total worker–management relationship towards a high degree of cooperation or towards the opposite pole – that of hostility. Other plants, due to the inherent strength of individual occupational groups, tread a middle ground. They have less potential for noteworthy cooperation but also less inclination towards the open conflict type of situation.' He suggests that groups formed by different technologies exhibit different behavioural characteristics which influence the industrial relations of individual plants. In particular they differ in the methods they evolve to solve day-to-day problems, their response to management and supervisory behaviour, and the type of people they elect as leaders. It is these responses which produce the patterns forming the fabric of industrial relationships. As part of his novel theory, Sayles went on to classify the groups into four types.

The first type is *apathetic* groups with little skill and few grievances, who participate in union activities only sporadically. Common denominators are limited, there is practically no use of pressure tactics, and a lack of clearly identified or accepted leadership. Examples of workers forming such groups are floor sweepers or cleaners.

Secondly there are *erratic* groups. These consist of members with a high rate of interaction on the job, who make homogeneous crews, work on short assembly lines, with job descriptions and rates matching nearly perfectly, and the work is worker- rather than machine-controlled. Characteristically, these groups are easily influenced and inconsistent in behaviour, often with tightly centralized leadership, and are quickly converted to good relations with management. Examples include assembly-line workers.

Thirdly, *strategic* groups. These are shrewd pace-setters, articulate on every weakness in order to gain results; they have better jobs than the groups already mentioned but not the best within the plant. The job does not always have individual operation, and the operative element is important (they may be welders or pressers, etc). Their behaviour involves continuous pressure, well-planned and continuous grievance activity, a high degree of interaction, and sustained union participation.

Finally, the *conservative* groups are self-assured and successful, with a moderate internal unity. Their behaviour is to show restrained pressure for certain higher specific objects, and to manifest activity–inactivity cycles in terms of union activities and the plant grievance procedure. Examples of such workers are skilled craftsmen.

This thesis throws light on the industrial relations in certain industries. For example, the vehicle industry contains many erratic groups, which helps to explain the frequent unofficial activities of car workers which, according to Sayles, are inherent in the technology of the industry. This may be an important reason why the vehicle industry in many countries suffers from industrial unrest. On the other hand, the hypothesis does not explain the differences in activities between similar groups in various plants. It does not tell us, for example, why one motor company has better industrial relations than another, nor why the quality changes over time. The theory concentrates too much on technology and the resulting group structures, ignoring other factors – the quality of management, geographical location, attitude of the unions concerned, individual motivations, which all influence the behaviour of work groups. In addition, Sayles' research methods are not entirely convincing, for he relies on interviews only, adopting no corroborative methods such as questionnaires or work diaries. Even his interviews are suspect, since in about half the firms interviews with union officials were refused by management. His work, however, is a presentation of hypotheses, which he freely admits.

Work on primary groups has been taken further by James W. Kuhn.[3] He does not isolate one variable and attribute overriding importance to it for, in his analysis, other factors are thought significant in affecting group attitudes. For example, he draws attention to:

(a) The services offered by the union, which can either help groups in grievance bargaining, or be so poor as to make little contribution. This encourages groups to act either officially with the union or unofficially without it.

(b) The traditions of industrial relations within the plant. For example, a tradition of using sanctions can cause pressure groups and stewards to continue applying them.

(c) The presence of Communists. This can accentuate problems in industrial relations, although Kuhn insists that, in his experience, they catalyse rather than cause problems.

(d) The nature of the industry. For example, there are industries in which redundancy is likely, such as ship-building, or those in which the labour market is tight, such as printing, or where profits are high and the capital–labour ratio also high, as in oil refining. All are important in determining the behaviour of work groups.

(c) The quality of management. It is important whether they recognize problems or are slow to do so, thus inducing frustration among work groups.

Kuhn believes that technology is also important, but thinks it is only one factor influencing the behaviour of work groups. This appears more accurate, since similar technologies may produce different group reactions, which must be accounted for. Kuhn feels that, together, these factors determine the nature of in-plant group activity, which largely influences how shop stewards behave. He notes that the local union, meaning the plant organization of the union, is a political body and partly the creature of the work groups. Its authority could crumble if it resists the groups too strongly. Since he believes that, consequently, shop stewards bargain as *leaders of these groups*, they may embrace unofficial activity and strike action because of the groups' behaviour. This view is relatively novel, it being often assumed in this country that shop stewards are primarily union officials able almost to dictate to members and having considerable personal freedom to manoeuvre. Under full employment, much attention has been focused on shop stewards, but until Kuhn's book was published in 1961 there was no major emphasis on shop stewards as, partly, prisoners of the structural determinants in the workplace. Arguing from the American collective-bargaining structure, Kuhn suggests that, to prevent unofficial action, certain topics should pass into the purview of lower-level representatives – shop stewards – instead of belonging to full-time officials or convenors. This would be important in those technologies most conducive to plant bargaining.

These technologies, he notes, have four aspects: they subject many of the workers to continual changes in work methods, standards, or rates, as they work at individually placed jobs. They allow workers considerable interaction with others in their technological groups. They group most of the work force into several, nearly equal-sized, departments. They require continuous sequential processing of material into one major product. These categories are somewhat vague, and Kuhn does not specify exactly why they are so important. However, he argues that local representatives should discuss with foremen such subjects as rotation of jobs, overtime arrangements, seniority procedures, and other departmental problems. He believes this would help workers to obtain meaningful control over their jobs, and preclude attempts to secure it, except through official bargaining. The subjects he suggests for departmental bargaining omit major factors such as wage rates, but perhaps such problems must be included for workers to obtain a *real* measure of control over their jobs.

This, too, is an interesting thesis which has much to offer, but it can be said at once that it contains one obvious drawback. It assumes that shop stewards are *necessarily* acting democratically as leaders of small groups. This does not always follow. The personality of the steward or the particular question at issue (evoking apathy in the group, thus leaving the steward comparative freedom of action) – may produce autocratic rather than democratic leadership. Kuhn is assuming that work groups, existing in workplaces and often consisting of few workers, naturally produce democratic leadership. This is, of course, an easy assumption, and many advocates of democracy, and of democratic organization, have also made it. Democratic theorists say that the smaller the unit, the easier is democracy, and the less likely is autocracy to develop. This is arguable, however, as a leading theorist of group behaviour reminds us: 'this word "democratic" may not be easily applicable to small groups ... to talk about the "democratic" atmosphere or way of life of a group often leads away from careful reasoning, so ill defined are these terms, and it makes dictators happy by further muddying the meaning of "democracy", a result that they themselves have done their best to accomplish. The fact is that leadership in a group may be at one time abrupt, forceful, centralized, so that all the communications originate with the leader, and at another time slow, relaxed, dispersed with much communication back and forth between leader and followers. Each mould is acceptable, appropriate and effective, but each in different circumstances.'[4]

Given the varied circumstances of group formation, attitudes, and behaviour, it is impossible to generalize about stewards as work-group leaders. On occasion, stewards themselves may formulate what the group accepts as its best interests; on others, they may be largely responsive to the group's wishes. The incidence of decisions made by the leader or the group will vary greatly according to its nature, whether 'apathetic', 'erratic', 'strategic', or 'conservative'; the personality of the steward, forceful or easy-going, and the type of issue involved, important to the group, which will therefore insist on making its wishes known, or of little interest and therefore left to the leader. W. E. McCarthy quotes the evidence of Dr G. Clack who took part in unofficial strikes when engaged in research. Clack notes that, generally, stewards were a restraining influence, although 'they could not afford to get out of touch with the feelings of the shop'.[5] Professor H. A. Clegg[6] points to evidence which demonstrates that in the printing industry 'not every chapel is wholly group centred' and that, in some cases, the Father of the Chapel has a great deal of power in real terms and sometimes acts as the leader of work groups. This evidence conflicts, to some extent, with the arguments of Dr A. J. M. Sykes, who suggests that the Chapel Father is strictly subordinated to the decisions and customs of the group, but the shop steward is expected to act as a *leader* rather than as a delegate and, once elected, the initiative lies in his own hands.'[7] Clegg notes further that the surveys of the Royal Commission do not support the view that the shop steward outside printing occupies such a leadership role for they reveal that two-thirds of the sample of trade union members reported that the majority generally decided what action should be taken over a complaint or a claim and also that less than half of the sample of shop stewards felt that they could *always* get members to see things their way.[8]

T. T. Paterson has shown that different leaders may emerge in work groups according to the circumstances of the situation, and he offers a useful classification in this area which categorizes the various leadership roles which are to be found. These leadership roles are as follows:[9]

1. *Exemplar.* This role is concerned with representation of the group-opinion norm and the holder exemplifies the group. In our culture he is usually neither vociferous nor bellicose. The members of the group usually pay great attention to his opinion.
2. *Exdominus.* This is concerned with external relations between the group and other groups. The holder of the role is usually relatively vociferous and bellicose and is often regarded as group spokesman.
3. *Indominus.* This role is concerned with internal relations among group members. The holder is relatively vociferous but not bellicose and he makes sure that the group conforms to its norm and holds together. He would be, for example, a good committee man.
4. *Eccentric.* The holder of this role is concerned with expounding belief and behaviour which is outside the norms of the group but acceptable to the latter when performed by the role holder. He points out views that are considered by the group to be worthy of its consideration and, therefore, his views may eventually become representative of the group.
5. *Mimetic.* All who follow the exemplar and domini roles take up this role. Some members of the group may only fill mimetic roles.
6. *Isolate.* This is not a group role since the holder does not conform to group norms and takes no part in group life.

It is important to note, as Paterson does, that whilst the roles are permanent the role takers may well vary with the

situation since the valuation of the role alters with the needs
of new situations. Thus the mantle of leadership may well be
handed round to individual members of the work group.
Thus even where shop stewards apparently effectively
represent the group or groups in collective bargaining, they
may sometimes be reporting the arguments of someone else
a situation not exactly unknown in this area! In practice, it
is impossible to use stereotype descriptions of group behaviour or group leadership behaviour.

Despite this, Kuhn's theories are accepted by industrial
relations experts in the UK, being the foundation of their
approach to plant bargaining problems. For example, Mr A.
Marsh[10] remarks that 'All current investigations into the
workplace situation tend to lay stress on the notion that
work groups find it natural to evolve norms or standards of
behaviour and to produce leadership of their own whose
principal aim is to defend these standards. Workers may well
be content to follow the directions indicated by management
until their norms are disturbed. Working pace, levels of
earnings, allocations of work, methods of work, ideas of just
treatment of individuals – all these considerations may, in
varying degree and in different circumstances, seem to be of
prime importance to work groups.' Marsh suggests that
stewards reflect the wishes of the work groups, when he
writes '. . . Nor do they [ie, recent writers] appear to doubt
the position which the shop steward tends to hold in relation
to the work group and its norms. He tends to be not merely
a workplace representative but also a work-group leader or,
in more informal circumstances, merely recognized by the
work group.' He does give another reason for the *effectiveness* of the steward: 'If the role of the steward can only be
explained, at bottom, in terms of the work group, his
effectiveness in that role and more recently his rapid rise in
authority over the economy as a whole can only be explained
in terms of general labour scarcity. Until recently the work
group has only in exceptional circumstances been able to
apply its working rules to the workplace so as to make its
bargaining position felt by management.' Marsh stresses that

the steward's position as a work-group leader is good reason for encouraging the growth of workplace bargaining and, like Kuhn, is concerned that work groups, left out of workplace bargaining, may act unconstitutionally.

These views of primary-group activity envisage them participating in collective bargaining, formally or not, and thereby acting in opposition to management. Some writers suggest that they can be brought into *cooperation* with management, if encouraged to act as groups in consultation on matters of mutual interest with management. For example, J. A. C. Brown[11] writes, in his interpretation of the Hawthorne experiments, 'There are two lessons to be learned from this part of the Hawthorne research. Firstly that no collection of people can be in contact for any length of time without such informal groupings arising and natural leader being pushed to the top. Secondly that it is not only foolish but futile to try to break up these groups; a wise policy would see to it that the interests of management and worker coincided to such an extent that the collection of informal groups which make up a factory would be working towards the same goals instead of frustrating each other's efforts.' This argument will be examined in the next section.

Some criticisms of primary-group theories

One serious fault in interpreting the Hawthorne experiments is to read them as suggesting the feasibility of absolute co-operation between the work groups and management. The remarks of J. A. C. Brown above provide one example. Another can be found in the work of Stuart Chase, who says,[12] 'the worker is driven by a desperate inner urge to find an environment where he can take root, where he belongs and has a function; where he sees the purpose of his work and feels important in achieving it'. Chase sees Hawthorne as proving that management must provide such roots and security by encouraging primary work groups in industry. These arguments are questionable, in implying manipulation of the work force in the interests of management. This is likely to arouse the opposition of work groups, shop stewards, and unionists as such and, at least in strongly unionized factories, will prove difficult. Additionally, such arguments assume that conflict can be ignored – surely unrealistic when economic and status conflict is the basis of collective bargaining. This does not mean that conflict must inevitably result in strikes, overtime bans, go-slows, etc, since it can be constructively channelled. Moreover, even strikes are partially constructive, or at least not entirely destructive, sociologically. Indeed, a strike may be acknowledged 'necessary' by management as well as men. The conflict inherent in our system of industrial relations cannot be ignored. Kuhn realizes the implication of the conflict theory, suggesting that the groups be brought into the collective-bargaining process as a counter to management's strength, and that conflict be channelled through the groups. This viewpoint, taken up in the UK by, for example, Flanders and Marsh, appears to be more realistic than the 'cooperation school'.

A second criticism of shop-steward-related work-group theories is that writers of this school tend to refer to stewards as leaders of work groups, as if each steward was elected only by his work-group constituents, representing them only in collective bargaining. This is unlikely, for two reasons. First, because work groups, certainly at the primary level, can be very small; several, probably, make up the constituency of most stewards. Evidence from a detailed study of nineteen shop stewards in six different factories, five in the London area and one in North Wales, supports this. The study was carried out by one of the writers by interviews with management and shop stewards, observation on the shop floor, and work diaries kept by the stewards during two months. Altogether, six months was spent investigating each plant. A variety of trade unions were covered, including the AEU, T & GWU, NUGMW, HDEU, NGA, and ETU. Technologies covered included process production (oil industry) and batch production (print, photography, synthetic fibres, and engineering). This research showed that the median number of groups under each of the nineteen stewards was five. One steward represented ten different primary groups and another nine and, excluding these, the mean average was three. Therefore, it is more plausible to count shop stewards as leaders of work *groups* rather than as work-*group* leaders. However, the research also revealed seven cases of informal leaders of individual primary groups putting pressures on the stewards, in two cases going over their heads to the factory convenor. Thus, some stewards may not even act as group leaders, being regarded as unsuitable for this role in not belonging to that work group. Other leaders may be 'appointed'. An excellent example of a *de facto* change in union leadership in a plant in changed circumstances is given by A. W. Gouldner in *Wildcat Strike*.[13] Here, he shows how an aggressive local union plant leader took over the leadership from his less forceful superior at a time when the members felt militancy was necessary. The second reason for rejecting the argument that stewards are acting as leaders of clearly defined work groups is that, as Professor H. A. Clegg points out, 'it is not always possible to pick out clearly defined work groups'.[14] He uses the example of a bus garage to show that whilst usually a driver and conductor work together as a team, both are part of large groups. Drivers have interests in common and for some purposes all the drivers may be said to constitute a single work group, and all the conductors another. Alternatively, since many busmen work on shifts, the drivers and conductors on one shift may have their own view of a particular issue. At other times the whole of the road operating staff may act as a single unit. There is still the inside staff, consisting of skilled mechanics, semi-skilled workers, cleaners and so on, each forming a group of their own for some purposes, perhaps coming together for others. Usually there is a single union delegate or representative for the operating staff, and one or more shop stewards for the inside staff. Clegg suggests that it is appropriate to see shop stewards as leaders of complexes or coalitions of work groups. The picture is, therefore, more complex than suggested by the work-group theorists, and it may be difficult or impossible to bring the work groups effectively into the collective bargaining process simply through shop stewards. In a recent study of the motor industry, Turner, Clack, and Roberts[15] note the emergence of the 'unofficial–unofficial' strike, ie, one not approved by the official union hierarchy, and also not first approved by the shop stewards. They also observed in a series of strikes at a car-assembly plant 'the shop stewards, and particularly the senior stewards' committee ... attempting to control a number of pressures to which they are subject, including those from the management and outside union officials, but *especially including pressures from particular groups and sections of work people themselves* ... The stewards appear as attempting to minimize trouble; but when trouble seems inevitable, they *attempt* to assert their leadership, in order to maintain their authority over the operatives.' 'Stewards themselves had to be goaded into reluctant action by their electorates' (our italics).

Stewards may not know sufficiently well the tasks of the work groups to represent them effectively in collective bargaining, and may even lack sympathy with the attitudes of some groups within their constituencies. Conversely, stewards may represent one group, eg, in representing a small homogeneous group of maintenance craftsmen. More work is needed on this subject before the establishment of valid general theories. The evidence from our inquiries among the nineteen shop stewards also suggests that the importance of group activity can be exaggerated. Of the nineteen, fifteen were leaders of work groups, and were subject to little pressure from those they represented. None of the stewards at Photography felt such pressure, and even H, himself aggressive and dealing with an uncooperative manager, was responsible to ten apathetic groups and seized on individual not group problems. I (90 per cent of whose constituents were women) and J also dealt with apathetic work groups, covering individual not group matters. At Synthetic Fibres,

K and L represented apathetic groups and again dealt with individual problems. Neither N, O, nor P at Precision Engineering had anything but apathetic groups to deal with and at Printing, groups under O and S were not active. E, F, and G at Wharfage, representing white-collar workers, had apathetic groups, and finally, at Refining, C was in the same position.

This would not of itself disprove the thesis of Sayles and Kuhn, had these groups been naturally apathetic. However, in about half the cases, this was not so. The groups under H should have been erratic, since they manifested all the characteristics of this Saylesian type – high interaction, lower skill type, pay about middle range, short assembly lines, worker element important to the job. They were, for example, spirit preparers, magnetic strippers, and ammonia processers; J also represented such 'erratic' groups of film slitters, perforators, packers, and labellers. At Synthetic Fibres, K represented groups with exactly the same 'erratic' type characteristics in workers who were mixers, viscose cave attenders, mercerizers, and grinders. At Precision Engineering, P had 'strategic' groups of welders and pressers and so had O in mostly semi-skilled inspectors. At Printing, Q and S represented 'strategic' groups, doing jobs which often had individual operation with the operative element important in the job, with the job relatively important to the plant though not the best in pay or status within the plant. These men were compositors and letterpress operators. These seven stewards represented groups which should have been active but were not. Management and union officials confirmed that this impression gained during two months was typical. The stewards were not regarded as acting as representatives of the groups beneath them, but as taking up problems for *individuals*.

Thus, at Photography, H dealt with the following matters: bonus queries for two individuals inquiring about their own job; he himself reported a door needing repair, nobody approaching him; again, he himself reported a faulty drinking fountain; he dealt with individual complaints about the attitude of one of the shift foremen; he answered two individual inquiries about a more senior job open to promotion; he answered an inquiry from an individual about the prospects of redundancy; he dealt with an individual's holiday query, and finally tried to answer a question from a constituent about the future of his job in the department.

J spent his time collecting subscriptions, answering two bonus queries affecting individual constituents, and attending a discussion of the application of work study to a new (individual) job.

At Synthetic Fibres, K dealt with an objection by a constituent about how the work load was distributed, and an individual's complaint of not receiving a day off in lieu of having worked during a holiday; he collected subscriptions and visited a man who was ill. On one occasion, he did discuss a problem of abnormal filtration affecting the viscose cave attenders – one of his work groups. But this was the only time he acted as a work-group spokesman. Certainly, at monthly shop steward meetings he discussed problems affecting the whole plant.

At Precision Engineering, R handled no departmental problems during this period, but dealt with matters of overall concern: the need for a new grievance procedure; a training scheme for apprentices, shift payments, a new sick scheme, a forty-hour week. O dealt with similar matters, since the shop stewards' committee was meeting with members of management to discuss new plant policies. But he also dealt with matters in his department. These included the problem of a man not doing sufficient work, according to the departmental manager, two individuals often absent, and one concerning a bad timekeeper.

At Printing, Q, a full-time FOC, dealt with seventy-seven individual items. Suffice it to say that his constituents approached him as individuals with matters affecting themselves. One complaint about draught did affect part of the work group in one section, and the steward was therefore representing part of a work group. But this was untypical.

For the rest, he dealt with complaints about the quality of individuals' work; two operators complained about bad paper and one of the discourtesy of a deputy overseer to himself. S dealt with ninety-seven separate points, here again being pressed by individuals in his department. He had only one problem entailing the use of the grievance procedure, otherwise carrying out the routine administrative duties of the full-time FOC, including correspondence, absenteeism, and typing out notices.

The lack of activity of the other eight stewards' groups may be explained in their being either apathetic or conservative types. N, at Precision Engineering, represented skilled craftsmen with the best job status and pay in the plant (conservative), while F, at Photography, had as 90 per cent of his constituents women who were reported as very apathetic. The three Wharfage stewards represented white-collar workers who appeared, for the most part as too management-orientated to press the stewards.

The groups of stewards A, B, D, and M were active since there was a special common factor. All represented craftsmen operating as maintenance workers in process plants. At Refining, the three craft groups under A, B, and D (respectively, engineering maintenance men, riggers and crane drivers, and ventilating engineers) were concerned about pay differentials between themselves and process workers. A few highly skilled operators earned more than the craftsmen's consolidated rate. Although this was due entirely to the shift differential, the craftsmen were unhappy and pressed the stewards to effect a change. This involved group activity by the constituents. Similarly, the groups were concerned over demarcation problems. Stewards were very careful to negotiate to protect the spheres of activity of each group of craftsmen. During this period, problems arose between riggers and management at Refining, over the rights of a rigger to accompany rigging equipment in transit. Also at Refining, ventilating engineers insisted on performing work which had, till then, been done by pipefitters. Similar activity existed at Synthetic Fibres, where the pipe-

fitters and the engineering craftsmen were in dispute over
who should do certain work on extruded piping. Again, the
engineering craftsmen were worried about pay differentials,
since some skilled process workers could, with shift differentials, earn more than the engineers' consolidated rate.
Here group activity occurred, as the engineering craftsmen
pressed the steward very hard into getting an increase to
rise above the few process workers earning more (before
overtime) than they were. These examples illustrate the
exclusive and jealous attitude of craftsmen described by
Professor H. A. Turner.[16] With craftsmen, therefore,
stewards may act as work-group leaders on occasions, but
evidence suggests this is confined to groups whose status is
being threatened.

In conclusion, it is impossible to accept the generalization
about work groups without considering carefully the activities of groups in actual factories. A more realistic and inclusive theory of work-group activity must take account of
more varied behaviour than present theories appear to.
With these provisos in mind, it is proposed to examine the
implications of primary-group theories in relation to collective bargaining in the UK.

The significance of primary-group theories to shop stewards: some observations

Assuming the theories discussed are accurate in some cases,
then on sociological grounds explicit plant bargaining is
advantageous, as Kuhn suggests, for without it groups may
act unconstitutionally. In the USA, a 'shop steward's'
responsibilities for bargaining on grievances arising from the
plant contract are often narrowly circumscribed by it, and
stewards usually cannot bargain above the level of departmental foremen or departmental management. Traditionally
in the UK, stewards have been less constrained and their
functions have rarely been limited by formal plant agreements with disputes procedures explicitly eliminating
stewards at an appropriate stage, except in so far as they in-

form full-time officials of the facts. Most stewards have responsibilities limited only by custom and practice, the policy
of management, which may encourage them to develop their
responsibilities, the policy and structure of the union, plus
other factors of greater or lesser importance from industry
to industry. Generally, stewards in the UK are thought to
have had great power within their work units and some
writers have argued that it should be curbed. Certainly,
many stewards have acquired power to negotiate on a
variety of matters, some, such as piece-rate schemes or the
overtime permitted to individuals, being extremely important in determining earnings. Probably, in practice, many
stewards' powers have not been as great as has been suggested. Milton Derber shows[17] from research done in 1955 in
ten firms federated to the Engineering Employers' Federation that the bargaining powers of stewards vary from union
to union. He concluded that union influence depended on
the degree of steward organization, while the steward's
position varied with the union. He found, for the AEU, that
stewards formed powerful groups and appeared largely
self-sufficient in dealing with management. They utilized
the services of full-time officials only when the procedure
required their presence, though other unions' stewards were
subordinate to them. Derber found that the T & GWU
influenced stewards more directly, noting that the local
organizer of the T & GWU frequently contacted his members at branch and stewards' meetings, often gave advice
to senior stewards, and occasionally met management to
negotiate wage and other issues. Among the reasons for
this closer control are higher membership and steward
turnover, since labour mobility among semi- and unskilled
workers is often higher than among craftsmen. Therefore,
full-time officials check on new stewards to see that membership is kept as high as possible.

It should be noted, though Derber omits to, that this was
in a period of exceptional labour shortage, 0·5 per cent
being the overall unemployment average in the Birmingham
area where the firms were situated. This probably increased

stewards' powers *vis-à-vis* management, possibly overemphasizing their typical nature. Even in the case of the AEU, which gives its stewards a large bargaining role, if there is relatively high local unemployment then managements may be less prepared to bargain with shop stewards.

The NUGMW also restricted the bargaining powers of stewards, being known to expel stewards who take unconstitutional action and restricting its stewards' activities to those in its handbook. In this union, the district secretary plays a large part in factory negotiations, while the NUGMW also has full-time branch secretaries as active negotiators.

The BISAKTA has also expelled stewards for breach of its rules, and indeed its rulebook limits their powers through the branch. Among other unions acting similarly are those in the printing industry. The T & GWU has about 30,000 shop stewards according to one estimate (see Research Paper 10 for the Royal Commission on Trade Unions and Employers' Associations, p 10), the NUGMW about 20,000 (see GMWU Journal July 1971, p 4). If the works representatives in BISAKTA and FOCs in the printing unions are added, then the number of stewards with bargaining activities subject to relatively close surveillance by their unions would reach nearly a third of the total number for the UK. Arguably, in workplaces with a multi-union structure, stewards from these unions would have more freedom of action, following the example of, say, unions like the AEU. But there is no evidence to support this; indeed Derber's evidence challenges it. Possibly, also, the lack of common interests between craftsmen and non-craftsmen might inhibit close cooperation, leading to an accretion of bargaining powers by non-craft stewards. In several cases known to us, stewards have complained of lacking the bargaining responsibilities of other stewards in their plant.

Of course, the advent of the Industrial Relations Act may change the power situation in which most stewards find themselves. The major implications of the Act for stewards are dealt with in some detail in Chapter 10. Suffice it to note here that stewards of registered unions have such powers as are allowed them in the appropriate unions' rules and that stewards of unregistered workers' associations cannot induce breach of contract without exposing themselves or their unions to possible legal penalties. In some fundamental respects, therefore, the power of stewards has been reduced.

Yet group theories still have important implications for the behaviour of shop stewards within the plant. They imply, for erratic and strategic groups, that stewards' behaviour may be due to group pressure. Thus, it is unrealistic to condemn it without first studying the group concerned and the problems leading to specific actions. Of course, not all stewards' behaviour derives from full group activities since, as stated above, not all primary-group activity is democratic. However, often stewards are pushed into activity by a group, their behaviour not necessarily reflecting their own views. These considerations should be balanced against approaches seeking to deal with stewards as culprits. Such policies could be positively harmful to industrial relations, easily exacerbating problems by leaving basic causes untouched, creating martyrs, and adding to bitterness in disputes. Similarly, the removal of particular stewards, eg, by dismissal by management, is not necessarily effective in 'solving problems', though it may be a necessary prelude. The removal of one 'culprit' may lead to the election of another, the group choosing as leader that person who best reflects their mood. Bad management creating distrust and resentment is likely to produce a succession of militant stewards.

Where there are apathetic or conservative groups, and in unstable situations, stewards may have more freedom of manoeuvre, and forceful leadership and demagogy may well produce the results desired by the leader. However, many other factors may affect steward behaviour. It would be inequitable to condemn stewards because their groups are apathetic, for the service offered by the union helps determine the activities of local leaders. The logic of this group analysis supports the creation of methods of investigation into the causes of disputes to forestall similar disputes in the future. A body capable of such depth investigation already exists in the form of the CIR and it has investigatory functions to perform. Perhaps its role could, however, be enlarged to enable it to seek out those organizations in the industrial relations system which suffer a great deal from the use of sanctions, make a detailed analysis of the problems of such organizations and suggest changes. Whether, in the last resort, it would be helpful to make these suggestions legally binding is a question which would engender much dispute: certainly, however, before final judgements are made such investigations are needed, it being too easy to make remarks, on superficial evidence, which can only be damaging. Without such opportunities for investigation, we must rely on the evidence of the two sides, which is naturally likely to be biased. Rarely do newspapers or broadcasting services record the views of those involved in dispute. Accusations of irresponsibility directed at trade-union officials or managers must remain doubtful until depth investigations have taken place.

The formalization of stewards' roles

If the work-group theories are accepted as applicable, the responsibilities of many stewards should be increased to bring the work groups they represent into the process of collective bargaining at plant level. This could be done in various ways. Perhaps the best way to recognize local situations, would be to define shop stewards' duties and responsibilities in a plant agreement which took account of the nature of the groups. Thus, the roles of stewards would be formalized in plant agreements, giving work groups an acknowledged position within the bargaining system. They could be drawn up by a committee of full-time officials, eg, branch and/or district officers, plus managers and stewards aware of behavioural patterns and plant structure. This would make more democratic the process of formulating grievance and bargaining machinery. As the structure of groups changes, eg, with advances in technology, the plant agreement can be revised and the role of the shop steward amended. Possibly, most managements would not wish to grant stewards such explicit rights, although some evidence on managements' attitudes[18] suggests that they prefer dealing with stewards rather than with full-time officials. However, they may prefer to leave such bargaining on its present basis. Dr McCarthy[19] suggests four reasons why management prefers to avoid formal recognition of shop stewards' *de facto* facilities and privileges.

(*a*) For example, managers felt that *de jure* recognition would add to stewards' status, their role being guaranteed by letter rather than acquired by custom or bestowed by privilege.

(*b*) Even if the present incumbents did not abuse the extension of *de jure* rights, managers were worried what advantage their successors might take.

(*c*) Some managers felt it better to confine stewards' rights as at present, for concessions over that might simply encourage even broader demands, to be extended *de facto* before consolidation.

(*d*) '. . . Management, particularly at board level, would not be prepared to admit publicly that they had been forced to accept such modifications in their managerial prerogatives and formal chains of command. For example, acceptance that no work change could be introduced without the prior agreement of shop stewards, or that a senior steward had immediate access to the works manager whenever he wished.'

From his experience, Dr McCarthy concluded that generally stewards 'do not seek to deny that their influence and status would be in some way advanced by a measure of modification of *de facto* procedural channels, one being quoted as saying, 'of course we would like to have the rules of our side – who wouldn't?'

Objections might be expected from some full-time officials, loath to agree extended and formalized bargaining authority to their stewards, implying a somewhat reduced role for themselves. Their objection might be to the act of formalization, since it could involve their exclusion from areas of bargaining they might prefer to retain. Moreover, the approach of unions to the extent of stewards' bargaining activities varies, making it difficult for district officials to agree between themselves on the procedural rights of their stewards. Unless the officials could agree, management might recoil further from the formalization of existing practices.

Yet many full-time officers are overworked and cater for thousands of members. Evidence on this point from the Royal Commission research produced the following figures:

Table 4.1

*Number of Members for whom a Sample
of Full-time Officers was Responsible[20]
(All figures are in thousands)*

	All Unions	T & GWU	AEU	NUGMW	ETU	AUBTW
Total No of Members	1,345	648	316	277	127	27
Average No per Officer	7·5	6·5	15·8	7·1	9·1	1·8

The research also revealed the number of plants for which

officers were responsible and the following table presents these findings:

Table 4.2

Average Number of Plants for which
Officers in the Sample were Responsible[21]

All Unions	T & GWU	AEU	NUGMW	ETU	AUBTW
102	68	193	105	197	145

It is, perhaps, not surprising in the light of the above figures that the mean number of weekly hours worked for all officials in the sample was sixty.[22] In spite of this situation there is little evidence that, generally speaking, unions are sufficiently rich to appoint more full-time officials. Evidence from the latest (1970) Report of the Registrar of Trade Unions and Friendly Societies certainly suggests that this is so. The 326 registered unions (accounting for 9,277,000 trade unionists) had funds equivalent to £14·50 per member and these funds were, of course, to cover all eventualities and hardly form the basis from which to increase the general supply of full-time officers. Thus, if full-time officials are to spend more time on the important aspects of their job, they might be advised to delegate, where necessary and possible, responsibility to their stewards. This would overcome the problem of giving better service to their members, while being unable to persuade them to pay adequate union dues to provide it. By allowing stewards to provide more services, unions need not recruit more full-time officials of the old style. The extra resources obtained from increases in dues might supply research and information locally, for example by the appointment of district research officers to assist full-time officials and steward bargainers.

This would effectively reform trade-union activities within existing practice in collective bargaining. It could be accomplished quickly and efficiently, not needing sweeping changes in structure or methods of financing, and would have the advantage of bringing union activities close to the

membership. Also, since most members who show themselves apathetic about trade-union branch meetings, etc,
tend to regard the stewards *as* the union, our proposals
might encourage non-unionists to join. They would see the
benefits of membership at first hand, rather than regarding
trade unionism as something centred beyond, and remote
from, their workplace.

But, in conclusion, more research is necessary on the role
of stewards in relation to work groups before anything definitive can be said. Clearly, this relationship varies, with
many factors rather than one overriding one. From our
review, however, shop stewards cannot be categorized
universally as work-group leaders, there being wide variations in constituents' pressure and in their acceptance of the
stewards' leadership. Sometimes work groups may throw up
informal leaders to challenge the steward, or they may be
comparatively uninterested in his activities. If work groups
are to play an active part in determining industrial relations
within a workplace through their representatives, the
stewards *must* retain their confidence and support. Evidence
suggests, particularly in large plants, that as stewards become
accepted by management, and as they develop bureaucratic
tendencies within their own stewards' associations, the
senior ones become dissociated from the work groups they
nominally represent. The fuller acceptance of stewards by
management, and the definition of their enhanced status in
agreements, stimulates greater interest in their activities by
the rank and file. However, a means in the workplace for the
regular expression of constituents' views and for more
frequent reporting back by stewards will clearly be necessary
if they are to remain representative and avoid this potential
divorce of interests.

References

1. *The Fawley Productivity Agreements*, Faber & Faber, 1964,
   p 140.

2. Sayles, L. R., *Behaviour of Industrial Work Groups: Prediction and Control*, John Wiley and Sons, London, 1958, p 118.

3. Kuhn, James W., *Bargaining in Grievance Settlement*, Columbia University Press, 1961.

4. Homans, G. C., *The Human Group*, Routledge and Kegan Paul, 1962, p 419.

5. Royal Commission of Trade Unions and Employers' Associations, Research Paper No 1, *The Role of Shop Stewards in British Industrial Relations*, HMSO, 1966.

6. In *The System of Industrial Relations in Great Britain*, Basil Blackwell, Oxford, 1970, p 22.

7. See 'The Cohesion of Trade Union Workshop Organization', *Sociology*, May 1967.

8. Clegg, *op cit*. pp 22–3.

9. Taken from *Glasgow Ltd*, CUP, 1960, pages 171–2, and *Morale on War and Work*, Max Parish, London, 1955.

10. Marsh, A. I., *Managers and Shop Stewards*, Institute of Personnel Management, 1963, pp 15–16.

11. Brown, J. A. C., *The Social Psychology of Industry*, Penguin Books, 1961, p 82.

12. Chase, Stuart, in *Men at Work* and *The Proper Study of Mankind*, quoted in Brown (Reference 11), pp 72–3.

13. Gouldner, A. W., *Wildcat Strike*, Routledge and Kegan Paul, 1955.

14. In *The System of Industrial Relations*, *op cit*, p 24.

15. Turner, H. A., Clack, Garfield, and Roberts, Geoffrey, *Labour Relations in the Motor Industry*, George Allen and Unwin, 1967, pp 222 and 214.

16. Turner, H. A., *Trade Union Growth, Structure and Policy*, George Allen and Unwin, 1963, Sect 3–2.

17. Derber, Milton, *Labour–Management Relations at Plant Level Under Industry Wide Bargaining*, University of Illinois, 1955.

18. Clegg, Killick, and Adams, *op cit*, p 175.

19. Royal Commission Research Paper No 1, *op. cit*, para 50.

20. See *Workplace Industrial Relations*, *op cit*, p 57, para 3.23. The sample consisted of 183 full-time officials 'who played an active part in workplace bargaining' (p 53, para 3.2).

21. *Ibid*, para 3.24. The authors note that in some cases 'plant or establishment' was difficult to define.

22. *Ibid*, page 55, para 3, 18.

Chapter Five

The Duties, Responsibilities and Attitudes of Shop Stewards

A study of primary work groups reveals an important source of pressure on shop stewards. We now turn to the duties and responsibilities of shop stewards as they appear in practice.

The most comprehensive survey of shop stewards appears in the *Government Social Survey of Workplace Industrial Relations*,[1] which was published in March 1968. It is our intention to present some of the more significant findings from this research, and then to present a summary of such findings from our own, much more limited, sample.

The findings of the Government Social Survey

Background of the sample
This part of the survey took the form of structured interviews with 1,161 shop stewards. The T & GWU, AEF, NUGMW and ETU contributed 98·5% of the total number, the NUR and the AUBTW making up the remainder.

Industrial distribution of the sample
Table 5.1 presents this aspect.

The authors of the survey point out that, compared with the total industrial distribution of workers, stewards in certain industries, such as engineering, are over-represented

Table 5.1

	ALL UNIONS	T & GWU	AEU	NUGMW	ETU	AUBTW
	%	%	%	%	%	%
Engineering and electrical goods	24	13	42	18	25	3
Vehicles	11	13	26	—	5	—
Transport and communication ..	12	25	3	6	7	4
Gas, electricity and water	9	2	3	16	20	5
Metal manufacture and goods.. ..	7	4	9	8	7	12
Public administration and defence ..	7	7	3	15	5	3
Chemical and allied	5	8	3	5	4	3
Food, drink and tobacco ..	5	8	1	3	3	1
Professional and scientific	5	5	1	6	5	3
Construction ..	3	1	1	1	9	61
Distributive trades	3	9	—	—	2	—
Shipbuilding and marine engineering	3	4	3	3	2	—
Bricks, pottery, timber, etc. ..	2	1	1	5	3	4
Textiles, leather, clothing	1	*	1	3	1	1
Other industries ..	3	*	3	11	2	—
Total	100	100	100	100	100	100
% base	(1,068)	(306)	(269)	(178)	(241)	(74)

* less than 0·5%

The AEU stewards were concentrated in the engineering and vehicles industry and the AUBTW stewards in construction, but otherwise stewards were spread over a wide variety of industries.

in the sample and stewards in other industries, such as textiles and clothing, are under-represented. They note that the industrial distribution of the sample reflects the various types of work groups represented by stewards in any of the six unions.

Size of plant
47% of the sample were in establishments employing 500
or more people. 29% were in establishments employing
100–499 and 22% in those employing less than 100. The
authors note that these figures are in line with the national
distribution of establishments by size.

Sex and age
Women constituted 6% of the sample (most of these were in
the NUGMW). The average age of respondents was 45
and the age range, by union, was 40 in the ETU to 49 in
the NUGMW.

Educational qualifications
81% of the sample attended secondary modern and ele-
mentary schools (compared with 70% of the general popula-
tion). One-third of the sample had experienced part-time
further education, although in the ETU the figure rose to
60%. A quarter of the stewards had served a full industrial
apprenticeship, with the proportions low in the general
unions, 61% in the AUBTW, 53% in the ETU and 46% in
the AEU.

Membership of other associations
31% of the sample belonged to such associations. This
included 17% who belonged to a political party – a surprisingly small percentage, perhaps, given the political aspects
of the shop steward's image! 70% replied that they paid the
political levy – which means that nearly a third did not!
Only just over half the respondents (54%) from the
NUGMW paid this levy.

Length of membership in the union
Nearly a third of the sample had been in their union for
more than twenty years, a third from ten to twenty years,
and just over a third for less than ten years. Only 4% had
been in their unions for less than two years and, on average,
stewards had been in their union for about fifteen years and

had represented their constituents for about six years. Thus it would appear that a steward normally has a number of years of rank-and-file membership in the union before taking on the job of shop steward.

Some aspects of the research findings

Average size of constituency
The average constituency of shop stewards in the six unions sampled was sixty. McCarthy and Parker note, however, in Research Paper 10 for the Royal Commission on Trade Unions and Employers' Associations,[2] that 'since these unions tend to operate in larger establishments, the overall average constituency size may be nearer 55, with 350 for senior stewards'. From this basis they went on to calculate numbers of stewards in Great Britain.

Numbers of stewards
In Research Paper 10, McCarthy and Parker estimate that in 1968 there were about 175,000 and that this represented an increase of about 15% over the previous ten years. If this trend has continued since 1968 then there may well be 185–186,000 shop stewards in Great Britain at present.

The duties and responsibilities of shop stewards
Table 5.2 presents the research findings in this area.

Each row represents a separate question put to stewards, and the columns cannot, therefore, be added down. The right-hand column represents proportions who *ever* discussed and settled each issue. The difference between these proportions and 100% consists of stewards who either *could* not discuss the issue (since it did not arise in their workplace), or *did* not discuss it.

The table demonstrates that certainly before the Industrial Relations Act began to make an impression, many stewards were performing a wide range of duties and participating in a great deal of bargaining activity. These findings

Table 5.2

Stewards' Range of Bargaining

DISCUSSED AND SETTLED

	EVER	AS STANDARD PRACTICE	RARELY EVER	DISCUSSED AND SETTLED (GROUPED)	AS STANDARD PRACTICE (GROUPED)
	%	%	%	%	%
(a) *Wage issues;*					
piece-work prices ..	28	20	8		
other forms of bonus payments ..	43	25	18		
plus payments for dirty work, etc. ..	39	19	20		
job evaluation ..	33	20	13	83	56
allowances of any other kind ..	36	20	16		
merit money ..	33	17	16		
up-grading ..	45	24	21		
(b) *Working conditions;*					
distribution of work	43	25	18		
pace of work ..	38	22	16		
quality of work ..	39	27	12		
safety questions ..	72	54	18		
health questions ..	60	40	20		
manning of machines ..	33	21	12	89	73
transfer from one job to another ..	56	33	23		
general conditions in the work-place ..	74	56	18		
introduction of new machinery/jobs	39	23	16		
(c) *Hours of work;*					
level of overtime ..	47	34	13		
distribution of overtime ..	48	34	14	75	49
breaks in working hours ..	39	23	16		
stopping and starting times ..	44	24	20		

Table 5.2 (cont.)

	EVER	AS STANDARD PRACTICE	RARELY EVER (GROUPED)		AS STANDARD PRACTICE (GROUPED)
DISCUSSED AND SETTLED					
	%	%	%	%	%
(d) *Discipline;*					
reprimands by the foreman ..	54	26	28 ⎤		
suspension ..	42	22	20 ⎬	67	34
dismissals ..	49	23	26 ⎦		
(e) *Employment issues;*					
taking on new labour	40	24	16 ⎤		
number of apprentices	13	10	8 ⎟		
acceptance of upgrading	35	21	14 ⎬	67	43
short time	24	15	9 ⎟		
redundancy questions	36	20	16 ⎦		

Note A small number of stewards said they also discussed and settled holidays or annual leave and a few other issues, but since these points were not put to all stewards no figures are shown.

are corroborated by the answers given by the samples of works managers and personnel officers (319 of the former and 121 of the latter) to a question on shop stewards' duties and responsibilities. This activity is at least partially reflected in the time spent in what, after all, is a part-time job. The following table deals with time spent.

Table 5.3

Average number of hours per week spent as stewards

	All unions	T & GWU	AEU	NUGMW	ETU	NUR	AUBTW
Hours per week	6	8	5	5	4	15	4

These times included an average of 4 hours spent in working time or during breaks, and 2 hours in the stewards' own time. Amongst the industrial groups, stewards in transport spent most (7·5 hours) and stewards in public administration least (3·5 hours).

Stewards' relations with other actors in workplace bargaining and with their members

Placing duties and responsibilities of stewards together with time spent, the evidence suggests that many of them are performing important tasks for their members, their unions and for management and that this situation appears to be appreciated. Thus, of the sample of union members interviewed (494), 86% felt that there was no one in the constituency who would make a better steward, and 69% felt that their stewards usually managed to get satisfactory settlements with management (5% said that they did not and the rest either answered 'sometimes' or 'don't know'). Of the sample of trade-union officers (this sample consisted of 183 full-time officers, all of whom played an active role in workplace bargaining), 'most officers rate the work of stewards highly' (p 64, para 3.60). 80% of the sample of managers (319 works managers and 121 personnel officers) replied that stewards were either 'very efficient' or 'efficient' as workers' representatives, and 96% of the sample of works managers regarded them as being either very or fairly reasonable people. From the sample of shop stewards, 13% stated that they had been victimized but 83% replied that management's attitude towards trade unions at their place of work was 'reasonably fair'. 93% of stewards considered their management 'reasonably fair' in dealing with workers who break rules and disobey orders. 35% of the sample of shop stewards said that managers were 'very reasonable' in the way they dealt with issues and 52% said that they were 'fairly reasonable'.

Shop steward training

Although stewards appear to be generally accepted by other participants in plant industrial relations systems, they appear to have received little assistance in terms of training courses which were aimed to help them as *stewards*. Figures produced by the research were as follows:

Table 5.4

Stewards who had participated in training courses

	%
All unions	30
T & GWU	40
ETU	29
AEU	23
NUGMW	22
AUBTW	18

Many stewards are thus not receiving the training back-up that the importance of their position warrants. This situation was commented upon by the sample of full-time officers. Only 7% of that sample thought that enough stewards had training for their job as stewards. 22% said, however, that training was available for stewards but they did not use it.

Arguments used to obtain increases
The need for steward training is demonstrated, at least to some extent, by the arguments which they stated that they used to obtain increases. The following table presents these results:

Table 5.5

Arguments used:	UNPROMPTED	PROMPTED	MOST IMPORTANT
	%	%	%
Comparison with other workers in different places of work ..	13	52	9
Comparison with other workers in same place of work ..	14	55	13
Change in the nature of the job	21	66	15
Change in/abnormal conditions of work	22	66	18
The cost of living	9	40	12
The level of profits	3	29	4
Amount of work done/produced	18		8
Ability, skill, quality, increased responsibilities	17		6
Job evaluation	10		6
Other answers	10		3
Don't know/not answered ..	—		6
Total	137%		100%
(Those who increased earnings)	(683)	(683)	(683)

(Both open questions and a series of prompts were used. The prompted list appeared to recall to some stewards arguments that they had forgotten they used.) In order to pursue such arguments effectively many stewards would need both the accurate information upon which to base their arguments and the skills necessary to utilize such information.

Shop stewards and strikes

Perhaps in spite of this poor servicing less than half the sample had experienced a strike[3] since becoming a steward; 40% had experienced at least one strike at their place of work since becoming a steward. This was made up of 16% who had had one strike, 20% who 'seldom' experienced them, and 4% who experienced them 'frequently'. 59% of the sample had used other forms of pressure. 42% had used overtime bans, 30% threats to strike, 28% working to rule, 12% go-slows and 6% other pressures. The majority of respondents (62%) felt that they could not obtain quicker or better results from their managements by using strikes or other forms of pressure. 28% said that they could. This compares with figures of 43% and 55% respectively for the sample of full-time officials. From this evidence it looks as if stewards, on the whole, have less confidence than the full-time officials in the efficacy of strikes and other sanctions.

Stewards' influence over members

The apparent mildness of stewards in the negotiating situation must be seen in the context of the fact that they almost invariably have to persuade their members to agree with them before taking any particular form of action in this area. Stewards' replies to a question about their ability to influence their members emphasizes their difficulties. The question was put to the sample as to whether they could always get their members to see things their way when a particular dispute arose, and get them to do what they (the stewards) believed was right. 43% said that they could, 17% said that they could sometimes and 37% said they could not.

It is interesting to compare this situation with the full-time officer–steward and full-time officer–member relationship. 87% of the sample of full-time officers felt that they had sufficient influence over the activities of stewards and members in industries for which they were responsible. The proportion was at least 80% in all unions. From these figures it appears that the influence of the full-time official is more readily accepted, in most instances, than that of the steward, and this helps to underline some of the difficulties faced by shop stewards.

E

Desire for Promotion

Is the apparent reluctance of many stewards to revert to sanctions a result of their desire for promotion within the company? The statistics suggest that in many cases it is not. 58% of stewards said that they were *not* interested in promotion. 28% stated that they were interested in becoming foremen (which title included other positions such as supervisor, charge-hand or section leader).

Ambition in employment appears to be connected with ambition in the union: 61% of those who wanted to serve the union in another capacity (34% of the sample said that they would like to do so) were interested in promotion, compared with 39% of those who did not want to serve the union in another capacity.

Whether these ambitions are realistic or not is, of course, an important factor in this context. 56% of those who wanted promotion thought that there was no reasonable hope of getting it, and 38% thought that there was such hope.

Shop stewards and their unions

Stewards' relations with managers appear, on the whole, to be good, but what of their relations with the trade unions? First, there appears in many unions to be close contact between stewards and local full-time officials.

Table 5·6

Steward/local officer meetings
Average number of meetings in last 12 months

T & GWU	15
AEU	7
NUGMW	11
ETU	5
AUBTW	15
All unions	12

Most stewards in the sample appeared to be impressed with the part played by local full-time officers in local negotiations. 68% felt that their local officer played a 'very important part', 27% a 'not very important part', and the rest of the sample gave other answers. 34% of the sample said that they would like their officer to play a more important part and most of the rest said that he already played an important part. ETU stewards were the most insistent that officers should play a 'bigger part'. 44% of the sample from this union expressed such a view.

Those stewards who favoured a more important role for their officers stated that in such an eventuality, the following benefits would accrue:

Quicker or better results; more responsive or cooperative management; make good steward deficiencies; make things easier for the stewards.	48%
Meet criticisms that officers are not sufficiently active; satisfy members that officers are doing their share; improve understanding between officers and workers.	16%
Strengthen the unions; draw more members; secure better participation by members.	12%

Most stewards also kept closely in touch with their unions through the branch. 44% of the sample attended all, or nearly all, branch meetings. Only about 15% were completely out of touch with their branch meetings. The average number of attendances in the last twelve months for all respondents was 13. 63% of stewards sometimes used their union branch as a place to *discuss* workers' grievances and claims, 24% did so very often, 19% fairly often, and 20% seldom. 32% of respondents sometimes used their branch as a place to *decide* workshop policy, 13% did this very often, 11% fairly often, and 8% seldom.

Thus stewards serve a useful purpose as communicators within trade unions. The importance of this aspect of their role is reinforced by the answers given by the sample of full-time officers to a question on their communications with members. They were asked how, other than through branch meetings, they did so communicate to discuss grievances and claims. 87% of the sample said through shop stewards, 83% said through correspondence, 79% said by means of the telephone, 75% mentioned workplace meetings, and 63% said by private visits to individuals. Thus the vast majority of full-time officers appear to use stewards as a means of communication.

In the light of these various findings it is, perhaps, not surprising that 70% of stewards thought that they had enough say in their union's policy at *local* level. Only 31%, however, were satisfied with their say in the union's policy at national level.

Stewards' desire for the job

In spite of the apparently good relations and high degree of mutual acceptability between stewards and managers, and stewards and unions, many people had to be persuaded to take on the job of shop steward. 40% of the sample replied that they had had to be persuaded to take the job, and 36% said that they had wanted it but had had to be asked to take it on. These findings were in line with those on elections, where it was found that 71% of the sample of stewards replied that they took on the job without having to go through any form of election. Interestingly, the sample of full-time officers did not entirely confirm the impression of no one else wanting the job of steward other than the man who took it on. Only 6% of the sample said that the *main* reason why stewards took on the job was because no one else wanted it.

Even though many stewards stated that they had had to be persuaded to take the job, the vast majority of the sample stated that they found the job rewarding and satisfying. 81% reported in this vein. The replies to a further question, on sources of satisfaction, showed that the major source was helping members in their place of work and negotiating on their behalf. The authors of the survey note that, in terms of job satisfaction, the largest group of stewards fell into the member-orientation category rather than the negotiating-orientation category or the management-orientation category.[4]

Reasons for resigning as shop steward

In view of this high level of satisfaction it is not surprising to find that 82% of the sample replied to the effect that they wanted to continue as shop stewards. Where stewards do give up there appear to be two or three major reasons. Some of these emerged from a question asked of full-time officers. 42% of the sample of such officers said that lack of cooperation from members was a major reason; 24% mentioned lack of cooperation from management, and 14% mentioned personal and domestic reasons. The two former reasons were also given prominence by the two hundred ex-stewards who were interviewed. The sample of shop stewards indicated another reason, however. When asked how the previous holder came to give up the job, 56% of the 838 stewards replying stated that he either left the firm, was promoted, or transferred to another department. The survey found that 13% of stewards were replaced each year (this calculation was based on replies given by the samples of works managers and personnel officers).

Importance of stewards to unions and members

Certainly it would appear that both members and unions need shop stewards. Most unions have too few full-time officials to cope adequately with the problems of members. Evidence of this situation can be found in the survey. 68% of the sample of full-time officers felt that their union ought to have more full-time officers. Returns varied – with

100% in the ETU saying this, 95% in the AEU and, at the other end of the scale, 57% in the T & GWU.

From the point of view of members, the survey shows that the steward is second to the union journal as a source of information about the union for its members – a further indication of the significance of the steward for constituents.

A factor analysis of stewards' responses

Finally, from the evidence taken from this extremely thorough survey, it is useful to present the factor analysis of stewards' responses. This analysis compares answers to questions under three headings – extent of union activity, experience of militancy, and steward satisfaction. The following table demonstrates the 'loadings' of each question on the factor. A high figure under the loading headings means that the particular answer to any question is quite strongly associated with the other particular answers in that factor. For example, 'think management efficient' is quite strongly associated with 'satisfied with facilities'. 'Think helping management' is not strongly associated with 'think management efficient'.

The authors of the survey draw three main conclusions from the analysis. First, with the exception of employers' association membership, the ways in which the stewards in the two groups of unions answered the questions were broadly similar (as indicated by the factor headings), which suggests that stewards tend to have the same general circumstances and views irrespective of the type of union. Secondly, tendencies for stewards to be both active and militant overlap and, thirdly, the level of steward satisfaction is not related strongly to activism or militancy. (For a more detailed discussion of this analysis see *Workplace Industrial Relations*, *op cit*, pp 46–7.)

Table 5·7

Factor analysis

	Loadings	
	TGWU & NUGMW	AEU & ETU
'EXTENT OF UNION ACTIVITY' (Factor 1)		
Much time spent as steward	·73	·65
Large constituency	·71	·47
High branch attendance	·64	·45
Senior steward	·52	·53
(a) High range of bargaining	·48	·55
Trained as steward	·41	·54
(b) Increase members' earnings	·26	·35
(c) In employers' association	·23	−·09
(d) Act for other unions	·10	·41
Think helping management	·42	·46
Refused to raise an issue	·24	·45
'EXPERIENCE OF MILITANCY' (Factor 2)		
Engineering industry	·75	·64
(d) Act for other unions	·61	·27
Large plant	·58	·63
Much experience of strikes	·58	·61
Much experience of other forms of pleasure	·54	·44
(a) High range of bargaining	·52	·40
(b) Increase members' earnings	·31	·50
(c) In employers' association	−·24	·53
Think get quicker or better results from strikes	·33	·24
'STEWARD SATISFACTION' (Factor 3)		
Think management efficient	·68	·68
Satisfied with facilities	·66	·71
Think management reasonable	·66	·63
Think management's attitude to unions fair	·62	·51
Do not wish to discuss other questions	·53	·58
Satisfied with opportunities to contact members	·50	·50
Think foreman efficient	·47	·45
Do not think get quicker or better results from strikes	·41	·37
Think helping management	·32	·29
Think management fair towards rule breakers	·31	·22
Not interested in another union job	·30	·23

(a), (b), (c), (d) = items loading on two factors.

The East Midlands survey

The results of the Government Survey indicate the general significance of the steward to constituents, trade-union officials and managers. However, the results presented above are related to one survey only – albeit by far the most comprehensive so far undertaken. For purposes of comparison we present a summary of the results of our own survey which was carried out by questionnaire, in 1966–67, into the roles of one hundred shop steward respondents, all of whom worked in the East Midlands. Respondents belonged to the AEF, NUR, NUGMW, BISAKTA, DATA, ASTMS, Hosiery Workers, NUM, ASW, NUSMW & C, T & GWU, ASMU, NACODS, ETU, NGA, and ASPD. The sample is heavily weighted towards establishments with more than two thousand employees.

The mean average size of constitution was sixty, and the duties and responsibilities of the sample can be seen from the following two tables.

The duties and topics covered are numerous, but stewards concentrated on a few. It would appear, from the tables, that they spent their time dealing mainly with matters of pay, hours, policing agreements made with management, on problems of hygiene, on questions arising from joint consultation and on attending branch and steward meetings.

Other important duties include production queries and dealing with complaints about management. One often forgotten element of the steward's job which appears in both tables is that of members' welfare problems. Many members regard their stewards as a source of assistance on welfare matters, especially those which relate to social-insurance benefits. In many cases stewards supplement the role of welfare officers in this area.

The average time spent on duties by stewards of all kinds was 10·7 hours, with 5·9 hours being spent at work and 4·8 hours being spent in their own time.

Our respondents were subject to only limited opposition

Tables 5·8 and 5·9

Importance of main duties according to stewards questioned*	
Duty	*No of times mentioned/100*
Pay problems	36
Observance of agreements	33
Joint consultation	28
Safety	19
Union membership	15
Production queries	12
Complaints about management	12
Welfare problems	12
Branch meetings	11
Steward meetings	10
Hours	8
Branch committee meetings	7
Redundancy	6
Overtime	5
Demarcation	5
New works agreements	4
Apprentices	3
Discipline	3
Job performance	2
Victimization	2
Shift work	2
Holidays	2

Range of shop steward duties	
Duty	*No of times mentioned/100*
Pay problems	82
Hours	53
Observance of agreements	43
Hygiene (factory cleanliness, etc)	34
Branch meetings	32
Safety	29
Joint consultation	28
Production queries	28
Complaints about management	26
Steward meetings	26
Union membership	23
Overtime	19
Welfare of constituents	17
Holidays	14
Dues	11
Redundancy	9
Job performance	8
Work study	7
Discipline	6
Victimization	6
Shift work	6
Staffing	6
Apprentices	4
Suggestions scheme	1
Terms of reference	1
Supervision of work	1
Demarcation	1

* Respondents were asked to list the seven duties they regarded as most important in order of priority. However, many listed less than seven.

in elections. 73% were subject, in theory, to regular re-election; 23% were opposed at the first election and 24% at subsequent elections. Replies to a question on replacement, however, show a large number of *potential* stewards, although in many cases these do not, apparently, contest elections. 64% of our sample thought that there was someone to replace them if they resigned as stewards. It may be that, in many cases, although prospective opponents will not challenge the incumbent they are prepared to wait until he retires. The returns showed an average of 6·5 years spent, to date, as a steward, and this may indicate that many stewards retire voluntarily – since their span of office gives plenty of time for opposition to manifest itself. This does not, of course, imply lack of opposition to the policies of existing stewards since, as suggested in Chapter 4, informal leaders may emerge temporarily.

Relations between stewards and departmental managers appear to be good – 69% of the sample stating that they got on 'well' or 'very well' with such managers.

Finally, most stewards appear to be in close contact with their trade unions. 51% of the sample met full-time officers at least once a month, and 88% of all respondents attended all branch meetings.

Conclusions from the surveys

The results confirm the by now widely held belief that stewards deal with important matters of job regulation such as pay, policing agreements, union membership, etc, and they also underline the breadth of steward activities at the place of work. The quality of relations between stewards and managers, and between stewards and trade unions, appears to be good and most stewards, contrary, perhaps, to their public image, do not appear to have frequent recourse to, or experience of, strikes. This situation exists in spite of the fact that there is a paucity of educational and training provision for shop stewards. No doubt more help in this key servicing area would be appreciated by stewards and would help to make them more effective in doing their job.

Perhaps such education and training courses could be aimed at providing stewards with skill in adjustment to the conflicting expectations and pressures which affect them. The essence of a steward's difficulties is often the role conflict with which he is faced.[5] Members of the steward's role set will often have different expectations of him. Management may well see the steward either as providing a link in the communications chain between themselves and employees or as a spokesman for union members. To the union a steward is often primarily an administrator (recruiting, collecting dues, etc) and communicator. Many unions also see stewards as informal negotiators – informal because the negotiating role is usually not mentioned in the rulebook (see Chapter 3). To the members the steward is usually the only point of contact that they have with the union and they will look to him to settle their problems. Stewards are, of course, directly responsible to workers and must conform to their wishes – even if these wishes are to allow the stewards to use his own discretion. The steward himself will tend to see his role in the light of his perception of the role expectations of other members of his role set and of the impact of such variables as the socio-technical systems of the plant; the tradition of industrial relations in the plant; the services offered by the union; the quality of management (can managers quickly see and diagnose problems?) and the degree of change (organizational and technological) which is occurring, etc.

From this analysis it can be argued that stewards will experience inter-sender conflict. Pressures from one role sender will oppose pressures from another. It is also possible to imagine a situation of 'role overload'. A steward will be asked to perform a number of tasks simultaneously. In both cases he has to decide which pressure to accede to.

How a steward reacts to such pressure will often be related to his original motivation in standing for election. If he was pushed into taking the job he may resign; if he is ambitious he will seek to satisfy whichever need is most clearly related to his own ambition; if he is ideologically motivated he may attack those members of his role set whose expectations he is unable to meet. In such situations in which stewards often find themselves, it may help for the various members of the steward's role set to discuss their general relationships with each other and, perhaps, some identification of demands can be made by the parties concerned. Whatever is done, however, the personality of the steward will be an important variable in shaping his responses.

Education and training courses might well help the steward to perceive more clearly the nature of the pressures operating upon him as well as the nature of the variables which he must take into account when planning strategy and tactics. Additional comments on the education and training of shop stewards can be found in Appendix B.

References

1. *Op cit*, pp 10–52. The survey was carried out in 1966 and consisted of personal interviews with samples of the major actors in workplace industrial relations. The interviews were based on a large number of scheduled questions to shop stewards, ex-shop stewards, full-time union officials, works managers, personnel officers, foremen, trade-union members and non-unionists. Different question schedules were used for each group, although in many cases similar questions were asked of different groups.
2. HMSO, London, 1968, p 15, para 56, fn 1.
3. A strike was defined in broad terms as any withdrawal of labour. The question asked referred to stewards' experience of strikes *at their place of work* – not whether they themselves had been personally involved
4. See Miller, D. C. and Form, W. H., *Industrial Sociology*, Harper, New York, 1957, pp 265–8.
5. Role is defined on pages 5–6 above. Role set is defined as those offices which are related to each other within an organization. Each member of a role set has role expectations of other

members and will communicate these expectations to the role holder. Each role holder will also have a perception of his own role as well as what other role holders 'send' him. For a fuller discussion of these concepts as they apply to the roles of shop stewards, see 'The Challenge from Below: An Analysis of the Role of the Shop Steward in Industrial Relations', by Alexandra Warren, *Industrial Relations Journal*, Vol 2, No 3, Autumn 1971.

Chapter Six

Shop Stewards' Organizations and Hierarchies

Earlier, we examined the influence of both union rulebooks and constituents on stewards' activities. To this must be added the nature of relationships *between* stewards, and the influence of the organizations they have formed. Again, the picture is that of an unstructured and uneven proliferation of *ad hoc* arrangements being indicative of the inadequate response of traditional systems to recent developments. The inadequacy is that they largely failed to anticipate or incorporate new forms of workplace organization. Consequently, workplace bodies have emerged meeting indisputable needs while being beyond external regulation. Perhaps most stewards' organizations emerged to augment services provided by unions, but many now challenge and may undermine union functions. They illustrate the challenge from below to the nature of both unions and collective-bargaining arrangements, also showing that these are no longer – if they ever were – structures with single sources of authority and decision-making.

Certainly, the activities of stewards' committees may not be complementary to the unions' nor to their agreements with employers' associations centrally, although some unions have attempted to integrate internal and external union action. However, even where this link exists, the connexion appears more systematic on paper than in reality. In practice, preserving the union 'chain of command' currently

relies on appeals to loyalty as much as on processes valued
by stewards on utilitarian grounds. The increasingly internalized regulatory process produces workplace arrangements between stewards, which possess their own institutional interests, to be defended against membership as
against management and unions. They are almost embryonic
company unions, though drawing strength from access to
the larger 'parent' bodies outside. Availability is everything,
though usage may be minimal. Consequently, the role of
external unions and joint machinery has declined in relative
if not in absolute importance.

The need for workplace organization, as distinct from
workplace representation, has emerged with increased
numbers of stewards and their experience of common
problems. Stewards, usually either lacking or explicitly denied permission by unions, have formalized inter-union
relationships in the workplace. Their formality varies;
much informal interaction between stewards takes place,
reaching high levels during crises over issues affecting all
stewards and members, reverting otherwise to regular
though infrequent meetings. Sometimes there is no stated
basis, contact being informal; at others inter-union and
inter-work group rivalry may inhibit cooperation.

A close analogy can be drawn between inter-union
stewards' organizations and the TUC. Membership is
voluntary, and some representatives, eg, of white-collar
workers, stay outside. Secondly, individual freedom of action
is little regulated by the centre, whose disciplinary powers
are slight. The leadership of officials of the joint organization may be accepted or rejected, their policies being
subject to approval by other stewards who can opt out.
Yet the convenors' influence can be considerable, particularly on plant-wide topics where all unions have
similar interests and where convenors have good 'records'.
Finally, management, like the Government, may often
negotiate successfully with the joint organization's officials,
but occasionally exaggerate the sway these officials have.
So, the danger exists of the leading stewards' interests

being different on occasions from those of the work groups.

Pressures have led to works-based organizations, often incorporating seniority and precedence, many being unacknowledged by the unions. Although cooperation between stewards does not always take committee form, particularly in small establishments, they are found through out the manufacturing industry, especially in large metalworking sections. Variations are legion, so we must begin our analysis by classifying the committees.

Types of shop-steward committee

(1) *Single union, single department, or plant*
This type, with membership restricted to those in a single union, is the simplest, involving fewest problems for a union. The committee may consist only of stewards, meeting to exchange information and to coordinate their activities. They may elect a senior steward or union convenor. Stewards of one union in a large factory may form their own departmental committees as well as a factory-wide single union committee, this being unnecessary in smaller works. In other cases, the shop committee may contain not only accredited shop stewards, but also rank-and-file members who act as a check on those representatives. Alternatively, the whole committee may negotiate with management, rather than leaving it to individuals.

Some unions, eg, the Hosiery Workers, do not base their workplace structures on representatives, but rely on shop or factory committees. Other unions regard workplace organization of stewards as secondary to workplace representation; indeed few union rulebooks allow for such organization. Among the few, the ETU encourages steward committees while the AEF rules have recognized shop committees since 1930. In both, the committees can elect a convenor, thus strengthening their stewards against those of other unions, and emphasizing membership of a union as the basis of organization and the focus for loyalty. Other variations in organization can be found. For example, the Foundry Workers, the Tailors and Garment Workers, and others initially allow for individual representatives, but stress shop committees which include those representatives and rank-and-file members.

The incidence of intra-union workplace committees has been estimated in the AEF, Marsh and Coker finding about one steward in ten a convenor,[1] ie, a senior steward among AEF stewards. This ratio suggests about 3,000 convenors among all AEF stewards. It is not known how far employers accept this role, though informally it seems widespread.

Perhaps the best example of workplace, single union *organization* is in printing, an orderly system of single union chapels having long been established. Each union chapel, ie, all members, elects chapel officials, including an FOC to act as senior representative in the department or establishment. This structure is closely integrated into each union in the industry.

(2) *Multi-union, single department*

These committees are found formally in relatively large establishments. Stewards of different unions from the same department form a joint shop committee to coordinate activity, face management, or act jointly in the plant-wide committee if departmental loyalties occasionally supersede union affiliation. The joint departmental committee may elect a convenor as representative at convenors' meetings.

(3) *Multi-union, whole plant*

This inter-union joint committee is perhaps the most usual form of steward organization, being known as the Joint Shop Stewards' Committee (JSSC) within a factory. Membership derives simply from being a shop steward. A committee of all union representatives is thus formed irrespective of union affiliation. When an over-large committee hampers the conduct of business, the JSSC may elect a convenor and an inner committee as the executive body. In smaller plants, the necessity for a further committee between the total body of stewards and the convenor, normally secretary of the JSSC, is less likely. However, other officers, eg, treasurer or representatives on management/employee committees, are still necessary. For example, the employee side of Joint Works Committees at Ford's consists of stewards elected by and from the stewards in each plant.

Variations in nomenclature make identification and understanding of function difficult. For example, Works Committees were established in federated engineering establishments under the 1919 agreements, still being found today. They were joint management/employee bodies with a specific but optional part in disputes procedure, to settle issues unresolved at shop-manager level, and prevent them from getting to works-conference stage. They were not originally part of internal steward organization, though consisting invariably of stewards. Stewards who are members of the Works Committee in federated establishments can meet in works time and usually form the executive of the JSSC. The secretary of the JSSC, the convenor, is normally secretary of the workers' side of the Works Committee, and is normally[2] responsible to the JSSC. Other worker representatives on the Works Committee may also be responsible to the JSSC and/or steward committees based on union affiliation or on a departmental basis.

Inter-union JSSCs focus union activity within a plant, especially if it is small. Here the whole committee negotiates on inter-departmental interests. Otherwise, an inner executive headed by a convenor acts on inter-departmental issues or in formal meetings with management. Electoral rules may allow the convenor powers to negotiate on behalf of all members, irrespective of union, and this practice may be tacitly acknowledged by management. Tactically, however, the convenor often prefers at least one other steward to accompany him.

Thus, the common multi-union stewards' committee seeks to overcome some disadvantages of union structure, and the unions' failure to adapt internal organization to the needs of workplace activity. Though performing a function, *formal* recognition by unions and management is minimal. Management particularly may recognize a convenor *de facto*, but neither has been anxious to stimulate powerful JSSCs. Both sides may attempt to ignore their existence.

(4) *Company-wide combine committees*

A shop stewards' combine committee is one of stewards from different establishments of a multi-plant firm. A common employer creates such committees, which frequently run counter to the district basis on union organization. Where branch factories are close geographically, the committees are more cohesive, those at Rootes, Morris Engines, and Standard Triumph International factories near Coventry being good examples. If organized in multi-product firms, the committee also cuts across different 'industries', and possibly industry-wide bargaining institutions. Usually such a committee comprises a few stewards from each plant, depending on size, normally including the works convenor. Organization of stewards within the same company but at different locations grows to meet the situation, eg, a dispute, where a convenor at one plant contacts another at a different plant. This contact may evolve through correspondence to informal meetings, and to a loose framework. It may remain *ad hoc*, or develop into a company-wide combine committee with its own, usually part-time, officers, funds, a written constitution, and regular minuted meetings.[3]

Such combine committees are most easily found in large firms, eg, BMC where formal meetings take place in different towns every two months. The Rootes Group Stewards' National Committee meets monthly in London, the directors having occasionally met the full committee. In Ford's, meetings were once secretive, but the committee has been acknowledged by senior management who now meet the plant convenors twice a year. Such committees exist in most large companies, and are not restricted to the 'engineering' industry. For example, shop stewards at ICI have links through the so-called ICI National Joint Committee, but this body is not recognized by the company. Meetings are usually supplemented by correspondence where distance inhibits regular contact. As stewards at different plants of one firm exchange information for mutual advantage, so do combine committees, particularly those from firms in competition. For example, the Ford and BMC combine committees exchange information with other committees in the motor industry, while stewards from the new motor plants on Merseyside have had informal meetings. Despite this, there seems little contact between stewards' organizations in different firms in one area. A shared employer constitutes a stronger link than a local labour market.

(5) *Industry-wide committees*

National industry-wide committees are generally regarded as a challenge by existing unions and encounter more definite opposition, in contrast with the somewhat equivocal reaction to workplace and combine committees. Industry-wide committees of stewards occur in several industries, notably in electricity supply, engineering, building, exhibition contracting, and, until recently, in the motor industry. Similar industry-wide organization of workplace leaders is found in the docks, through the Portworkers Liaison committees. However, their formality, influence and degree of representativeness varies widely. Some committees are industry-wide, but are more accurately described as 'industry-based', their influence varying considerably by region. For example, unofficial site organization in building is stronger in London, through the London Building Workers' Joint Sites Committee, than elsewhere. During the last war, the Shop Stewards' National Council was influential in the aircraft industry, and subsequently throughout engineering. In the fifties, the BMC joint stewards combine committee created an industry-wide Shop Stewards' Committee, holding meetings attended by stewards from all major car-manufacturing companies. This committee had a formal constitution, and met regularly, but since the late 1950s it has disintegrated, though informal contacts are maintained.

The Engineering and Allied Trades Shop Stewards'

National Council has long existed and was particularly influential during the last war. Its present significance is arguable, but it was condemned by the TUC in 1960. The unofficial stewards' organization in the electricity supply industry seems stronger in London than elsewhere, emerging during national wage negotiations to put pressure on official negotiators. During negotiations in 1963, its call for a 'go-slow' was followed in some power stations. Though its leading spokesman was expelled from his union, the committee still exists and publishes a periodic newsheet, *The Power Worker*.

The titles of some bodies claiming to be national stewards' organizations are much more grandiose than realistic. Most lead a shadowy existence, spasmodically emerging during crises. During wage negotiations in July 1963, London stewards claimed that they had organized stoppages on building sites in London, Liverpool, and Manchester. Most cannot be regarded as permanent, national bodies. More accurately, they are groups of militants, frequently dominated by members and sympathizers of extremist political bodies. Attendance at meetings is left to individual choice, though workplace stewards' committees may pay the expenses of attendance. Officially, most unions dislike or prohibit participation; this may inhibit their development, but does not stop the flow of literature.

(6) *National and other committees, irrespective of industry*
Industry-wide stewards' committees retain at least an ostensibly advantageous organizational form, in their 'rational' industrial basis. However other, less theoretically justifiable, committees exist, eg, attempts to call national conferences or to form a national organization of stewards to challenge individual unions and the TUC in national policy. The TUC condemned 'the abortive conference in December 1959 convened in the name of the Firth Brown stewards'.[4] Others attempt organization by region, eg, the London Shop Stewards' Defence Committee. These bodies are less significant even than industry-wide committees, their purposes and sponsors being perhaps more suspect.

There is little evidence of formal organization between stewards of firms using the other's product. Where contact exists it has seldom evolved, in the absence of geographical proximity, beyond correspondence and exchanged information. Lerner and Bescoby[5] quote an example of a loose liaison between the joint stewards' committee of a Sheffield crankshaft firm and the BMC Combine Committee. Before the merger of Briggs Motor Bodies and Ford's, links between their stewards were close, because of geography, competition in the same labour market, and the dependence of one plant on the other.

The most authoritative evidence on the extent of shop-steward organizations and hierarchies available to date was gathered by the Royal Commission's survey, details of which are given in Chapter 5. Just over one-fifth of the sample of shop stewards were senior stewards, and over two-thirds of the stewards and the personnel officers questioned said there were senior stewards in their plants. The senior stewards spent an average of ten hours per week on their union duties, compared with the six hours spent by ordinary stewards. One per cent of the sample were 'full-time' stewards. Meetings of stewards, of a variety of forms, took place in the workplace of 66 per cent of the survey's informants. Almost half the stewards said meetings of stewards of different unions were held at their workplace, 12 per cent of the stewards said they had attended so-called combine committee meetings, and 42 per cent of the full-time officers said that at least some of their stewards had attended such meetings. Stewards' meetings in a single workplace were mostly organized by the stewards themselves but those of the combine type were organized about equally by stewards and by full-time officials.

The reasons for shop-steward committees

The emergence of steward committees has been encouraged by many factors, some closely associated with the advent of stewards themselves. Bargaining opportunities in the plant, the divorce of branches from the workplace, low branch attendance, and union structure are examples. However, other reasons explain the need for coordination between workplace representatives.

The size of manufacturing establishments and of companies has increased generally. In June 1961 over 48 per cent of employees in manufacturing worked in establishments employing more than 500 people, over a third in establishments of over 1,000.[6] Work in large plants obviously demands formal contact between stewards. Moreover, the distribution of stewards, in engineering at least, is disproportionately concentrated in large establishments,[7] and over recent decades representation has deepened. Increasingly large-scale manufacturing units, and more stewards per member, simultaneously make committees desirable, on numerical grounds alone.[8]

Tactically, there is an obvious logic for joint steward committees. The stewards of different unions face a single employer, whose policies affect them all. They have similar working conditions, consultative machinery, wages structure, personnel policies, and general practices. Unionism is steeped in ideals of fraternity and unity, the latter having repeatedly been of enormous strategic value. The unions recognize the need to meet employers collectively in industry-wide bargaining, either through a federation or an *ad hoc* negotiating committee. The effectiveness of united activities and policies is similarly apparent to stewards. Joint organization facilitates a concerted response to management, offsetting the often weakening effects of separate working policies.

Autonomous JSSCs may act on policies not uniformly supported by each union in the plant. However, it is more likely that such committees will take decisions on issues on which their unions have no predetermined policy, or formally offer no guidance. Thus, joint committees may not so much clash with union policies, as determine supplementary ones, though these may subsequently be repudiated officially.

Inter-union contact at workplace level is not only of tactical value, but is perhaps primarily induced by the search for information and the pooling of knowledge about the employer. It supplements information from branch meetings about conditions in other firms. Managements are sensitive to the activities of firms in the same labour market, privately exchanging information on such labour matters as earnings, holiday arrangements, shifts, discipline, etc. Management is also aware of dissimilarities between departments of the same plant and between plants. For the unions, the locality is covered by residence-based branches, but the absence of a union mechanism to exchange information about factory practices has led stewards to create their own organizations.

Sometimes, this latent organization has been impelled towards formality by various joint management/employee committees. Committees forming part of the procedural chain, or general consultative, production, safety, and other internal committees including employees bring together workplace representatives. Agendas must be formulated, and the secretary and members elected. If they discuss relatively significant problems, stewards endeavour to obtain seats on them. Since consultative and other committees discuss topics of specific union interest, as is the trend, management will require authoritative union representatives.

The development of productivity bargaining at establishment level in the mid and late 1960s saw the creation of *ad hoc* multi-union committees of stewards which, subject to outside ratification, negotiated with management at length and in detail over the introduction of changed working methods, etc. Such bodies, which appeared to overcome the difficulties of multi-unionism at plant level and to develop a functional working relationship between stewards and external full-time officials, were commended by both the NBPI and the Donovan Commission. Some of the early procedural reports of the CIR have recommended single plant or company-wide bodies, and the integration of plant negotiating and consultative arrangements into a single committee.

The difficulties of cooperation at branch level between different unions may be exacerbated by inter-union competition, which may extend to their workplace representatives. The numbers of unions and representatives in a plant also complicate workplace organization, however desirable to stewards. Despite this, the number of unions claiming representatives in a plant is often exaggerated by reference only to very large industrial firms. Marsh and Coker found that workplace union structure in engineering was relatively simple, eg, in establishments with fewer than 1,000 manual workers, on average less than four unions had stewards. The average figure for establishments in the 1,000–5,000 range was only six.[9] In the industry most frequently quoted to illustrate union structural inefficiencies, the organizational problem therefore appears manageable, in terms of the number of stewards to be brought together. The recent spate of union mergers, involving such formerly independent unions as the NUVB, ETU, PTU, ASW, CEU, DATA, etc., has no doubt reduced this problem.

The interdependence of work groups resulting from modern technology further stimulates joint organization within a firm. Action in one section has immediate repercussions on employment elsewhere. Joint organization does not prevent sectional action, but it aids support action or at least forewarning. This information centre may similarly mitigate undesirable repercussions, or reveal new means for settlement. Certainly, realization of interdependence has promoted the development of coordinating committees in firms.

The functions of joint shop-steward committees

The activities of joint stewards' committees could all be classified as coordination. In answer to a question in our questionnaire about the value of such a committee, the most

frequent justification was as a source of information about
events in the plant. Details of current problems and of
practice in different departments predominated at JSSC
meetings, respondents emphasizing the up-to-date nature
of the information, as against that from branch meetings.
Our respondents indicated that some committees met regularly each week, others quarterly, but most were 'monthly,
plus, as and when necessary'. Pooling of information about
current problems and practice was highly valued, presenting
a more coherent picture of managerial policy than was
otherwise available to individual stewards. For example,
one steward said, 'Every steward is in the picture about
management.'

· The committees were also considered important in uniting
aims, in allowing common policies to be developed and, as
one respondent put it, enable 'one approach to management
instead of four separate ones'. Others mentioned that they
revealed the consensus of opinion, and that they promoted
unity among union members. Thus, inter-union committees
do more than provide information; they develop common
policies for stewards of different unions. These policies were
related to all the workshop problems which stewards encounter, respondents specifically mentioning discussions on
pay, job rates, differentials, machine speeds, redundancy,
grading, holidays, shiftworking, safety, welfare, JWC
agenda, demarcation, union membership, overtime, and
work study. After similar investigation in engineering, Dr
Lerner concluded that 'these committees have provided
most of the initiative for extending the scope of factory
agreements.[10] Clearly, plant committees provide a forum for
discussion of stewards' current problems, and a mechanism
promoting common lines of approach. Such policy-making
is, in the strict union view, outside the scope of stewards,
taking place in a body beyond union control.

Most inter-union committees elect officials, and possibly
a smaller executive committee, to be concerned with plant-
wide issues. This executive, eg, a works committee, is
regarded as senior, assisting stewards in their union or their

area who have registered 'failure to agree' in early stages of procedure. They, in turn, often pass problems to the works convenor. Respondents noted, for example, 'the weekly meeting gets fairly rapid results through the convenor'. The committee may nominate candidates for management/ worker committees and, as from its own officers, will receive periodic reports. One respondent stressed that 'the formation of sub-committees to look into particular questions is useful', another mentioning that the work load could be shared. This division of labour suggests that policy formation has achieved some degree of refinement.

The JSSC also has an educational function. Many respondents mentioned that the committee enabled them to 'air problems and get good advice'. Others stressed the help of experienced stewards in advising their younger colleagues. The meetings gave stewards an opportunity to raise problems, and they valued the advice they received. Again, the committees fill a gap left by the unions, this time in 'training'. This has important implications, practices tending to be perpetuated, the stewards' functions being subject to equalizing pressures irrespective of union. The influence of more experienced stewards is probably extended at the expense of full-time officials. Some senior stewards mentioned the committee as a valuable communications system for passing information to constituents. Some committees published newsletters for factory circulation, financed from JSSC funds. Some managements provided facilities, in other cases it was done less openly.

Committees raise funds through raffles, sweepstakes, and levies. These funds have many uses, eg, administration and secretarial assistance, publication of bulletins, compensating stewards for loss of earnings when not otherwise provided for, expenses of such committee officials as delegates, such welfare benefits as funeral wreaths and donations, and other activities.

While their functions vary, one major activity is providing information before bargaining, discussing bargaining priorities, consolidating aims, and coordinating action.

Committees widely attempt to standardize practices among departments, and management is made to feel vulnerable if its policies are applied inconsistently. Even slight variations over small issues, eg, the number of times late before a warning, provoke claims for uniformity of treatment. More significant are similar equalization claims on such topics as piecework and bonus rates, overtime distribution, etc. There are, almost inevitably, inconsistencies in piecework prices to be used as a lever, and the joint committee can reveal them. These are exploited by appeals that, in fairness, similar jobs should receive similar rewards, the equity of sharing overtime equally, 'why aren't maintenance men warned for bad timekeeping', etc. As one steward put it, 'anomalies arising on the shop floor can be ironed out.' The use of comparability, and managements' sensitivity to it, enables concessions in one department to be transmitted throughout the plant, and regenerated by appeal to customary differentials. Pressure is exerted in vulnerable departments or plants for improvements, and the gains spread across the plant by intra-plant whipsaw tactics. Management in large plants faces an enormous communications problem if it is to contain this form of advance, as do multiplant companies in face of a combine committee, for their techniques are essentially similar. The building industry affords another variation on this form of pressure. Organization between stewards on large sites is often better than that between different subcontractors on the site. Here the comparisons bargaining technique is applied to each employer in turn, 'original' pressure being directed against the most vulnerable subcontractor from time to time. Firms whose contracts contain penalty clauses may be especially open to workplace pressures and, with no coordination between the firms, this ratchet advance can be perpetuated. Similarly, strong workplace organization prevents management transferring work held up by a dispute, outside officials having difficulty in discovering the truth.

Company-wide combine committees

Company-wide combine committees' opportunities for fruitful comparison are largely limited to those afforded by management. Owing to difficulties, their principal communication concern is with major conditions, eg, earnings, manning production schedules, discipline, hours, grading, etc. In engineering, where the national agreement makes no provision for fringe benefits such as retirement pensions, sickness benefits, redundancy payments, etc, some combine committees have been preoccupied with this topic, although others are also frequently discussed. Transfers of work to new plants in Development Areas have caused anxieties in the older motor factories, and have been discussed by the Combine Committees.

Companies whose wage structure is relatively simple, eg, those based on time rates for few grades in a job evaluation scheme, as at Ford's, or in the chemical industry, or where there is centralized control, plainly limit their scope. In contrast, companies with complicated payment systems, with large incentive components, and a high degree of decentralization, provide endless opportunities for plant pressure on the grounds of 'fair comparison'. Conversely, regular contact between stewards from different plants probably inhibits management from attempting to take advantage. Managements do not oppose variations in principle, eg, in earnings, as in different locations this may be consistent with an adequate labour force. Their acceptance of standardization is partly the result of union, and partly steward pressure.

Having studied earnings for six categories of workers in several branches of engineering. Lerner and Marquand[11] concluded that combine committees equalize earnings upwards through multi-plant firms. This hypothesis may explain the absence of correlation in most regions between high or low earnings, and high or low labour demand. The strength of the committees is a factor in transferring earnings improvements, in time, from high labour-demand areas to others. Similarly, companies with interests in different sub-branches of an industry or those whose interests spread in conglomerate form across industries may find it desirable – for internal policy reasons or because of combine-committee pressure – to develop uniform company-wide wage structures. In this way, increases perhaps justified by reference to productivity improvement in one plant or product division may be transmitted to workers of similar skills, and union membership, in other sections of the firm. Such mechanisms in a firm's internal wage structure can have important implications. Both 'industry' and 'district' earnings statistics figure prominently in union and steward arguments for improvements locally, and so the committees' activities stimulate reactions outside the firm concerned.

Employers also undertake wage surveys, noting conditions provided by competitors in the industry, and in the same locality. This criterion for granting or rejecting claims for improvements is often used by employers in negotiations, inducing stewards to obtain similar information. On the local criterion, stewards are often informed through their branches or district committees. AEF stewards complete a detailed report on workshop conditions and rates every quarter, to be discussed at the quarterly district meetings of stewards. The gap in information about their company left by union organization regionally is partially remedied by combine committees, while communication between stewards in competing firms further supplements bargaining material. Some unions, eg, the T & GWU and NUVB in the Midlands motor industry, have sought to recover supervision of this activity by organizing meetings of stewards from one large firm, and from competing firms.

Combine committees are seldom recognized by unions or management, but Ford's has sought to associate the committee with its internal communications system. Periodic meetings between convenors and company (as opposed to plant) management are conducted 'consultatively', giving convenors accurate information and management opportunities to clarify policies and kill rumours. Other companies tacitly acknowledge combine committees by listening to points raised by stewards known to be influential on them, or by providing them individually with information.

Company-wide combine committees thus occupy an anomalous and necessarily unofficial position, but their proliferation has not thrown up as many problems for the unions as might be expected. They coordinate JSSCs, gather and disseminate information, and act as pressure groups on both management and official union negotiators. Their activities, methods, and perhaps policies stem from the failure of multi-plant firms to develop comprehensive, company-wide machinery, although many provide such channels on a plant basis.

Convenors and senior stewards

The variety of stewards' workplace organizations is reflected in the different bases for the election of convenors and chief or senior stewards. For example:

(a) In large plants, workplace organization may be based on a hierarchy of shop committees, each electing a shop convenor, he in turn representing them on a plant-wide convenors' committee which forms the executive body of the JSSC. This shop committee may have a multi-union composition.

(b) Stewards of one union may elect a senior steward or convenor from amongst themselves, to represent their union in plant-wide discussions.

(c) Collectively, the stewards in a plant (or shop convenors or single union convenors) may elect a works convenor, who will represent stewards across the whole plant. Always, the convenor is answerable to the body electing him, either within one or across several unions. He is normally subject to re-election, but many convenors continue in office as long as they retain the stewards' confidence.

The formality of procedures for the election of convenors can be exaggerated, but it tends to be more regularized than is management's attitude to the hierarchy of stewards. The Engineering Employers' Federation has not recognized convenors, though many federated companies do. The Confederation of unions formally acknowledged them in 1947, and has endeavoured to draw works convenors into its structure. Managements usually recognize convenors or senior stewards informally, but some avoid these terms. They acknowledge that a certain steward, eg, the convenor, is influential and has a wider brief than others, but will not acknowledge the role as such. Thus, recognition *de facto* is common, but *de jure* definition of the office avoided. Some firms accept the convenor *de jure*, though understating the extent of his officially acknowledged functions. Other firms fully accept the situation and provide such facilities as office, telephone, and possibly clerical help for the works convenor.[12]

Thus, management wavers between grudging recognition and enthusiastic assistance. Many purposely leave the position flexible for fear the present convenor may be replaced by someone less acceptable. Thus, liberal facilities offered to one convenor, eg, freedom of access throughout the plant and to senior management, can, it is thought, be limited if his successor shows signs of abusing them. For this reason, most firms insist that convenors retain some connexion with the job they nominally hold, by working the start of their shift, or by clocking in as if for their nominal job.

In large plants, a works convenor may come to spend most or all his working time on his representative duties. Clegg *et al* (1961) note that in Birmingham 'local employers and trade-union officers seem prepared to agree that about fifty convenors (or other representatives) spend more than half their time on union business, and that most but by no means all are in the engineering industry'.[13] The question of payment is handled in various ways. Management may agree to pay the convenor an agreed salary as a convenor, though more usually he is paid the average earnings for his work group or, rarely, the basic rate. Whatever the practice, the joint stewards' committee usually makes up any loss of earnings from their own funds. It is not unknown for members' contributions to make up a convenor's entire earnings.

The degree to which management recognizes a works convenor will influence his role. Some withhold recognition totally, restricting him to internal administration among the stewards. Much more often, however, management acknowledges his influential position, and attempts to utilize it. The convenor enables management to discuss problems common to many unions within the factory, reducing the number of occasions when solutions wait on not readily available external officials. His presence allows more problems to be kept domestic, if both sides desire this. Also, managements may dislike local union officials, therefore channelling negotiations through convenors and stewards. The reverse can also apply, management sometimes seeking to restrict the role of workplace representatives in favour of district or national officers, or to maintain management prerogatives. A T & G W U national officer has claimed that at Ford's '. . . nearly every matter which was likely to become a dispute was within the field in which shop stewards were not allowed to negotiate. They were not allowed to discuss merit pay, line speeds or labour content, work standards and movement of labour'.[14]

Often the works convenor is an experienced unionist, and is regarded by both sides as an elder statesman. In our experience, senior positions in steward organizations, convenor or works committeeman, are often held by one person for long periods. A convenor's ability to influence his fellow stewards is valuable to managers, permitting ready consultation on plant-wide topics, avoiding duplication and saving time. Such topics are frequently raised by management, and the presence of a convenor facilitates a quick and convenient reference for management if the interests of work people are affected by a change. In a case study of one factory, Alan Fox notes that the 'convenor', who was branch secretary of the workplace-based branch, was

'. . . a pivotal figure in the whole pattern of management–union relations . . . Nominally he was a leading hand in the warehouse and received the rate for the job, but came to spend the whole of his time on union business. In negotiation and discussion, his complete authority over the men meant that if a matter was cleared with the convenor it was cleared with them all. His behaviour was not only that of the redoubtable fighter for the workers' rights and interests, it also carried some of the flavour of an auxiliary to management. This was an outcome not of sympathy with management or Company, but of identification with Milton as a working community.'[15]

In large plants there are difficulties of contact between stewards and management. A convenor, trusted by his committee, will facilitate frequent contact and the growth of confidence between the senior steward and management. Many managements seek to establish cordial personal relationships, emphasizing their availability to the convenor, who is rightly thought important in determining the attitude of stewards. An established convenor adds continuity to the conduct of labour relations, especially where turnover of shop stewards is high.

However, the works convenor is not always universally accepted by work groups, which limits his influence and the unity of the factory labour force. Working solidarity may be achieved only if the convenor is accompanied by a deputy works convenor of a different union. If a convenor is generally accepted by other stewards, he is asked to advise them individually on problems, tactics, and possibly policy. A long-established convenor is particularly useful for his knowledge of plant practices and precedents, for these are seldom written into agreements. Additionally, he is expected to protect the interests of members temporarily without a steward, and often supervises elections. Thus, he is generally thought of as advancing the interests of *all* employees, being free of sectional bias, almost in forgetting to which union he belongs. The works convenor's position is like that of a steward adviser, a day-to-day coordinator on issues referred to him by stewards. He may take a part in the progression of grievances, depending how far an individual steward has gone, procedural practice within the firm, the importance of the issue, etc. He may limit himself to issues which run across union membership or departments, or problems with policy implications, or new issues. Management may regard him as a trouble shooter, and expect him to influence other stewards in observing procedure and to use his expertise and experience to calm troubled waters and prevent hasty action.

The research reported by Clegg, Killick, and Adams included twenty-eight completed questionnaires from convenors, though not distinguishing shop, union, and works positions. Consequently, there are limitations to the conclusions which can be drawn. For example, average size of constituencies was 978, but excluding those convenors responsible for less than 100 members, the average constituency becomes 1,648. One respondent said he was personally responsible for 18,000 members. The results showed that the convenors spent, on average, eighteen hours of working time, and five hours of their own time on union business per week. They spent much more time in negotiations with management above foreman level than at that level, time spent with senior management being five times greater than with shop-floor supervision. Such negotiations took just over one-third of all the time spent, while 'discussions with members and stewards', presumably strongly weighted by the latter, accounted for another third.

These averages obscure individual variations, and certainly hide the convenor who is concerned with industrial relations nearly full-time. It is difficult to say how many convenors fall into this category, for the informality of practice leads to underestimation. Rigid interpretation of 'full time' leads to similar understatement. Thus, Clegg *et al* guessed at more than 500 full-time convenors, or their equivalent, in this country. Not all are in manufacturing industry, and of these by no means all in engineering. 'The number giving half their time or more to work of this kind might be as high as two thousand.'[16] This is little less than the 2,500 figure given for ordinary full-time union officers and is certainly rising more rapidly, indicating their importance and potential as works-based 'full-time' union representatives.

Convenors and the unions

In contrast with salaried union officers, shop and works convenors elected by multi-union committees are not accountable as convenors to any union executive. Integration is possible only where the unions are linked through federation or, less likely, where all unions accept the primacy of a works convenor over other stewards, allowing his union to exercise supervision. It is extremely unlikely that this will be accepted by other unions or stewards, as it implies subordination of interests to one union, perhaps a union without the majority of members. The best contemporary arrangement is found in the building industry. The National Federation of Building Trades Operatives has wide powers over its member unions. A federation steward is appointed on each site, being responsible to the Federation. He is normally accepted as senior by stewards of other unions, and can convene meetings to decide issues affecting members of more than one union. Also, the Federation has monthly meetings of stewards of affiliated unions, attended by federation stewards. The NFBTO comes closest to formal integration of 'chief stewards', being allowed by member unions to exercise some coordinated control.

In large printing establishments, an Imperial Father is sometimes elected to coordinate issues affecting members of several chapels. However, traditions of craft differentiation, separate union organization, and the weakness of the Printing and Kindred Trades Federation at workplace level have limited the development of this office.

The Confederation of Shipbuilding and Engineering Unions adopted a link with convenors in 1947, recognizing Joint Shop Stewards' Works Committees and giving Confederation credentials to the chairman and secretary of these committees. These confederation stewards 'shall act on behalf of and be responsible to the Confederation District Committee'[17] with direct access to the Confederation's district secretary, a full-time official of one union. In addition, the forty-eight district committees hold quarterly meetings of the chairmen and secretaries of stewards' works committees. Thus, the framework for communication and control exists, but the authority of the Confederation has not developed, the term 'confederation steward' being little used. As stated, the Engineering Employers' Federation has not recognized these offices. Secondly, the Confederation has minimal autonomy from its constituent unions locally, and the machinery for control remains largely on paper. Unions within the Confederation have not altered their rulebooks to allow for this provision, and such rulebooks are still the primary reference for stewards.

Limitations on steward committees

So far, we have discussed both intra-plant and inter-plant joint steward committees, emphasizing the reasons for their existence and the value stewards attach to them. However, there are contrary pressures militating against them, currently perhaps being a greater check than any formalized system outside a powerful federation.

At plant level, the unions may be in sharp conflict, eg, over membership or work allocation, which inhibits co-operation between stewards. Certain sections may advance their own interests while ignoring others', and may positively injure the interests of members of other unions. At BMC's Coventry plant in 1966, production workers of one union struck in protest against the unofficial activities of internal transport workers organized by another union, because the latter's protracted action limited their piecework earnings.[18] One union's members may be harmed by the advance of others, particularly over demarcation and manning, as during the introduction of the web-offset process in printing.

Certain groups of workers may not feel they have much except information to gain from cooperation, eg, maintenance workers in relation to production workers, staff union representatives and manual workers. Small unions fear their interests would be submerged in any association, independence being preferable, although stewards' committees seldom infringe the freedom of action by 'affiliated' stewards. This view is commonly held by skilled maintenance men, who seldom fully accept non-craftsmen as convenors. As noted, unions often refuse to allow convenors from other unions to negotiate for their members.

Personalities and politics also enter the undercurrent of stress dividing stewards. Local full-time officials may take a strong line over participation in inter-union committees. Certain sections may be considered to be benefiting disproportionately from joint organization. Shift working makes meetings difficult, and infrequent contact leads to suspicion. This infrequency is especially important in inhibiting combine committees between remote plants. Further, the interests of different plants are not identical. For example, the location of extensions may be influenced by the labour relations in various branches. In difficult times, work allocation between units makes some more vulnerable to short-time working and redundancies. Further, there may be suspicion that the convenor is utilizing his position to advance the interests of members of his union, while neglecting those of others. Thus, inter-union competition over membership, composition of joint stewards' committee, and other problems limits the cohesiveness of workplace committees. Combined committees may be particularly hampered by lack of funds, lack of data implied by the absence of full-time assistance, changes in personnel, and the difficulties of attendance. Indeed, having recently surveyed the motor industry, Turner, Clack and Roberts concluded that national firm-wide committees had had little effect, and that 'the effectiveness of the stewards' associations seems roughly in inverse proportion to their distance from the workplace'.[19]

Committees, unions and bargaining

Joint shop stewards' committees are patently considered useful by stewards, but they have created opportunities for independent action. They may challenge existing union policies and the established machinery for regulating relationships. Despite this, their relationship with the unions and management has not, in the main, presented major difficulties. Some notorious, but exceptional combine committees or JSSCs have ignored established trade unions and collective agreements, interposing themselves between the rank and file and union officials. Examples were those at Briggs Motor Bodies, London Airport, and Ford's in the late fifties and early sixties. Court of Inquiry Reports documented the financial strength, independence, and extremism of these committees, indicating the attractions of these powerful 'private unions' to men dedicated to industrial disruption for political reasons.[20]

The unions are aware, as the TUC put it, that 'some joint arrangements between stewards have been harmful', to unions as to employers. Further, 'cases of muddle, duplication and even conflict have arisen through these bodies acting as though they were independent of union obligations'.[21] The *potential* freedom of action within contemporary union workplace organization is well attested by the TUC's view. Initial union coolness to joint steward committees has not prevented their appearance. The unions must now live with them, and find ways to influence them.

Certainly, present trends suggest the continued growth of stewards' committees, highlighting the problem of lack of a mechanism for drawing these bodies into official union organizations. Present union rules do not allow for their development and so they grow through expediency to meet day-to-day requirements. The dynamic of modern manufacturing and the urgency of many problems demand rapid decision-taking. Reference to external union bodies is time-consuming, and it is likely that the periodic meetings specified in federation rulebooks are devoted to previous events, rather than to determining new policies for the future.

The Donovan Commission felt that the reform of collective bargaining through the development of comprehensive plant or company agreements would provide a means of drawing multi-union shop stewards' committees closer to official union hierarchies. Such committees were thought likely 'to have an important part to play in the negotiation and administration of satisfactory company and factory agreements . . .' (para 695). The Commission noted that the majority of full-time officials covered in its survey thought there were advantages from their point of view for stewards of different unions to meet in the workplace, but felt it desirable that the full-time officials should become more closely involved in such meetings. In particular, the unions should provide official committees to perform many of the functions now carried out by these unofficial gatherings. Full-time officials should attend the meetings, discuss the formulation of shop-floor policy and the way to handle multi-union grievances and claims with leading stewards. It was also suggested that union executives should authorize the establishment of *ad hoc* consultative committees at national level 'to cover the more important multi-plant companies – especially those where the stewards themselves have found it necessary to develop their own unofficial contacts through informal "combine committees"'.[22] Both suggestions offer ways of increasing the contact between joint stewards' bodies at the workplace and joint union bodies outside, which would presumably be of benefit to both. The feasibility of such arrangements depends largely on the willingness and ability of the unions to deploy resources – in particular the time of their full-time officials – to this, and on the unions being able to agree on the composition of *ad hoc* inter-union arrangements for supervision and co-ordination at local level. The role of stewards and stewards' committees in the conduct of formal plant or company negotiations along Donovan lines is discussed further in Chapter 10.

In the absence of reformed bargaining structures, however, intra- and inter-factory stewards' committees will continue to present problems to both unions and management. They generate and disseminate information for use in bargaining, yet their 'unofficial' status makes it difficult for either management or unions to verify and confirm the information. It may be inaccurate, but once believed on the shop-floor it is difficult to remove and may be a source of discontent. Management recognition of the JSSC or combine committee may be the only way to combat misinformation. The emergence of productivity bargaining and the greater involvement of senior stewards, particularly in long negotiations over new payment systems, etc, has meant that managements have given more and more information to leading stewards. Indeed, in such cases, the role of the senior stewards has often changed from one of simple opposition to management to one of seeking to 'sell' the new arrangements to their members, once the stewards themselves have been persuaded of the advantages. There are obvious dangers here in that the senior stewards may become associated with the advocacy of management policies. In the context of the motor industry Turner, Clack and Roberts felt that stewards' organizations operated as a 'buffer' between employers and operatives.[23] This implies the balancing of immediate sectional interests against the broader factory and longer-term interests of the stewards and their organizations and thus the leading stewards could themselves begin to experience the difficulties of control faced by any 'establishment' in the unions.

References

1. Marsh, A. I. and Coker, E. E., *op cit*, p 177.
2. The name 'works committee' is a source of confusion. It is now more commonly applied to a committee of senior stewards with explicit and preferential negotiating arrangements with managements, rather than to the joint seven-a-side management/steward committees of the 1919 Agreement.

 3. See Lerner, Shirley W. and Bescoby, John, 'Shop Steward Committees in the British Engineering Industry', *British Journal of Industrial Relations*, July 1966.
 4. *TUC Annual Report, 1960*, p 129.
 5. Lerner and Bescoby, *op cit*, p 163.
 6. *Annual Abstract of Statistics*, No 102, 1965, Table 139.
 7. Marsh and Coker, *op cit*, p 189. Their sample showed that two-thirds of AEF stewards in federated engineering firms were in establishments employing over 500 manual workers.
 8. *Report of the Joint Labour Council for the Motor Industry* into disputes at the Rover Company's assembly plant at Solihull, December 1965. This Report showed that with a total labour force of 5,204 there were 240 shop stewards, ie, an average constituency size of 22. Of the unions involved, the NUVB had 121 stewards, the T & GWU 80, and the AEF 21.
 9. Marsh and Coker, *op cit*, p 187.
10. Lerner, Shirley W., 'Factory Agreements and National Bargaining in the British Engineering Industry', *International Labour Review*, January 1964, p 6.
11. Lerner, Shirley W. and Marquand, Judith, 'Regional Variations in Earnings, Demand for Labour and Shop Stewards' Combine Committees in the British Engineering Industry', *Manchester School*, September 1963.
12. The CIR Report on shop stewards' facilities is referred to in Chapter 10.
13. Clegg, Killick, and Adams, *op cit*, p 179.
14. Report of Court of Inquiry, HMSO Cmnd 1999, 1963, para 78.
15. Fox, Alan, *The Milton Plan*, Institute of Personnel Management, 1965, p 19–22.
16. Clegg, Killick, and Adams, *op cit*, p 180.
17. Confederation Minute, Quarterly Meeting, February 19th, 1947.
18. The *Financial Times*, April 15th, 1966.
19. Turner, H. A., Clack, Garfield, and Roberts, Geoffrey, *Labour Relations in the Motor Industry*, George Allen and Unwin, 1967, p 22.
20. HMSO Cmnds, 131, 608 and 1999.
21. *TUC Annual Report, 1960*, pp 129–30.
22. Donovan Report, *op cit*, para 86.
23. Turner, Clack, and Roberts, *op cit*, p. 222.

Chapter Seven

Workplace Bargaining and Shop Stewards

Collective bargaining between employers and unions has evolved through several stages. In the late nineteenth century, agreements between unions and employers were characteristically by district, but in this century increasingly gave way to industry-wide settlement, applicable by all employers in an industry who belonged to the employers' association. This change was deliberate, but recent developments have been less so.

During and since the Second World War, bargaining activities have shifted, for though the traditional machinery remains the 'centre of gravity' has moved away from industry-wide committees. Such bodies retain former functions; they no longer represent all bargaining, and in many industries their importance has been considerably undermined. This movement has not been conscious decentralization, but unplanned and until recently unannounced. As industry-wide bargaining is characteristic rather than universal, so there are variations in the extent of workplace bargaining. Perhaps its greatest development is in engineering, but similar trends appear in most manufacturing and to a lesser extent in the service sector. Workplace bargaining has altered the role of the steward; he is no longer a guardian of national agreements, but is concerned to improve them, now widely exercising influence on the conditions of employment of his constituents. He is a rule maker and a negotiator as well as a custodian and rule enforcer. The changing scope of industrial relations has broadened the issues regulated jointly in the workplace. While many are small, detailed and complex, cumulatively they influence both earnings and costs. Their multiplicity taxes, if not exhausts, the capacity of traditional machinery and its union officials.

Workplace bargaining was not designed, but just happened. Its scope is obscured by its informality, and its recently recognized importance has not yet provoked adequate institutional response. Indeed, this delay in adjusting the existing structure, which emphasizes external regulation of employment relationships, is responsible for many problems of present concern.

The value of industry-wide negotiating procedures

Traditionally unions, employers and governments have supported a voluntary system of industrial relations, the two sides regulating their relationship as they wish. Government intervention has intended to stimulate growth of voluntary joint negotiating machinery, to protect unorganized workers or provide further means of reaching peaceful solutions after the exhaustion of voluntary procedures. More recently, Government intervention has reflected a different view, that settlements are no longer of purely private interest, but also affect those of both the public and the Government. Indeed, in the House of Commons in November, 1966, the then Minister of Labour said that the public interest was of overriding importance. Recent Government policy has repeatedly reflected this tripartite view of collective bargaining.

Historically, the unions stressed the equity of workers of similar ability performing similar jobs being paid similarly. They were concerned with the 'rate for the job', seeking to equalize it throughout industries and occupations. Industry-wide rates also promoted union solidarity and the development of common interest amongst union members. It prevented competition between workers unfavourably affecting the wage paid, being particularly valuable in periods and areas of high unemployment, a national standard being more easily defended than numerous district rates. The standard rate increased members' dependence on the union, while centralized bargaining facilitated the extension of union organization throughout an industry or occupation. Moreover, it conserved union resources, and enabled the unions' experienced officials to conduct negotiations.

The employers also felt it offered strategic benefits, notably in restraining undercutting wages and 'unfair' competition. Individual employers were protected from special claims, nationally organized unions could be matched, and some balance of power achieved. Industry-wide bargaining reduced the risk of a firm being strikebound while its competitors still produced, thus protecting its share of the market. Simultaneous wage increases similarly preserved the relative position of firms. If increased wage rates resulted in higher unit costs, all firms could raise prices in coordination.

The organization of bargaining over *major* conditions on an industry-wide basis inhibits disputes over these issues in individual firms. The time-consuming negotiations involved can be left to specialists in the employers' association, and being remote from any one firm, do not jeopardize relationships within it. Moreover, negotiations being external, collective and centralized, employers are free from 'inspection' by outside union officials not subject to the company's sanctions. Inevitably, negotiations are generalized, and the individual firm is shielded.

However, multi-employer collective agreements generally allow employers to supplement their terms locally if necessary. Employers may want their own wages structure, they may want a direct incentive, for example, and generally prefer flexible rather than rigid national agreements. Industry-wide negotiations allow unions to obtain improvements for some members which might not be possible in local labour conditions. But, with labour scarcity, or other favourable conditions, members can supplement the standard rate, taking 'two bites at the cherry'. Thus, in new employment conditions since 1945, centralized wage bargaining has not inhibited unions' bargaining opportunities elsewhere. National bargaining is a valued part of a dual system, particularly in unevenly organized industries, in 'marginal' firms, and in safeguarding the position of senior union officials.

Reasons for the development of workplace bargaining

(1) *Full employment*

The growth of workplace bargaining cannot be wholly explained by the state of the labour market, but undoubtedly full employment since 1945 has been crucial. Scarcity is no longer exclusive to skilled labour, but applies generally, thus enhancing labour's bargaining power. This emerges in national negotiations, but more profoundly in the extension of bargaining to the workplace. Stewards have secured improvements on national agreements, employers have had to pay more to recruit and retain labour, and to maintain industrial peace. A tight labour market has induced regular comparisons and competitive bidding between employers, while buoyant product markets, greater process interdependence, etc, have increased the force of stewards' sanctions. Similarly, employers' sanctions have lost much of their edge. In short, the balance of power is tilted in favour of labour, and this greater bargaining power has been channelled into the workplace and into the components of earnings determined there, eg, bonuses, merit rates, overtime, etc. Greater pressure is also applied to non-financial issues.

(2) *Procedural facilities*

Procedural means for passing on complaints and claims in the workplace are provided for in collective agreements, which allow representatives to progress issues by recording failure to agree at successive internal stages. This process makes issues collective, and its impersonal nature prevents managements from handling issues individually, as they might for unorganized workers. Thus, an open-ended avenue is provided for workplace representatives. Procedural machinery may be used without limit, although managements occasionally refuse to discuss certain topics as non-negotiable, but evidence suggests it is increasingly used. Marsh and Jones[1] found a doubling of hearings at works-conference level in the Engineering Procedure between 1956 and 1963. This is surprising when workplace parties evidently desire to keep issues domestic, and when many firms operate informal procedures supplementing those in national agreements in order to encourage it. However, Marsh and Jones quoted an 80-per-cent chance of settlement at this semi-domestic level.

(3) *Collective agreements*
Industry-wide collective agreements are not usually accepted as providing terms which cannot be supplemented. They are more typically regarded as minimum guarantees to be improved upon, though conventions in some employers' associations have discouraged this from being done openly and directly on basic wage rates, length of the working week, length of holidays, etc. Secondly, collective agreements often omit subjects of joint interest, and often fail to define the rights of the two parties comprehensively. For example, basic wage rates, premium rates for overtime, public-holiday rates, shiftworking allowances, the length of the nominal working week, and holidays are normally specified, but do not regulate shift rotation, discipline, engagement and dismissal, distribution of working hours, spacing of breaks, redundancy, pay methods, supervision, etc. If these topics are mentioned it is for guidance only, most national agreements being totally silent. These gaps leave scope for workplace regulation, assuring workplace representatives an influential role. Moreover, the standardization of industry-wide terms does not reflect company variations in productivity, profits, labour supply, orders, etc, all these being

exploitable at company or workplace level. District officials having wide responsibilities may be preoccupied with problems elsewhere; but stewards are ever present, have a narrower brief, and often form inter-union committees to overcome structural handicaps.

(4) *Fixed-period agreements and Government intervention*
It has not been customary to agree termination dates in industry-wide agreements in Britain, but fixed-period agreements enjoyed a certain popularity in some major industries, especially in the mid 1960s. Indeed, in October 1965, 27 per cent of employees were covered by such agreements.[2] By restricting national claims for several years, these agreements transfer attention to the workplace. Future national improvements are assured, and national officials' hands are tied, but stewards can exploit local opportunities. The tendency for improvements to be more easily achieved locally also reflects coercive Government interest in national agreements. Workplace improvements are less publicized, being small and numerous, and thus are not susceptible to the same scrutiny, particularly in small firms. This point is especially relevant in periods of stringent incomes policy as applied in the 1966–70 period, as Government policy can more easily be evaded at local level than in industry-wide settlements.

(5) *Payment by results*
Payment-by-results systems are significant in local improvements. While national agreements customarily stipulate an incentive rate at a level enabling a worker of average ability to earn a minimum ratio of the basic rate, the schemes are usually supervised at workshop level. This is not invariable, eg, the cotton-textile and some sections of the boot-and-shoe industries have district price lists, but even here workplace representatives can exercise influence over their constituents' earnings. Changes in production, in layout, working conditions, quality standards, etc, stimulate renegotiations, usually resulting in higher earnings. Work-measurement

techniques are insufficiently accurate to prevent discrepancies, exploitable by stewards. In April 1961, 42 per cent of manual workers in manufacturing worked under incentive schemes, a figure exceeded in several industries in which stewards are active. They covered 62 per cent of wage earners in shipbuilding and marine engineering, 52 per cent in vehicles, 47 per cent in general engineering and electrical goods.[3]

(6) *Consultative procedures*

During and after the Second World War many companies established joint consultative machinery, generally to aid efficiency and cooperation through improving management–employee communications. In the workplace, these committees dealt with domestic problems such as production, safety and welfare. Although negotiations were explicitly prohibited, management often failed to maintain fine distinctions between consultative and negotiable topics. Many accepted the change in function of joint consultation, others resisted it. Practice varies, but the evidence suggests that pure joint consultation is declining.

(7) *Management's preference for shop stewards*

Some managements prefer to deal with stewards, resisting the participation of full-time officials, of both unions and their employers' association, in workplace problems. Many consider it a failure, as well as a loss of control, to call in outside officials. Stewards may be similarly inclined to restrict the access of full-time officials. Unlike officials of an employers' association, company managements must live with the solution obtained from external machinery, and suspect that the association's officials will allow precedent and their wider concern with other members to influence settlement of a problem. Moreover, it is common sense to solve a problem as low and as early as possible. Stewards are subject to the firm's sanctions, are readily available, better informed of facts, views, and members' probable reactions. Personal relationships between managers and stewards may be better than those with outside officials, and may be enhanced by keeping topics domestic. Moreover, the volume of issues may make it expedient for management to deal with stewards rather than the officials of several unions.

(8) *Personnel specialists*

Another development in workplace bargaining is the introduction of specialists by management, eg, work-study officers, labour-relations and personnel officers. The largest post-war growth in members of the Institute of Personnel Management, absolutely and in percentage terms, is found in engineering, including vehicles and aircraft.[4] And here, stewards have perhaps reached their highest density and development. The expertise of some firms in labour relations exceeds that of employers' associations, while their knowledge of the intricacies of a problem, and of management policy, means they are often better equipped to handle the management case. A similar comparison holds between experienced stewards or convenors and full-time officials. The emergence of company-wide steward combine committees also reflects the trend for increasingly domestic industrial relations activity. It may be suggested that active workplace bargaining will increase the importance of labour-relations specialists within management and they may promote an 'internal' policy.

(9) *Informality*

Most workplace agreements are informal and unwritten, which affords both sides some advantage in flexibility of operation. Management may prefer this uncodified system, thinking it will allow downward reinterpretation in better circumstances. However it is arguable whether 'custom and practice' is more vulnerable than a written agreement, or whether purposely bad memories are less provocative than overt bad faith, on either side.

The influence of stewards on the pay, working conditions, and terms of employment of union members is widespread, substantial, and increasing. Modification of this generalization is progressively less necessary. The absence of incentive schemes no longer precludes workplace bargaining on financial issues. For example, Dr McCarthy found that 'stewards in such trades as confectionery, or in services like gas, electricity and local government, can base an effective system of workplace bargaining on obtaining local improvements in the rates of work'.[5] One rota representative in a municipal bus undertaking felt that the rigidity of the national agreement prevented local negotiations on wages and earnings. He therefore acted to protect members' working conditions, making life (as he said) 'cushier' by resisting reductions in services and in running and journey times, etc.

Workplace bargaining, or at least regulation of the many components of earnings, is often loosely assessed by reference to the gap between earnings and wage rates. Thus, before examining other aspects of workplace bargaining, wage drift must be examined.

Wage drift

Wage drift refers to the tendency of earnings, excluding overtime, to rise more rapidly than negotiated wage rates. It has been the subject of much dispute in academic literature, not least because of problems of measurement. 'Pure' wage drift has been authoritatively defined by Professor Phelps Brown, who states 'the essence of drift is that the effective rate of pay per unit of labour input is raised by arrangements that lie outside the control of the recognized procedures for scheduling rates',[6] ie, negotiated agreements, awards, or statutory orders. Dr Lerner adds that 'drift can occur in two ways: a worker's earnings may increase outside the terms of the recognized collective agreement, but no change occurs in the degree of utilization of his labour; a worker's earnings may remain constant between scheduled rises, but his labour is under-utilized as compared with the period when the recognized collective agreement was negotiated.'[7] Thus, because of variations in labour inputs it cannot be said whether increases in earnings under payment-by-results schemes do or do not constitute pure drift. Similarly, overtime earnings cannot be automatically classified as drift. Loose piecework rates, unadjusted to improved techniques, increase earnings per unit of labour input and constitute drift. Conversely, greater application of labour inputs by workers in speed and effort in unchanged conditions, resulting in higher earnings, is not drift in the sense defined by Phelps Brown. Thus, changed labour inputs and occupational movements bedevil the accurate measurement of wage drift.

It is comparatively easy to measure an 'earnings gap' statistically, but it is not drift. Moreover, Ministry of Labour classifications do not coincide with bargaining units, but a few examples illustrate the widening gap between basic weekly wage rates and average weekly earnings. In June 1967, the consolidated national time rate in engineering was 221*s* 8*d* for skilled fitters and 187*s* 4*d* for labourers. Average weekly earnings for fitters on time work ranged from 417*s* in marine engineering to 515*s* 6*d* in motor vehicles, and for fitters on piecework from 456*s* 1*d* in electrical engineering to 540*s* in motor vehicles. Labourers' earnings on timework ranged from 309*s* 10*d* in electrical engineering to 360*s* in motor vehicles, and on piecework from 331*s* 9*d* in mechanical engineering to 365*s* 9*d* in marine engineering.[8] In April 1967 the minimum weekly wage rate for adult male workers in the tobacco industry was 235*s* 6*d*, but average earnings of all adult male manual workers were 444*s* 7*d*.[9] In the municipal bus industry the NJIC basic weekly rate for drivers in July 1967 was 257*s* and average weekly earnings 446*s* 5*d*.[10] Figure 7.1 provides a more general impression.

Essentially, wage drift is associated with two forces in the workplace:

Fig. 7.1

Weekly rates of wages, average weekly earnings for manual workers, average salary earnings and retail prices, 1958–71.

Average 1955 100

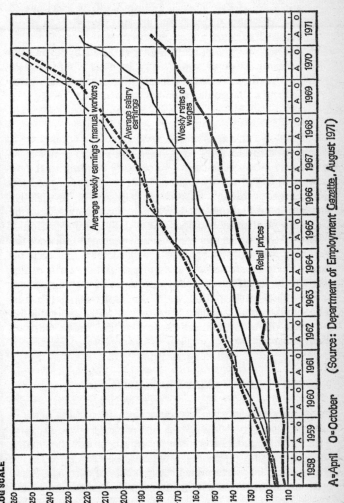

LOG SCALE

A=April   O=October   (Source: Department of Employment *Gazette*, August 1971) (*a*) Stewards or their equivalent press management to increase earnings above the scheduled rate. This pressure may be applied initially at strategic points, or be associated with gradual improvements by pieceworkers (primary drift). This is followed up by pressure to re order the wages structure in response to these initial disturbances (secondary drift).

(*b*) Management may grant higher earnings by raising the scheduled rate or, more likely, by contriving increases in overtime, failing to revise piecework rates, introducing or improving bonuses, artificially regrading jobs etc.

Ultimately, management is responsible for arranging its wages structure to fulfil its policies, within the limits of its employees' ideas of fairness. A company wanting to reduce wage drift has primarily to accept that some loss of production does not always exceed the alternative prospective increase in unit labour costs. Wage drift is generally less, the closer the control by management of daily administration of of the agreement. In this way, management can influence the role of stewards, for wages systems, structures and controls help determine stewards' bargaining activities. Drift is also likely to be less if the company negotiates its own agreement rather than participating in multi-employer agreements. The avoidance of payment by results reduces opportunities for wage drift, as these schemes often undermine management control.

Financial topics in workplace bargaining

Bargaining over issues of payment is a vital activity of stewards in industry, movements in earnings beyond rates nationally agreed giving *some* indication of this. Normally, such bargaining supplements national basic rates, covering many workplace-determined components of earnings. Stewards are, however, active in improving occupational or job rates, especially where multi-employer agreements only loosely categorize jobs. For instance, the engineering agreement is concluded for adult men principally in terms of skilled fitters and unskilled labourers, and though mentioning *some* sub-groups among the skilled, it does not contain even minimum rates for semi-skilled grades. Thus, it fails to outline differentials between many occupational groups found in the industry. They are, thus, left to workplace agreements. Specific occupational groups, eg, sheet-metal workers, submit claims at works level, which *may* be settled early and internally by stewards. Different groups of semi-skilled workers, eg, inspectors, may seek to restore their position, similar sectional claims being presented by their stewards with external officials only asked for ratification. Periodic 'domestic' claims by sub-groups constitute open bargaining at works level, and management eager to settle them may do so without directly involving external union officials.

A claim for a domestic sectional increase is perhaps the most obvious example of a steward's bargaining role, but stewards do bargain on other money topics. Indeed, wage-rate bargaining may be precluded by the nature of the agreement, and the conventions of union and occupational organization in the workplace. However, such factors are a lesser obstacle when payment-by-results systems are present.

(1) *Payment by results*
Payment-by-results schemes are a major vehicle of wage drift. It is no accident that 'in the engineering, metals and vehicle industries ... shop stewards devote more time to negotiating incentive rates than to any other function of industrial relations'.[11] Opportunities for wage drift under such schemes are numerous. Continuous repetition makes an operator more proficient; he can thus earn more for the same effort. Small but cumulatively important changes in layout, handling methods, etc, are introduced constantly, though each by itself may not warrant a restudy of the job. The inconsistencies of work measurement, as well as small method improvements, lead stewards to complain of the

tight rates – while defending loose ones. Cohesive work groups, where restrictive group norms influence individual earnings, hide slackly rated jobs. Changes and discontinuities in production permit new negotiations, eg, between different jobs in a jobbing factory, over the introduction of new machinery which increases output without increasing labour inputs or over movements of labour to new jobs. Loss of earnings militates against labour mobility, and so management often provides compensatory allowances or favourable retraining rates. Changes in materials have similar effects, and understandings need to be reached on the quality of materials, on quality control standards, and arrangements for reworking faulty pieces. Agreements also are necessary on shortages of materials, the condition of equipment, procedure during breakdowns, and the size and composition of group incentive schemes. Almost any change initially induces defensiveness in shop-floor workers, though also affording bargaining opportunities. Innovation is a topic on which stewards seek consultation, and on which their duty to advance their members' interests is well developed.

Concessions in one section of a plant provoke restorative action elsewhere. For example, existing relativities between pieceworkers' and timeworkers' earnings will be upset unless the latter are safeguarded by having a built-in ratio to pieceworkers' earnings. Failing this, timeworkers' representatives claim, on grounds of equity, increases in lieu of bonuses, which management may concede to avoid trouble. While primary and secondary drift can be isolated in theory, in a complex factory with different work groups and frequent work changes it is difficult to specify which claim starts the cycle. A wage structure may always appear anomalous to *one* group, and differentiation of the labour force leads to multilateral bargaining.

Stewards in factories with incentive payment schemes can help determine the rates *ab initio*. Stewards' books of rates, extending back over long periods, are known to pass from a steward to his successor. The steward's knowledge of prices, times, and precedents, may exceed management's. Not all jobs can be referred to previous standards. Work study is not universal and can be challenged in any case, while new jobs may run without timing and guesswork is still widespread among shop-floor supervision. A recent investigation into a piecework dispute in a large motor plant revealed '. . . that supervision at the company has to rely considerably upon shop stewards for its facts and figures in relation to the booking of new and untimed work. At the same time the information so provided is a major factor in determining a piecework time to stand perhaps for many years.'[12]

(2) *The effort bargain*

Unlike payment by results, timework offers fewer opportunities for stewards to influence directly their members' pay. However, as the price per unit of input is the basis of negotiations under incentive schemes, so it is on timework, though the process is different. The process is described as an 'effort bargain', as against the 'money bargain' on incentive schemes. A man's earnings may not be threatened by changes but job content and effort may alter. Generally, this issue is less immediate and less easily measured than a piecework price, but timeworkers' stewards are no less conscious of its importance. The problem here is manning, or labour content. Stewards in timeworking motor plants keep logs of assembly-line speeds, existing manning quotas are defended, and attempts to speed up the track or reduce manning are resisted. If management successfully re-allocates or reduces labour, then unless the technology prohibits it, the remainder may induce overtime. British industry is widely thought to be overmanned, certainly if some prominent management consultants are to be believed, but this problem has been attacked by productivity bargaining and by the 'shake-out' of labour during 1970 and 1971.

(3) *Overtime*

Where incentive schemes are not applied, overtime is the principal way of raising short-term earnings. Only 40 per cent of wage earners are paid by results, but for them overtime is an additional opportunity to supplement weekly earnings at premium rates. Traditionally, these premia were applied to discourage employers asking workers to work outside normal hours. It was accepted that the exigencies of production, seasonal fluctuations, urgent orders, increased output, etc, might occasionally demand overtime working, but employers were to pay premium rates to offset the inconvenience. This original concept does not reflect contemporary attitudes to overtime, though it may apply to individual cases. Overtime has become systematic in many industries and firms, being relied on by management to achieve production schedules, and by employees as a regular source of income. With labour scarce, and if employers adhere to their association's conventions to respect established wage rates, overtime is a method of adjusting rewards to meet the market. Indeed, the length rather than the brevity of working hours is frequently used by firms in recruiting. Retention of overtime is induced by other firms adopting the same policy.

A prospering firm short of labour will extend labour supply by lengthening working hours, both to increase production and attract new workers. However, if the latter is more important, the atmosphere during overtime hours may not lead to much extra production. Men may simply be marking time. One effect of systematic overtime, commonly complained of by management, is that it induces absenteeism on normal working days. Further, if men prefer increased income to leisure, the availability of overtime may affect their job performance in working hours – a job may be spun out to create overtime. Briefly, premium rates provide an incentive to maximize overtime, particularly as overtime working is not compulsory, and can be accepted or refused by the individual. Spinning the work out may be deliberate, or induced by an atmosphere that accepts the availability of overtime.

In 1938, actual hours worked in industry were less than the usual standard working week, ie, 47·8 compared with 48. From the end of the Second World War until the mid-

1960s, actual hours worked did not fall much, despite periodic reductions in nominal working hours to 40 for most manual workers. Overtime pay thus increased as a proportion of weekly earnings, although the level of overtime working has fallen in the years since 1965, as Table 7.1 shows.

Table 7.1

Average weekly hours worked by men operatives in manufacturing industries

1938 October	47·7	1957 October	48·0
1943 July	53·1	1959 October	48·2
1945 July	49·4	1961 October	46·8
1947 October	46·2	1963 October	46·8
1949 October	46·6	1965 October	46·1
1951 October	47·6	1967 October	44·3
1953 October	47·9	1969 October	45·7
1955 October	48·7	1971 October	43·6

Source: Department of Employment *Gazette*

Overtime worked varies, but reaches very important levels in certain industries. For example, in 1966 the average hours worked in road haulage were 57; for production workers in bakeries average hours were 51½, though there was nominally a 40-hour week.[13] Overtime working has widely become customary; attitudes towards it vary, but the impression is that it is sought rather than avoided, and in certain industries relied upon. Professor Turner concluded that 'variation in average hours seems more closely, and of course inversely, connected with the wage levels of particular trades than with their activity. Overtime has clearly become a systematic method of raising lower male wage rates.'[14] Of the twenty-one manufacturing industries where average hours worked by adult males in October 1967 exceeded forty-seven, only two equalled the manufacturing industry average hourly rate of pay, despite their heavy loading with overtime premiums.

While premium rates paid for overtime, usually a proportion of the wage rate, are included in national agreements, its level and distribution are regulated in the factory, stewards rather than full-time officials protecting members' interests. Customarily, stewards are most concerned with the distribution of overtime opportunities, striving towards fair shares, often by means of a rota system. However, in the writers' experience, they may also seek agreements guaranteeing overtime working. Such pressure reveals both the gulf between long-term official union policy and the short-run views of members, and the uncertainty induced by large but inevitably unreliable overtime earnings.

The *upward* consolidation of overtime working by stewards is described by Flanders in his analysis of the Fawley productivity agreements.[15] He notes that initially overtime was increased to deal with specific circumstances in different departments at different times, but that the level was maintained by a ratchet effect. That is, 'the almost automatic adjustment in work habits and behaviour. Everyone comes to count on it for the completion of tasks.' Then 'notions of equity' came into play, accusations of favouritism were made, and stewards demanded fair shares in overtime distribution. 'To meet such charges management began to collect statistics and broadly accepted the principle of equal opportunities. In consequence, although decisions about the working of overtime nominally remained with supervision, the stewards, acting as guardians of the principle, came effectively to control its distribution. Moreover the application of the principle was pressed to increasingly fine limits ... equalization reached the point where the stewards, on a week-by-week basis, wanted to see their men working within an hour or two of each other.' This situation is widespread in British industry. The fair-shares principle has, in our experience, been applied by stewards to different shifts, within and between departments, and between different crafts.

Stewards apply it less to different local factories, but loss of labour may obviate the necessity.

Systematic overtime remains discretionary for the individual, but employers cannot shed the burden so easily. Considerable overtime working has its own momentum. To the worker, overtime is lucrative, to the steward it is an area of joint regulation, over which management has lost unilateral control. This may not apply when management wants to increase overtime, though some collective agreements restrict this,[16] but a downward revision is usually resisted. The elimination of high levels of overtime is accepted as a negotiable topic, for which compensation must be paid. Indeed, the negotiated reduction of overtime in return for compensating increases in basic wage rates was a prominent feature of many productivity agreements in the 1960s, most notably in the electricity supply industry.

Stewards also try to regulate the incidence of overtime, in stating when it will be worked, for how long, what notice shall be given, etc. They may favour at least one hour a night, no overtime on Fridays, and try to substitute Sunday for Saturdays. As management normally require the concurrence of stewards, and as overtime is voluntary, management's bargaining power is relatively small. Overtime affects internal wages structures, particularly if opportunities to work vary between different groups. This stimulates restorative claims, not necessarily for overtime, by those who feel aggrieved. Professor Robertson's finding that 'unskilled workers quite generally appear to restore some of the gap in their relative earnings levels as against more skilled groups by working longer hours' has been widely confirmed.[17] Conversely, not all workers seek overtime. This is especially true of women and the obligation to work a 'reasonable' amount of overtime contained in some agreements is for them a dead letter.

(4) *Other financial topics*

Multi-employer bargaining arrangements imply that the results arrived at will not suit equally all the firms concerned.

The terms are necessarily broad, being possibly appropriate to only less prosperous firms in relatively favourable labour markets. Firms may want to adapt their wage structure for such purposes as rewarding long service, special responsibility, or skill, and compensating for unpleasant working conditions, marking status, building in a promotional element or progressive scale, adopting their own incentive scheme, etc. Generally, a federated firm trying to apply individual policies increases the amount of bargaining within the company, and thus almost necessarily involves its stewards in workplace bargaining.

Over the past decade or more, many firms have introduced job evaluation, by which jobs are graded into a few categories according to their content, thus reducing the number of different pay rates. Often stewards, particularly convenors, are actively involved in implementing job evaluation, sitting on appeals committees, etc. Clearly, disputes arise over job gradings, particularly with production changes, and stewards may advance complaints. However, if it replaces payment by results, job evaluation reduces the scope for workplace bargaining. It often produces individual rather than collective complaints, for claims on behalf of one grade automatically imply changes in all. Day-to-day haggling is generally much reduced. Job evaluation is found most extensively in the chemical industry, being applied in the national agreement. It does not eliminate disputes but, once introduced, involves less debate. However, it does not eliminate wage drift, for specious grading, eg, raising the pay of scarce categories of skill beyond that indicated by the principles of the scheme, is essentially the same as purposely loose piece rates, or 'manufactured' overtime.

Some companies, particularly those paying on a time-rate and/or job-evaluation basis, have built merit payments into the structure. The principle theoretically applied is to assess the operator rather than evaluate the job. Factors which can be objectively measured, eg, timekeeping, attendance, and length of service may receive special payments but are often included in merit schemes, together with such 'personal qualities' as reliability, job performance, cooperativeness, etc. The subjective nature of these assessments is the antithesis of trade-union principle of 'the rate for the job', and inevitably provokes accusations of favouritism. Stewards frequently oppose such schemes, press for equality of 'merit money' once introduced, and challenge the allocations. In turn, management may use merit money to reward the occupation rather than individual performance, particularly where the grading structure is too rigid for adequate recruitment.

The list of workplace- or company-determined supplements is a long one. Many engineering firms pay a 'company bonus', and 'house rates' are commonly negotiated by FOCs in the printing industry. Christmas bonuses are widespread in building and other industries, all supplementing nationally negotiated rates. Some payments are provided unilaterally by employers, others are the result of negotiations. Stewards help secure, defend, and apply special allowances. Some national agreements provide for them, with special payments for dirt, heat, danger, height, fumes, etc. Allowances are made for tools, walking, and washing time, etc, and many outlive their justification. One large firm found itself still paying a few men 'shutter money' fifteen years after the end of the Second World War. Many companies have schemes for sickness and pensions, and stewards seek more favourable principles in their administration, even if they cannot directly negotiate over the level of benefits. The provision of clothing by a firm, across the plant or to specific jobs, frequently involves stewards, while they and the labour market may partly account for the relative stability of canteen prices. The list is virtually endless. The national agreement may be silent, employers' associations may advise resistance, but inroads are made gradually by stewards in the workplace.

The range of shop steward bargaining

So far, we have discussed aspects of workplace bargaining directly affecting the price of labour, but stewards also help regulate its utilization within a factory. Some rulebooks, particularly those of the craft unions, charge stewards with 'defending the interests of the trade'. This gives them scope on topics such as job demarcation, labour mobility, discipline, manning, union membership, supervision, apprentices, dilutees, etc. Many assume such responsibilities without instruction. Some employers find stewards' attempts to extend joint regulation beyond the wage/price bargain irritating, for there is less acceptance of the legitimacy of the workers' desire to protect their interests on the work rather than the wage side of the employment contract.

Some unions with craft traditions have determined some aspects of entry, work performance, and content unilaterally, but these working rules are subject to pressures with technological and economic change, and the steward may find himself essentially on the defensive. However, the notion of property rights to and within a job is spreading among all workers, and attempts to extend it explain much non-financial bargaining in industry. The defence of protective working practices is appropriate to workplace representatives, as they are well placed to understand these often informal practices and to detect attempts to undermine them. The fact that such practices are often peculiar to one plant and not codified in union rulebooks or collective agreements stresses the importance of stewards, helping to account for the decentralized nature of 'productivity bargaining'. Clearly, the steward is able to build up and defend the customs protecting members from capricious change, and may be able not only to reduce members' vulnerability to sudden management decisions, but also gain acknowledgement that certain decisions are to be made jointly. Whether day-to-day pressures on aspects of work regulation are bargaining is debatable, for the processes by which workers gain more influence over their work environment can be both dramatic or scarcely perceptible. Marsh thus describes the general position: 'Stewards are prepared to bargain about anything which appears to affect the interests of their members in the workplace, and all situations appear to offer some opportunities for this.'[18]

While stewards cannot bargain on every issue they would like, they have neverthless secured agreements on various topics. After an inquiry covering forty-five works agreements in engineering in five cities, Dr Lerner made this list of subjects covered:[19]

Trade-Union and Shop-Steward Status. Employers' recognition of unions, stewards and (sometimes) works convenor; 100-per-cent union membership; the obligations and rights of stewards; payment to stewards for working time devoted to negotiations; works dispute or grievance procedure; stewards' meetings on works premises; use of bulletin board and other facilities.

Hours of Work. Starting and finishing times, meal breaks, teabreaks; distribution of overtime; guaranteed overtime; restrictions on overtime; choice of shifts, rotation of shifts.

Redundancy. Consultation with shop stewards; measures to keep dismissals to the minimum, eg, limit recruitment, work sharing, transfers, etc; length of notice; selection of employees to be dismissed; appeals; aids in securing other employment; severance payments; re-engagement.

Miscellaneous Provisions. Works rules; personnel records; physical examination; safety provisions; collections; leave of absence; promotions and transfers; joint productivity committees; joint consultative committees. These were the subject of workplace agreements, and would involve local full-time officials and stewards, though the latter would obviously raise the issues initially and supervise any agreements.

Dr Lerner emphasizes that the list is a summary, and can certainly be extended within and outside engineering. Moreover, it lists positive *agreements*, excluding topics on which stewards make representations but do not record agreements. For example, in our experience, stewards play an active role in works discipline, challenging specific cases of warning, suspension, or dismissal, and also reaching agreements over the general procedure.

There are, in timeworking production departments, agreements over labour content and production pace; workplace interpretations of what is meant by national agreement terminology, especially such indefinite adjectives as 'suitable', 'reasonable', and 'appropriate'. Stewards are concerned in the transfer of members, job rotation, and mobility of labour generally. Holiday arrangements, ballots over dates, distribution of holiday-period working, and staggering of holidays, *all* particularly involve maintenance workers' stewards. They are also concerned in demarcation issues, in such industries as shipbuilding devoting much time to this topic. Our questionnaire showed that stewards spent considerable time on factory hygiene and in discussions about improvements in physical working conditions.

It is not always clear whether an agreement exists. For example, an individual case may be resolved, but a management anxious to avoid setting precedents emphasizes its *ad hoc* nature. Failure to resolve a problem, particularly one in an area regarded as a management prerogative, still allows stewards to attempt attrition on the issue, thus gradually increasing their influence. Management may publicly proclaim its prerogative, but opposition by stewards may constrain its exercise in practice. Examples include subcontracting work, appointing supervisors, introducing new labour, and employing consultants, etc.

Our questionnaire and our experience suggest that stewards bargain with supervisors and rate fixers on the shop floor, but spend considerable time negotiating with higher management such as departmental, plant, and personnel managers. In many factories, the reference of major issues to foremen may be perfunctory. The supervisor cannot assess claims by stewards, and both will be aware that he must refer upwards. In these instances, stewards are anxious to reach the decision maker, and in time may bypass the supervisor.[20] Similarly, line management at departmental level may avoid time-consuming negotiations, particularly on plant-wide issues, passing the problem to higher levels or to specialist personnel departments. All this enhances the status of stewards, creating problems in the relationship between them and supervisors. Stewards as workers accept the foreman's authority, but as stewards may have contacts with higher management not readily available to foremen. The latter may resent their ambiguous situation, particularly if they are not informed about the progress of issues, and if their views are not canvassed by management about daily working discipline. Access to management may, independently, enhance the importance of topics raised by stewards. Conversely, stewards frequently serve as channels of information down from management. If management intends to 'tighten up' discipline, stewards often receive forewarning. Similarly, they may assist management, especially supervision, in handling difficult individual cases, in placing 'convalescent' employees, etc.

Most procedures, and unions, expect workplace representatives to handle complaints initially, to the stage when external officials must take over. Whether, in fact, the full-time officials can always do this depends on several factors, not least their availability and the willingness of management or stewards to involve them. District officials may place embargoes on stewards' discussing certain problems with management, yet the dynamics of a problem and simple expediency make implementation of this rule difficult. Moreover, some stewards resent the implication of lack of competence. If stewards decide to reject such limitations, eg, by a joint stewards' committee decision, the practical redress of full-time officials is limited. More topics are discussed, joint regulation of employment is extended, stewards can secure acceptance of new principles in the relationship, members' interests being advanced. The official limiting stewards to the traditional areas will be suspected of bureaucratic behaviour if he is unable to secure improvements more effectively than his stewards. On the other hand, if his bargaining skills are superior, his participation will be more frequently sought.

Somewhat surprisingly, in view of the fact that there is often thought to be friction between shop stewards and full-time officials over their relative power and influence, the Royal Commission's survey found little evidence of this in practice. The interdependence of their roles was acknowledged by both sides; the stewards had no desire to belittle the role of the full-time officials, and they in turn were broadly satisfied with their role in workplace bargaining. The officials were particularly appreciative of the job done by the stewards, and the vast majority (87 per cent) felt they had sufficient influence over them. Again surprisingly, 39 per cent of stewards said the full-time officials already played an important part in local negotiations, and 34 per cent of stewards said they would like to see full-time officials play a more important part.[21]

Bargaining techniques

The right of stewards to progress grievances is widely accepted, though not invariably protected by industry-wide agreements. Given this procedural channel, the steward's bargaining strength revolves around the support of his members, his ability to gain acceptance of new agreements, and to lead them collectively. The vulnerability of employers to these sanctions varies. A factory assembling components into one product is susceptible to any sectional stoppage. Conversely, firms can continue for long periods despite strikes in certain sections, eg, among draughtsmen. Firms dependent on overtime for normal production provide stewards with another weapon. Capital-intensive industries, where labour cooperation is crucial, illustrate technological and other influences on bargaining. Management, too, has its sanctions, though the classical lockout is now largely precluded by public opinion. Management can change its policies, apply positive and negative sanctions; it can redistribute labour, making life difficult for stewards by adhering to the letter of agreements, refusing very minor changes, and attacking informally acquired 'privileges'. For example, management may respond to an overtime ban in one section by cancelling it across the entire plant.

Stewards do not simply present demands, threatening action if they are not fully accepted, though this can happen. Experienced stewards pride themselves on their negotiating skill, and few persistently take precipitate action. Workplace bargaining, like all bargaining, involves tactics. Indeed, success depends on tactics, and however good relations are, both sides need to exercise skill to be sure of obtaining the best agreement. Honour has to be satisfied, usually by hard bargaining. Neither steward nor manager could feel he is adequately carrying out his duties if he depends merely on the goodwill of the other.

As negotiators, stewards employ various negotiating techniques, but particularly arguments of equity. Often, they appeal to ethical values, evaluating management by these standards; stewards and their members assess a firm, and especially its managers, personally. They examine the motives, integrity, and personality of managers they negotiate with, and frequently stewards and managers come to respect each other. Both appreciate the other's problems, but acknowledge the man as well as his role. Thus, mutual trust and the anticipation of reasonable treatment largely prevent the breakdown of relations. Such relations are established gradually, but can disappear rapidly if the expectations of one side are not reasonably fulfilled.

Among the criteria of fairness are those of equality of treatment, consistency, and comparability. Comparisons of conditions and terms are made between crafts, grades, departments, shifts, different plants of the same firm, local firms, and within the industry. Notably, the Engineering Industry's three-year agreement of 1964, trying to restrain workplace bargaining for that period, provided that, 'as regards domestic claims there shall not be any of a general character covering all or substantially all of the manual workers in an establishment. Claims on behalf of individuals or groups of workpeople within an establishment shall be permitted provided they are based on alleged anomalies or inequalities.' Once a disturbance occurs in a quasi-static situation, reference to comparability will spread its repercussions throughout and possibly beyond a factory. On wage and bonus issues, the reaction may be immediate; one group has 'got out of line' and regaining the *status quo* involves many adjustments. This argument of 'fair comparisons', especially referring to the immediate past, is accepted almost as much by managements as rough justice as on the shop floor. Inconsistency of treatment in similar cases, at different times or in different departments, provides stewards with bargaining opportunities, largely acknowledged as just by management. Thus, bargaining often proceeds by appeal to values both sides acknowledge, though to differing degrees. The degree of management acceptance of 'fairness', eg, comparability and consistency, helps determine the shop-floor view of management's 'reasonableness'.

Another standard used by stewards is that of custom and practice. This argument is used to challenge any changes management introduces which are not favourably received on the shop floor. Existing arrangements are greatly valued and change is resisted, for anticipated opposition may deter management from making proposals. The use made of 'custom and practice' by stewards illustrates the fear many of their members have of change, not only for security of employment. It also involves earnings, a particular job, and more broadly the security stemming from the routine of work and one's known workmates. However, defending old practices assists stewards in obtaining compensation for more permissive patterns of work.

Closely associated with 'custom and practice' is the use of precedent by stewards in bargaining. Actions by management are subjected to the criterion of previous practice, 'unfavourable' departures being challenged, eg, the degree of consultation taking place before changes. This technique particularly applies to discipline, where case law is often accepted by management as overriding the letter of works rules. Stewards are not constrained by the infrequency of negotiating meetings, being ever present. Agreements they reach are not as limited as those in most national agreements. Workplace problems are continuous, receiving daily attention. Managers, unlike national negotiators, cannot restrict negotiations to quarterly meetings on a previously determined agenda. Lengthy intervals to fix attitudes and consider claims are not available, though both sides occasionally use delay tactically.

Workplace bargaining is also influenced by the stewards' conception of their own position in relation to management. Both are concerned with power in the workplace, and tend to view the other competitively. Stewards seek to extend their scope and, however good their relations, do not allow their influence to rest simply on the goodwill of management. To define topics on which consultation is required is to define areas of joint regulation, reasserting the steward's importance in being strategic and 'non-bypassable'. Management may seek to restrict its dealings with stewards, or may elevate stewards to a position of interchangeability with outside officials. Stewards may exploit the difference between their constituents and the union. All this is part of a power game, as real when the rules are observed as when the weapons chosen breach the traditional morality. Briefly, stewards have become powerful, and often skilled negotiators – a position which management has on the whole fostered, and which the unions have been unable to prevent.

Workplace bargaining is diffuse, it has evolved spontaneously, and prior to the Donovan Report its nature and characteristics were largely unknown. The Report confirmed that it is pragmatic, continuous and often intensive, although its stage of development varies between and within industries. In some firms workplace representatives have successfully challenged basic rates, while in others bargaining is confined to non-monetary topics, though both have implications for production costs. Workplace bargaining may be partially measured by the extent of wage drift, the continuation of which in unfavourable economic conditions suggests that it has now developed its own institutional momentum. Thus over the post-war period management has found its independent pursuit of policy objectives progressively limited, its behaviour modified, and its prerogatives eroded by the presence of powerful union representatives in the workplace.

The Donovan Commission argued that the nature and characteristics of workplace bargaining were at the root of Britain's industrial relations problem, such bargaining being categorized and criticized as 'autonomous, fragmented and informal'. The Commission's proposals for reform, and the implications of reform along the lines it suggested, will be taken up in Chapter 10.

References

1. Marsh, A. I. and Jones, R. S., 'Engineering Procedure and Central Conference at York in 1959: A Factual Analysis', *British Journal of Industrial Relations*, July 1964.
2. Banks, R. F., 'Long Term Agreements and Package Deals', *Industrial Welfare*, Vol XLVII, October 1965.
3. Ministry of Labour *Gazette*, September 1961.
4. Chrichton, Anne, 'The IPM in 1950 and 1960', *Personnel Management*, December 1961. Membership of the IPM rose from less than 8,000 in 1966 to over 14,000 in 1971.
5. McCarthy, W. E. J., 'Shop Stewards at Work', *Aspect*, April 1963, p 31.
6. Phelps Brown, E. H., 'Wage Drift', *Economica*, November 1962.
7. Lerner, Shirley W., 'Wage Drift, Wage Fixing and Drift Statistics', *Manchester School*, May 1965.
8. National Board for Prices and Incomes, Report 49, *Pay and Conditions of Service of Engineering Workers*, HMSO, 1967.
9. HMSO Statistics on Incomes, Prices, Employment and Production, March 1968.
10. National Board for Prices and Incomes, Report 50, *Productivity Agreements in the Bus Industry*, HMSO, 1967.
11. Lerner, Shirley W., 'Strikes', *District Bank Review*, June 1963.
12. *Report of the Joint Labour Council for the Motor Industry*, Dispute at Standard Triumph International, Coventry, August 1966.

13. National Board for Prices and Incomes, Report 17, *Wages in the Bakery Industry*, HMSO, 1966.

14. Turner, H. A., 'Wages: Industry Rates, Workplace Rates and Wage Drift', *Manchester School*, 1956, p 113.

15. Flanders, Allan, *op cit*, pp. 57–64.

16. The Engineering Agreement limits this to 20 hours in any four weeks, but the qualifications provide sufficient loopholes in practice.

17. Robertson, D. J., *Factory Wage Structures and National Agreements*, Cambridge University Press, 1960, p 151.

18. Marsh, A. I., *Managers and Shop Stewards*, *op cit*, p 12.

19. Lerner, Shirley W., *International Labour Review*, *op cit*, p 14.

20. See Thurley, K. E. and Hamblin, A. C., *op cit*.

21. McCarthy, W. E. J. and Parker, S. R., *Shop Stewards and Workplace Relations*, Royal Commission Research Paper 10, HMSO, 1968, paras 121 and 207.

Chapter Eight

Shop Stewards and Industrial Conflict

The implicit basis of collective bargaining is a conflict of interest between the parties. Bargaining, in which shop stewards are increasingly involved, is concerned with reconciling divergent interests. However, it is clear that this is not always achieved peacefully. The very term 'bargaining' implies the availability of sanctions, and so the association between stewards as bargainers and the use of sanctions implicit in that role must now be examined. However, expressions of conflict in industry stimulate largely emotional reactions making it necessary to digress, temporarily, to look at the system which provokes one of the few manifestations of organized social conflict in this country.

The bases of industrial conflict

Despite areas where the interests of management and employees often appear compatible, and where cooperation commends itself to both in order to achieve their objectives, plainly the employment relationship involves many divergent interests. Thus, representatives of each group are concerned to manage this conflict, as far as possible preventing it from being damaging. The extent to which the conflict of interest is constructively regulated and peacefully channelled depends broadly on how well the values and behaviour of both sides conform to a mutually acceptable standard. It also depends on the skill and alacrity of the representatives in handling problems.

Conflict of interest exists most openly over payment, or more broadly over the distribution of rewards arising from the working relationship. There is no accepted formula for allocating a firm's profits between the various claimants. If labour persistently obtains a disproportionate return it may eventually destroy that employer. High costs mean un-competitiveness, lack of business, and jeopardized employment. Thus, even of wages it might be argued that in the long run interests are not incompatible, assuming labour is concerned with job security, acceptable alternative jobs being few. However, in the short run and in buoyant market conditions, management can pass on cost increases in price rises, or otherwise offset wage increases. Thus, limiting earnings rarely appears to employees as self-interest. Labour, then, seeks both higher earnings and a larger share of total returns, seldom regarding this as jeopardizing future employment.

There are other, less obvious, features of the work situation which are equally divisive. The division of authority, stemming from the primacy of managerial objectives, creates authority relationships, suggesting in sociological terms that some conflict is inevitable. The authority may be challenged, particularly on topics debatably within management's pre-rogative over which employees wish to exert some formal influence. Authority also creates real and perceived differences in status, causing conflict both within and between management and shop-floor groups. Examples of conflict stemming from the authority structure are commonplace, eg, discipline, but there are other less evident manifestations. For instance, management aims at an internal structure and production methods considered most appropriate. However, this formal system is subject to the reaction of employees, and their attempts to protect their interests. Management tends to regard labour as a necessary factor but also as a cost to be minimized, as against labour's view of the nature and purpose of employment. Clashes between the firm's impersonal objectives and the employees' personal values appear inevitable.

In employment, employees give up some freedom, implicitly undertaking to obey the management. Instructions emanate from managerial decisions intended to realize company objectives, eg, cost reduction, profit or production maximization, etc. However, the contractual element in the relationship is vague or even silent on the degree to which management can command. The national collective agreements or works rules seldom specify when management can act unilaterally, and the exercise of managerial authority becomes subject to traditions and expectations in the workplace. Thus, in fact, it is subject to joint regulation, formal or otherwise.

Employees try to reduce their vulnerability to unwelcome managerial decisions, and to extend their influence over their work environment. Probably, their attempts at such regulation, as well as attempts to limit managerial freedom of action, will run counter to management's view of its own interests. They may well inhibit the achievement of management's prime objective, efficiency. They may seem attacks on management's right to manage, and thus on management's status, to which many contemporary managements are very sensitive.

Other evidence supports the hypothesis of industrial employment as a conflict situation in which cooperation may be achieved, rather than as a basically harmonious system occasionally breaking down. In certain industries, the technology, ie, the types of jobs, production organization, and control systems, engender conflict. The motor-vehicle assembly line is frequently quoted to illustrate a managerial philosophy giving precedence to mechanical efficiency, to the exclusion of the social and other needs of employees. Possibly, here, the mechanically imposed discipline and repetitive short job cycles contribute to endemic disputes. Certainly, this technology appears likely to create frustrations, with concomitant aggression or resignation.[1]

As both manufacturing establishments and companies become larger, human-relations problems increase, for the individual worker's remoteness from the employer leads to impersonality. Often, the individual worker feels insignificant, and that the firm is indifferent to his personal employment. The identification with and personal commitment to a firm is usually less in large firms than in small, where there is frequent contact between employer and employee. Problems of communications between shop-floor and management are frequently cited as major background causes of industrial conflict. These shortcomings exacerbate problems, but their improvement alleviates rather than removes more fundamental causes of conflict.

The employment relationship is obviously one of interdependence, but it is also one of expediency. It is an economic relationship, the result of bargaining, in which both parties attempt to optimize what they derive from it. One writer[2] has summarized the conflict between employees and management as that between the efficiency-centred outlook of management and the security-orientated values of employees. In that these interests are incompatible, conflict can be anticipated. However, in many ways, the interests of the two parties are not inconsistent, ie, where providing security facilitates the achievement of efficiency. Perhaps the relationship may be usefully summarized as one of antagonistic interdependence.

To argue that conflict is inherent in contemporary industry does not imply that it is necessarily damaging. Its expression in established negotiating procedures is not generally considered harmful, compared with, say, unofficial strikes. Indeed, arguably, the conflict is constructive. When grievances on either side find a remedy, the relationship is adjusted to ensure continued cooperation. Attention centres on either party's dissatisfactions, and recognition of the constraints on the other allows agreement. The problem is then revealed as one of identifying areas of conflict, and of regulating the expression of conflict. It does not mean suppression or denial of conflict, but rather its relief through accepted machinery. Thus, the relationship of unionists and employers proceeds by identifying areas of conflict, and regularizing their expression procedurally, together with advancing the aims of both through cooperation where interests overlap.

A strike is an interruption in the flow of consent, an overt expression of conflict; as such it attracts attention. However, conflict may be less dramatically expressed, in restrictive practices, uncooperativeness, limiting production, overtime bans, go-slow, work to rule, and through labour turnover and absenteeism. The method of venting dissatisfaction varies with the situation, and with what is considered legitimate, or effective, or customary. The possibilities quoted reveal the myopia of the obsession with strikes, and the dangers of assessing industrial relations by reference to the strike record. In industry, a cold war can be more damaging than a hot one. Moreover, some evidence suggests that considerable organized conflict is not inconsistent with high morale,[3] and that certain strikes benefit work performance.[4]

The importance of unofficial strikes

Although the Department of Employment does not differentiate between official and unofficial strikes in its published statistics, it has stated periodically through the 1960s that 90 to 95 per cent of all strikes in the UK are unofficial. They also account for the major, if a somewhat smaller proportion of days lost. For example, in 1960–64, unofficial strikes accounted for nearly 60 per cent of days lost, though if the 'unusual' national one-day token stoppages are excluded the proportion is over 75 per cent.[5] Definitions, however, are crucial. Perhaps the most succinct is given by Knowles,[6] that 'an unofficial strike is one which is not recognized by the Executive Committee of a union'. Ambiguity arises, however, in a strike being official to one union but unofficial to another, and the position changes over time. Some begin unofficially, ie, not being called by a trade union, but subsequently receive recognition, as indicated by the payment of strike benefit. The Department combines these criteria in the figures given above, defining unofficial strikes as those 'not called or recognized by a trade union'.[7] A further distinction exists between unconstitutional and unofficial strikes, the former contravening an agreed disputes procedure. Most unofficial strikes are also unconstitutional, but not all, eg, action taken after the exhaustion of the procedure, but remaining unrecognized by the union. The Department of Employment notes that official strikes seldom occur before the procedure is exhausted.

Many initially unofficial strikes gain union support when the facts become known. In a survey of 445 strikes during 1956–9, the TUC reported that 'in about half the cases reported to the General Council where strikes began without official sanction, the unions paid dispute benefit. The other half were less spontaneous and included instances where strike action was taken or prolonged contrary to general policy and specific advice.'[8]

Unofficial strikes are often regarded as a post-war phenomenon, but while more frequent in the post-war decades, they are not novel. For example, Professor Phelps Brown, writing broadly about the later nineteenth century, observes that sudden outbreaks of strife surprised union officials, who condemned members for breaking agreements, the public blaming the leaders for being out of touch with the rank and file.[9] Before the Second World War, the Ministry of Labour estimated that only a third of stoppages in 1936–7 received union approval as evidenced by payment of strike benefit.[10] Further perspective on the importance of strikes is given by comparisons of days lost recently as against earlier years, and by contemporary international comparison.[11]

Unofficial strikes are frequently condemned for damaging the economy, exports, and individual firms. The usual criterion is 'working days lost', though this indiscriminating measure is, as Knowles observed, 'not unlike estimating air-raid damage by reference to the bomb tonnage dropped, irrespective of target or type of bomb'. This crude measure may distort the *real* loss of production. For example, to equate 'days lost' and 'output lost' may apply passably in service industries, but less so in manufacturing. In manufacturing, 'lost' production may be rapidly regained, though involving such extra costs as overtime. Employers do not *always* regret the loss of output, eg, if they are producing for stocks. In the motor industry, the number of working days lost directly in the fifties varied almost inversely with the number of strikes, strikes being commonest in high-demand periods and least frequent during recessions.[12] Again, not all stoppages are reported to the Department of Employment, and the figures exclude days lost at establishments other than that in dispute. This can reach important proportions. For example, it has been estimated that from 1960 to 1964, over 260,000 working days were lost per year in the motor industry at establishments other than where each stoppage took place, compared with 480,000 days lost *directly* through stoppages.[13] The figures may also understate the real loss of production from recurrent unofficial strikes in one firm. These may deter customers, suggesting unreliability to foreign buyers. Domestically, strikes may transfer demand to other companies or other goods and services. Further, the 'days lost' standard ignores the ability to continue operations without the strikers, or the delay before a strike has any effect. The effects of *threats* of strike action also count. These may not directly affect production, but may produce important management concessions. The presence of these sanctions forms the background to workplace negotiations, being a 'deterrent' to some management behaviour.

The number of days lost through strikes in this country is relatively small. Even in 1970, when the 'days lost' reached a post-war peak of 10·8 million, a crude measure would suggest that the loss to gross national product was less than a quarter of one per cent. If a year more typical of the post-war period is taken, for example 1965, and we examine those industries in which days lost per thousand workers was highest, the loss of working days due to industrial disputes was less than one per cent of total working time in each industry. Nevertheless, the *number* of strikes has increased over the period, and it was the effect this increase might have on management initiative and the introduction of change which the Donovan Commission found disturbing. The annual average number was 2,458 for 1955–66, an increase of almost 40 per cent on the 1945–54 figure. The 1967–71 average was about 10 per cent higher than the 1955–66 average. These figures obscure a particularly important trend, that is, the rapid increase in strikes outside the coal industry. This industry accounted for over half the strikes in each post-war year until 1962, its share falling continuously from 78 per cent in 1957 to less than one per cent in 1970. Thus strikes have become more frequent, particularly so outside what was formerly the most strike-prone industry. The number of strikes outside the coal industry rose from less than 1,000 throughout the 1950s to 3,746 in 1970.

Increased numbers of unofficial strikes provoke objections on ethical as well as economic grounds, and have also drawn into question the suitability of traditional procedures and institutions. Unofficial strikers are condemned for breaking formal agreements when they feel it advantageous, and for selfishly exploiting local conditions. Certainly, workers often press claims when the situation strengthens their bargaining power.

On the other hand, employers know that procedures allow them to change the *status quo* and then listen to objections from employees which can then be lengthily resisted owing to the delay in exhausting the procedure. Demand conditions may tempt employers to 'reinterpret' national or plant agreements and customs with this intention. Unhappily, moralizing criticism of unconstitutional strikes concentrates attention on their impropriety rather than on the circumstances of the dispute or the suitability of procedures.

Increasing unofficial strikes may reflect a changing moral and social climate, in which to breach traditional machinery is not regarded as seriously as formerly. But it also reflects changed collective bargaining, the different nature of unionists' understanding of 'joint regulation of employment', and the declining relevance of some procedures to contemporary problems.

The background of unofficial action

Unofficial action, characteristically taken by workers in a firm under the nominal leadership of a shop steward, has many facets, and is attributable to various 'causes'. It may be seen as a strategic weapon employed consciously by workplace leaders who assume the mantle of generals or conspirators. Unofficial stoppages have the military virtue of surprise. Another view is that unofficial action is a necessary explosion of pent-up frustration, released often by a trivial incident. Again, on other issues, immediate reaction may be necessary if the issue is not to be lost by the tardiness of negotiating machinery, eg, questions of conditions, allowances, closed shop, etc. Further, unofficial strikes may be seen as a rational exercise by unionists, from which benefits gained outweigh costs incurred. At one level, they may be a response to a specific incident, at another an outburst of unrest associated with social conditions at large. The great variety of unofficial strikes, their circumstances and their causes, may make any one of these descriptions accurate in a given situation.

As, usually, unofficial action is also unconstitutional, the question arises whether lengthy, industry-wide grievance procedures remain acceptable, particularly to rank-and-file members. Confidence in them on the shop floor may be minimal. Secondly, they may be impractical for some disputes, eg, the so-called 'perishable' issues needing immediate solution, or those on questions previously excluded from union influence, ie, management's refusal to negotiate on a particular topic. Thirdly, the procedure may be inappropriate to the changing nature of workplace disputes. Though successful in such traditional issues as wage claims, it may be inappropriate to changes in working arrangements, job content, or the treatment of individuals. Fourthly, the procedure may be insufficiently adaptable to new requirements, becoming inappropriate for the industries it covers, eg, the engineering industry procedure (1922) was applied to much of the motor industry.

The Donovan Commission (para 475) felt that a minority might want to make trouble, and irresponsibility or weakness were factors which contributed to the frequency of unofficial strikes. The Report stressed, however, that 'the root of the evil is in our present methods of collective bargaining and especially our methods of workshop bargaining, and it is in the absence of speedy, clear and effective disputes procedures.' One of the principal objects of the factory and company agreements which the Commission advocated so strongly, was to develop 'joint procedures for the rapid and equitable settlement of grievances . . . This is what is lacking at present, and this is the indispensable condition for reducing the number of unofficial and unconstitutional strikes.' The Commission endorsed the view that most of the issues raised in procedure were workplace issues, and relatively few arose from the application or interpretation of industry-wide agreements.

One criticism of existing procedures is that they are too slow. Marsh and Jones[14] found, accepting wide variations, that on average in 1959 it took about thirteen weeks to progress issues in the engineering industry procedure from the first works conference to central conference. However, they suggested that unions rather than employers were mainly responsible. Delay in using the external machinery can give tactical advantage to either side, while increased use of procedure overburdens union officials, thus involving delay.

Not all procedural delay stems from traditional machinery outside the firm. Procrastination by middle management causes discontent among workplace representatives, but may stem from the emphasis stewards place on precedent and uniformity of treatment. However, there are limitations to the view that small issues blow over, or that a 'cooling off' period is required. Postponement often exaggerates small issues into major problems, precipitating action. If this causes many disputes, the provision of speedier procedures should not be difficult. Some agreements already make provision for 'express routes', eg, in the tobacco industry, while others, eg, coal industry, limit the time for a problem to pass from stage to stage.

Unofficial strikes are occasionally described as 'strikes against the union'. The rank and file may feel that their officers are unable to interpret their problems, or to secure concessions. This is partly internal to the union, becoming more difficult as union size increases. Large unions have coordination problems dwarfing those of our largest companies. However, it may also uncover very *real* differences in outlook, for the district officer has to look beyond the short-term interests of a few members.

Unofficial action is occasionally used by the rank-and-file to draw the attention, usually of union officials, to problems at shop-floor level. It is thus designed to modify the behaviour of officials, making up for deficiencies in union communications. It may indicate a declining reliance on full-time officials. The official may be unavailable for an urgent problem, or his anticipated moderation and support of constitutional machinery may be discounted. He, personally, may fear repudiation by his members, or feel a strike justified, and be deliberately unavailable to management. Over a period, unofficial action may represent a desire by union members to re-order the balance of authority between them and the union. The power structure of a union, particularly in full employment, more closely resembles an inverted pyramid than an orthodox one, yet the formal structure does not acknowledge the transfer of bargaining opportunities. Increased unofficial action within the membership is predictable in that the formation of breakaway unions has been unlikely to succeed, given the hostility of established unions, employers, and the TUC Disputes Committee.[15] However, the provisions of the 1971 Industrial Relations Act will make it easier for disenchanted members to replace an established union. In certain sectors, disaffection with the established union and its organization is serious, eg, in the docks, but though less developed elsewhere, its causes are by no means absent.

Full employment and the general economic environment in post-war years have reduced the identification between members and their union. Some improvements in conditions are more closely associated with stewards than with outside officials and remote negotiating bodies. This reduced dependence, externally, appears particularly true of non-skilled men, against whom union sanctions are less powerful. Also, the constitutions of most basically craft unions provide for greater local autonomy. The Welfare State has reduced members' reliance on union friendly society-type benefits. Earnings are such that the loss of a few days' pay is not so strongly felt as formerly.

However, a basic change in post-war years has been increased bargaining at workshop level. The growing number of strikes has taken place beside a redistribution of union functions in favour of the workplace representative. Outside the coal industry strikes 'caused' by claims for wage increases have increased as a proportion of all stoppages in recent years.[16] If members do better under the leadership of stewards than the union, then the stewards will be most influential. Managements could seek to contain pressure in the workplace by avoiding haphazard concessions, or by refusing to concede to stewards something formerly denied to external officials. This is influential in determining the actual, as well as formal, attitude of the union to unofficial action. If managements create the impression that more will be achieved by surprise strikes than by negotiations, they invite employees to take such action as the only way to secure change. For example, 'BOAC admitted that over a long series of unconstitutional incidents the shop stewards had produced a run of successes as a result of which they had no doubt come to be regarded by the workers as astute leaders . . .'[17]

Union claims to discuss topics previously held by employers to be non-negotiable are generally resisted more firmly nationally than at plant level. As on earnings issues, progress here is often faster in the plant than nationally. Management may view such pressure as a battle over the principle of who is to control the factory, believing success necessary to preserve its control. The cost of an increase in piecework prices is easily calculable, and can perhaps be passed on to the customer. But an issue over, say, management's right to discipline unilaterally or to subcontract work involves deep principles. Management may question such challenges *a priori*, regarding them as part of the 'insatiable' demands of employees with only harmful effects on efficiency. Yet, the real ability of management to discipline employees is much modified by what its employees will accept. Consent cannot be ascertained, as the expectations of both sides are imperfectly known, but some companies have successfully clarified the position by acknowledging joint regulation where it already existed in practice.

Traditional procedures may be well attuned to usual grievances, eg, pay complaints, yet not sufficiently sensitive to new issues of importance on the shop floor. Lines of communication are a problem, but the *content* of information flowing upwards is also important. Selection at intermediate levels may distort information concerning 'new' problems. The responsiveness of the system to expected complaints, eg, on wages, hours, etc, may lead to frustrations being translated into an 'accepted' topic. This may yield agreement, without solving the real problem.

The behaviour of management may also lead to unofficial action. Delay in dealing with grievances, haphazard concessions, *ad hoc* solutions, hurried decisions, and failure to consult all contribute to unofficial action. On the other hand, individual employers are vulnerable to workplace pressure, for a stoppage at certain times affects their ability to meet delivery dates and obtain subsequent orders. Small strikes allow competitors to benefit, and make decisions to resist or concede extremely delicate. Often, managements rigidly emphasize the sanctity of agreements, valuing constitutionalism rather than examining the causes of a dispute.

Managers thus obscure any doubts they may have of the morality of their behaviour on the issue itself.

The role of shop stewards

Strikes in the UK are characteristically small, short, local, unconstitutional, and unofficial. They are usually against a single employer, and frequently restricted to one establishment or even one group of workers. The obvious implication is that they are led by workplace leaders, though not necessarily by acknowledged representatives, who have no union authority to initiate such action. This often reveals the disparity between formal authority and actual power, but does not necessarily mean that the unions are out of touch with their members, or opposed to the action. It may help officials in negotiations, and accelerate a favourable agreement. H. A. Clegg observes that 'union officials may sometimes inform employers that unless a certain concession is granted they cannot be responsible for the actions of their members. On occasion, officers have been known to suggest to shop stewards that a demonstration of the validity of this kind of statement by their members would be of assistance in negotiations.'[18]

To presume that stewards *lead* unofficial action is to oversimplify though, in the main, probably valid. However, often a steward is forced to defend unofficial action he has not instigated, and members reject his 'constitutional' advice, accepting the leadership of men with no union position. Similarly, men may strike without reference to their representatives, who may attempt to reduce stoppages as a long-term policy.[19] On the basis of extensive survey evidence, the Donovan Commission came to the view that trouble was often thrust on shop stewards, and that they were often striving to bring some order into a chaotic situation.[20] In particular, it was concluded that shop-floor decisions which generally precede unofficial strikes are often taken against the advice of shop stewards – a view supported by detailed research in the motor industry. This study suggested that 'strikes have been as common in plants where the stewards' organization is weak and divided as where it is strong, and there is more to suggest that senior stewards attempt to control the development of disputes and are pushed into stoppages from behind than that they lead workers into such crises'.[21] Unofficial strikes and other types of unofficial action were seen by the Donovan Commission primarily as the result of the failure to devise institutions in keeping with changing needs. The Commission's surveys revealed that over three-quarters of the works managers and personnel officers thought that shop stewards were either less militant than or only as militant as their members. In answer to a question put to rank-and-file members, viz, 'How ready do you think your shop steward is to urge strikes or similar action when he is trying to get management to agree over some dispute?', 72 per cent said 'not at all ready', and only 4 per cent said 'very ready'.[22] Thus the overall picture suggests that stewards, on the whole, are a moderating influence, but that if their advice is rejected by the members, they will then normally try to retain their influence by accepting the majority view, and thus may appear to take a leading part in the conduct of a stoppage. Potentially, however, the steward has unique opportunities to influence his union members. He may, if he is accepted, be regarded as a leader of opinion in labour–management relations. His position, contact with management, knowledge of union affairs, experience of negotiations, and access to information not available to his constituents all foster his leadership.

In the long term, the steward's behaviour appears likely to reflect the values of his constituents. In contested elections, the steward elected and his subsequent behaviour are circumscribed by his constituents' expectations, and views of the management. An elected representative is occasionally unable to lead effectively in changed circumstances. If he does not respond to a different situation, or the changed feelings of his members, his advice is likely to be ignored and he is, in practice, replaced as leader. Gouldner[23] describes how conciliatory union leaders, in a plant with deteriorating labour–management relations, were replaced in practice, though not formally, by more extreme leaders when members felt a strike necessary. Such examples are common on the shop floor, but are more publicized nationally when moderate leaders come under pressure from militant groups, amending their behaviour to retain actual as well as formal leadership.

This analysis of the steward's position suggests his leadership is subject to the discretion of his constituents. Failure to carry out his often ill-defined 'job description' to their satisfaction renders him ineffective or leads to his replacement. However, there are limitations to this. It assumes, for example, that there are individuals of different types, with different views, prepared to accept the position. This is not always so. Secondly, it assumes that constituents can express their feelings and opinions to the steward; this is seldom easy in the workplace, and mass meetings are not conducive to reasoned debate. Indeed, most members may be apathetic, making little effort to influence the steward. Thirdly, members may think it the steward's function to gain the most benefits, not being concerned if his tactics and style in so doing do not reflect their own views. Approval of the end may justify the means. A 'proved' steward, with a good record for improving the conditions of his members, may carry them with him repeatedly in unconstitutional action. This may well become accepted, especially if it is thought to be the only thing management understands. It is reinforced by union strategy of solidarity, and threats of social or other sanctions against nonconformists. Men often follow stewards in unofficial strikes in ignorance of the issues. Also, the rank and file often have a very hazy impression of the minutiae of procedure, their outrage at an evident injustice overriding their understanding of their obligation to follow established procedural methods.[24]

Thus, though the steward must have his members' confidence to retain his position, the pressures they apply on him may be weak and infrequent. An established steward can exercise his discretion. A militant steward can play on the fears of his members, and a political zealot may well extend overt action. Unconstitutional methods, once accepted as justified, may become habitual, and be difficult to remove. This is perhaps the greatest danger indicated by the upward trend of the strike statistics, corresponding to the experience of several large firms in which a strike has become a first rather than a last resort.

Leadership of unofficial strikes, and the threat to use them, is usually the principal objection to the activities of shop stewards. However, unofficial action is not confined to the unofficial strike. The impression is that, recently, such 'cut-price' weapons as the overtime ban or work to rule have been used more frequently, the strike being simply one of many sanctions. They suggest the leadership of men, presumably stewards, with some knowledge of tactics and the position of the firm, and discredit the 'spontaneous outburst' explanation of unofficial action. To estimate how much considerations of strategy are present in unofficial strikes is difficult. Statistical support for stewards viewed as tacticians planning campaigns against management is largely limited to wages and related topics, *in which the discretion over timing is in the hands of stewards.* For example, in an examination of the north-east shipbuilding industry, G. C. Cameron observed, 'Thus whilst insecurity provides the basic cause of such (wage) disputes, their timing is largely dictated by the state of the market for labour ... Fifty-six of the eighty-one (wage) disputes started when the level of unemployment was either at the lowest annual point or not greatly in excess of that point.[25]

Professor Turner considered that 'most strikes are not initiated in support of some new demand on the employees' part, but in immediate protest against some act of the management concerned – or against the terms on which it intends to implement a change'.[26] It is difficult to classify the principal cause of a strike as either aggressive or defensive, as the chain of causation is so involved, but many strikes appear to be responsive.

There is a danger of condemning all stewards for the behaviour of a few, but a small if well-publicized minority of stewards do sometimes persistently disregard established procedures, perpetuating strike activity as an end in itself in seeking to disrupt working relations, employment, and production. There is evidence of political groups committed to disruption establishing themselves among stewards, but little evidence of their success. There have been few well-documented situations where stewards might justly be accused of manufacturing grievances rather than managing them. Sometimes, stewards have pressed members unwilling to participate in recurrent unofficial strikes, in some areas fines being paid to stewards' committees. Abuse of the position of the shop steward undoubtedly occurs, but evidence is slight in relation to the large numbers of stewards.

A few unions have occasionally disciplined stewards, for example by removing them from office, for taking action in breach of union rules, policies and procedure agreements. BISAKTA has repeatedly asserted its authority in this way, while the T&GWU, the NUGMW and other unions have taken similar action, less consistently. Competition between unions for members, often with militancy as the cutting edge, has limited the application of this sanction, despite the advice of the TUC. Many union officials consider that expulsion not only creates martyrs and hostility to the union, but also removes offenders from the union's influence, while not preventing them from influencing union members. The Industrial Relations Act (Section 36) places a new responsibility on the parties to a legally enforceable collective agreement, making it an unfair industrial practice not to take 'all such steps as are reasonably practicable' to prevent breach of the agreement. As yet we have no judicial interpretation of the steps which might be regarded as 'reasonably practicable', but this could involve the loss of office or expulsion of the leaders of unconstitutional action.

Occasionally, in what have been called endemic strike situations, unions have almost completely lost their influence with shop stewards and strikes have persistently taken place against union advice. Given the nature of 'news' such cases are well publicized, and include such examples as Briggs Motor Bodies in the mid 1950s, Ford's in the early 1960s, BMC, and the London and Hull docks in 1965 and 1966. Although managements tend to look to union leaders to regain control, the officials appear unable – or unwilling – to do so.

Managements fear the consequences of imposing their own discipline, though feeling aggrieved at the open disregard of legitimately constituted agreements. Reliance on procedural rules may be justified, but it is often false to portray an injured management with no responsibility for the situation, or for correcting it. Appeals for unilateral union action have not generally been successful. Such situations have usually been relieved by management action, eg, at Ford, Rootes, and BMC, and/or by joint action to improve relationships by examining the fundamental issues. In future it will be open to managements in such situations to seek investigation by the CIR, either through the NIRC or on a voluntary basis.

Another important factor in the behaviour of stewards is their relationship with full-time officials. This may appear competitive, with both seeking to restrict the functions and information of the other, but in practice present relationships are usually regarded as satisfactory and the interdependence of the roles is widely acknowledged. Certainly stewards *could* make life difficult for district officials, particularly if management prefers to deal with stewards. District officials subject to periodic re-election may also find it difficult to oppose influential stewards in plants with a large membership. However, generally relations between the officials and stewards are good, each regarding the other as complementary, informal limitations on freedom of action thus being accepted voluntarily. Certainly, stewards value their contacts with the union; most are regular attenders at branch meetings. Many branch positions are filled by stewards.

The role of stewards in controlling rather than creating

conflict is often obscured by publicity given to the few who attract the headlines. However, this view is changing. The diagnosis of the Donovan Commission has been particularly influential, and the CIR has also emphasized the need for orderly internal representational systems, recommending, for example, that a convenor system should be established in the Merseyside plants of Joseph Lucas. The absence of accredited union representatives in certain industries, notably the docks, has been acknowledged as a weakness for both union control and orderly workplace relations. The T & GWU experimented in introducing stewards into the docks at Hull and elsewhere in 1966, to improve relations and union influence, although this proved difficult, as the cases before the NIRC in 1972 demonstrated.

The availability of sanctions is now accepted in day-to-day employment relationships. Both sides are aware of how their interests can be threatened. For example, stewards may support output limitations, sponsor an 'uncoordinated' disinclination to work customary overtime, or an open overtime ban. They may not attend normal meetings with management, or joint consultation, insist on the letter of previous agreements, or progress every issue raised by members with time-consuming conscientiousness, etc. Briefly, they can make changes in their cooperativeness very difficult for management to combat. As individuals, they may withdraw from what Kuhn calls the 'helper functions', in which stewards assist foremen in daily labour management, eg, absenteeism, poor performance, timekeeping, etc. 'A shop steward can talk to an offending worker as a fellow worker and defender, while the foreman is always suspect.'[27]

Moreover, McCarthy notes wide divergences in the value attached to established procedures by management and shop stewards.[28] He observed that management regards facilities for the progression of grievances as a concession, for which stewards should be grateful. Their gratitude should be demonstrated by invariably abiding by the 'no collective action before the exhaustion of procedure' clause commonly found in these procedures. Stewards regard the procedural and substantive contents of agreements as guaranteeing only minimal rights, which are to be improved upon. As such improvements are gained, they are assimilated into 'custom and practice' to be defended as stoutly as a written agreement. Moreover, management attempting to 'tighten up' is regarded as breaking plant agreements, and stewards feel free to respond similarly. Quite simply, the primacy of 'peace clauses' is not accepted equally by both sides. Moreover, situations arise where managers challenge representations made by stewards, as being beyond the stewards' brief. Such behaviour may be regarded by stewards as unreasonable, justifying the application of pressure irrespective of agreed procedure. Clearly, the evaluation of the 'morality' of managers' behaviour on a given issue often outweighs obligations to follow procedure.

If management fails, in stewards' eyes, to honour agreements, stewards may regard this as more grave than their own repudiation of a procedure they themselves did not negotiate. As workplace agreements proliferate, the parties acquire many obligations, and agreements made at one level *need* not be consistent with those at another. Unfavourable revision provokes accusations of bad faith with possibly immediate effects and long-term deterioration in relationships.

This emphasizes the leadership of stewards in defending understandings developed through the daily regulation of relationships. Stewards who have personal loyalties among their constituents have wide discretion in reacting to managerial behaviour, in being predisposed towards immediate action or caution. However, such strong leadership is not universal, stewards' advice may be rejected, and sometimes stewards find themselves following their members in actions they think inappropriate. Thus, it is impossible to define the role of stewards in conflict in generally applicable terms; different case studies demonstrate variations in the part they play. One recent strike, of which the writers had first-hand experience, illustrates this. A large multi-plant industrial company proposed to reallocate work among its factories, causing some redundancy at the factory in question. Manual workers' stewards, through the JSSC, announced, without calling a meeting of members, a one-day protest strike, which took place. White-collar stewards convened members to consider similar action, which was firmly rejected. After the stoppage, criticism of the manual workers' stewards by their members reached such a level that the long-serving factory convenor resigned, serious divisions appeared in the JSSC, and between its leaders and the rank and file, threatening to break up inter-union organization at the factory. It also weakened the stewards' hand in subsequent negotiations over transfers and redeployment. Clearly, stewards must 'beware marching too far in front of their army' if individuals are to retain their positions, and if management is not to exploit both their failure to represent their members and divisions within their organizations.

The increase in unofficial strikes and other workplace sanctions reflect the changes in the location and subject matter of employment regulation. In view of this structural change, challenging the framework of traditional institutions, it is perhaps not surprising that the present pattern of overt conflict does not fit into the traditional mould. Its causes are deeper than mere personalities, more complicated than advocates of punitive solutions suggest, and, as has been recently observed, more likely the result of local democracy than of local autocracy. However, the immediate impact of unofficial action is upon management. These effects and other repercussions of the internal representational system must now be examined.

References

1. Goodman, J. F. B. and Samuel, P. J., 'The Motor Industry in a Development District', *British Journal of Industrial Relations*, November 1966.
2. Flanders, Allan, 'The Internal Social Responsibilities of Industry', *British Journal of Industrial Relations*, March 1966.
3. Scott, W. H., *et al*, *Coal and Conflict*, Liverpool University Press, 1960.

4. Paterson, T. T., *Glasgow Ltd*, Cambridge University Press, 1960.
5. Ministry of Labour, Written Evidence to the Royal Commission on Trade Unions and Employers' Associations, HMSO, 1965, para 127.
6. Knowles, K. G. J. C., *Strikes*, Basil Blackwell, 1954, p 30.
7. Ministry of Labour, *op cit*.
8. TUC Annual Report, 1960, para 60.
9. Phelps Brown, E. H., *The Growth of British Industrial Relations*, Macmillan, 1960, pp 231–32.
10. Quoted in Turner, H. A., *The Trend of Strikes*, Leeds University Press, 1962.
11. See Appendix A.
12. Turner, H. A. and Bescoby, J., 'Strikes, Redundancy and the Demand Cycle in the Motor Industry', *Bulletin of the Oxford Institute of Statistics*, May 1961.
13. Ministry of Labour, *op cit*.
14. Marsh, A. I. and Jones, R. S., *op cit*.
15. See Lerner, Shirley W., *Breakaway Unions and the Small Trade Union*, George Allen and Unwin, 1961.
16. Goodman, J. F. B., 'Strikes in the United Kingdom: Recent Statistics and Trends', *International Labour Review*, May 1967.
17. Report of the Court of Inquiry at London Airport, HMSO, Cmnd, 608, 1958, para 62.
18. Clegg, H. A., *General Union*, Blackwell, 1954, p 133
19. See Turner, H. A., Clack, G. and Roberts, G., *op cit*, pp 224–229.
20. Donovan Report, *op. cit*, para 110.
21. Turner, H. A. *et al*, *op cit*, p 330.
22. McCarthy, W. E. J., and Parker, S. R., *op cit*, paras 111–112.
23. Gouldner, A. W., *Wildcat Strike*, Routledge and Kegan Paul, 1955.
24. See Scott, W. H. *et al*, *The Dock Worker*, Liverpool University Press.
25. Cameron, G. C., 'Post-War Strikes in the North East Shipbuilding and Ship Repairing Industry', *British Journal of Industrial Relations*, March, 1964.
26. Turner, H. A., *The Trend of Strikes*, *op cit*.
27. Kuhn, J. W., *op cit*, p 31.
28. McCarthy, W. E. J., *The Role of Shop Stewards in British Industrial Relations*, *op cit*, paras 36–45.

Chapter Nine

Implications for Management

The rise of stewards presents a challenge to individual managements, as well as to the existing institutions of industrial relations. Managerial behaviour is increasingly subject to close scrutiny by powerful internal union representatives. This position has often inhibited managements from initiating changes they think desirable, but which are not carried out through fear of their unsettling effects. While some managements are faced with obstructionism, post-war change in the location of union activity has not made management's task impossible. It is our thesis that management is best placed to affect the quality of human and industrial relations in its plants, and the emergence of stewards makes management's attention here even more pressing. Stewards may, in one sense, increasingly constrain managers, but they also enable management to manage, in another sense, with greater certainty.

The importance of shop stewards to management

Until recently, it was widely held by students of industrial relations that managers prefer to bargain with full-time officials rather than stewards. The reasoning was that management prefer the periodic attention of the stereotype 'knowledgeable, reasonable, and responsible' full-time officials rather than the continuous and 'irrational' approach of stewards. Additionally, it was felt that management would resent encroachments on its prerogatives, ie, the right to decide unilaterally, by stewards anxious to enlarge their spheres of influence. For managements, logically it seemed best to bargain with officials rather than their own employees, pressure from the latter having 'dangerous' implications of increasing industrial democracy, with all the ideological overtones this concept has in British industry. Arguments ran, therefore, that the duties of stewards needed confining and defining precisely to keep the majority of collective bargaining activities for the attention of full-time officials.

Recent evidence has, however, challenged this belief. The Government Social Survey sample of works managers and personnel officers showed a strong preference for negotiating with shop stewards rather than full-time officials. 70 per cent of the sample of works managers and 76 per cent of the sample of personnel officers expressed a preference for negotiating with stewards rather than full-time officers when either was equally competent to settle an issue.[1] Research by Clegg, Killick, and Adams on the attitudes of personnel officers to shop stewards also shows they prefer dealing with stewards in collective bargaining. Returns from their questionnaire show that 69 per cent of those officers in the survey preferred to bargain with stewards as against 17 per cent with officials, both being equally competent. The reasons given by the majority included stewards' intimate knowledge of the circumstances (expressed by half the 69 per cent), preference for keeping issues within the factory, better contact of stewards with members (or control over them), and the beneficial effect on relationships within the factory. While these were the expressed reasons, possibly others also apply. Managers, perhaps, feel that stewards may have less freedom of action than officials, being subject to the firm's sanctions, whereas the latter are not. In practice stewards have three roles to carry out – they are representatives of members, trade-union officials, and employees. In some circumstances the third role may intrude into the other two and the steward may find it difficult to forget that he is employed by those with whom he is bargaining. In some circumstances this may encourage more mildness, possibly making him less effective than he would like to be. Both positive and negative sanctions are available to management, although the former are much more likely to be used in a period of full employment. Thus our survey revealed that 49 per cent of the sample were interested in promotion to the job of supervisor, and this was probably sometimes an influence on them during bargaining. However, this figure should be contrasted with that provided by the Government Social Survey in answer to a question to managers as to whether shop stewards were more or less likely to be promoted than other workers in the plant. 76 per cent of the sample said that it made no difference that they were shop stewards, 16 per cent said that stewards were more likely to be promoted, and 8 per cent said less likely.[2] It is possible that some managers' attitudes towards their shop stewards may be seen as attempts to gain the benefits of 'quasi company unionism' by conducting most negotiations with lay union officials who are members of their own staff and excluding those with an outside, independent, status. Sometimes, however, a full-time official might be called in to act as a 'fire brigade' and, of course, not *all* managers prefer to deal with shop stewards. As a policy matter, or where they dislike a steward, they can always deal with full-time officials trying, wherever possible, to exclude the steward from bargaining. Dr McCarthy quotes an example of a paint firm which dealt directly with the local full-time official, even over piecework prices, the steward having little to do.[3]

Nevertheless, personnel managers may feel that the more they discuss and negotiate with stewards, the more their own status is enhanced. Their work load is increased and they have opportunities to participate in bargaining, as line managers often seek their aid by passing stewards on to them. They are thus given the opportunity of preventing disputes from breaking out, and this often enhances their own roles. Certainly, by completing negotiations in, as far as possible, a mutually successful manner, stewards and personnel managers are likely to enhance their reputations with management and trade-union officials. As far as many personnel managers are concerned, matters so settled are confined to the plant and such managers appear in a relatively favourable light as able to settle with their own employees without relying on outside intervention. Many personnel managers of our acquaintance comment favourably on not having to call for external assistance from either employers' associations or trade unions.

The managerial approach to collective bargaining

A major implication for managerial policy arising from relations with unions in general and stewards in particular is the need for objectives to be clearly thought out and policy goals firmly stated. Also, that there should be greater willingness by managements to bargain with specific proposals.

It has been aptly remarked that 'management, accustomed to consider the initiation of new schemes as an essential part, indeed the very core, of its job in all other aspects of industrial life, has been curiously slow to innovate in the field of labour relations. Traditionally, managements have waited for an approach to be taken by the unions rather than themselves assuming the lead.'[4] It is doubtful whether all management is accustomed to considering change to be the essence of its job. Indeed, many commentators point out that this approach is found in far too few, perhaps a minority of cases. Yet perhaps in industrial relations conservatism is more predominant than in other fields. This state of affairs is due to a variety of factors. First, traditions in collective bargaining are against such processes, as the quotation suggests, and since in bargaining, as in industrial relations in general, traditions are so important in determining behaviour, quick changes cannot realistically be expected. Secondly, the application of the line and staff principle to personnel departments means that they are largely advisory. Most important decisions in labour relations are taken by line managers concerned with production, whose time for labour matters precludes deeply conceived policies.

Thirdly, decisions about labour relations are often taken by employers' associations following negotiations with union associations. Minimum wages and working conditions emerge for large sections of an industry. Individual firms within the associations are not encouraged to be radical, innovations at one workplace being used by unions in attempts to spread them at others throughout the industry. Many marginally profitable firms could not afford to implement such a policy and, therefore, unless nationally agreed, innovations are unlikely to reach these firms at all. This situation enables unions to make the running in labour relations, the changes being made often originating with the union. Innovating employers are usually outside the associations, where they are 'free' to be radical without involving other firms. Employers' associations appear to militate against widespread changes in relations through collective-bargaining procedures. Some recent research in the neglected field of employers' associations suggests, however, that this point should not be over-emphasized. A Royal Commission Research Paper by V. G. Munns and W. E. McCarthy notes how difficult it is for employers' associations to maintain control over member firms, both in the sphere of wages and working conditions and over more general industrial relations questions. Their survey showed that 72 per cent of national association officials and 42 per cent of national federation officials considered that they made little or no attempt to influence the industrial relations activities and decisions of member firms. Only 14 per cent of all national officials said they tried to influence their members 'a lot'. Nevertheless, non-federated firms with formal responsibilities only to themselves have much more scope to innovate than federated firms. This supports the view that, more formal bargaining should occur at plant level.

Fourthly, implementing big changes at plant level involves large sums of money available only to firms with large resources. This is shown in the major productivity agreements achieved in the United Kingdom, the companies involved being usually large, the *quid pro quos* given to unions also being large. Of course, as is well known, the majority of such agreements occurred on a 'partial' rather than a comprehensive basis and in firms which did not command great resources. Nevertheless, even including firms that have concluded partial agreements with the trade unions, only about one-quarter of the national labour force was covered by some form of productivity bargaining in 1970 – after it had reached its peak – and the majority of British managements did not participate in this innovatory development. Indeed, as the National Board for Prices and Incomes pointed out, productivity bargaining has been undertaken by the 'reasonably efficient rather than the inefficient'.[5] One aspect of productivity bargaining has been that it has tended to concentrate 'efficiency skewness'.[6] The high level of expertise necessary to conduct productivity negotiations is only available to certain firms – those which have the financial resources to buy and/or develop the relevant specialist skills. There is therefore 'a financial "threshold" through which companies must pass if radical change, along productivity-bargaining lines, is to be introduced.'[7]

The defensiveness of many managements in collective bargaining is accompanied, in many cases, by a defensiveness in their attitudes towards shop stewards. This is shown by the Report of the Commission on Industrial Relations on Facilities Afforded to Shop Stewards.[8] Thus, for example, the Report notes that 'the facility to leave the job is less well developed for collective meetings between the steward and his constituents. Our studies indicate that in the majority of cases, stewards meet their constituents collectively outside normal working hours. Management usually feel no responsibility in this area.' The Commission commented fur-

ther, 'In our detailed studies there were few examples of
stewards from one individual union being given the facility
to meet in works time'. The Commission recommended that
stewards should be given leave from the job to perform their
agreed functions 'as a general principle', that permission to
leave the job should be sought from the appropriate management representative and that such permission should not
be unreasonably refused; leave should be given to the
steward for business of an industrial-relations nature and
that 'it might be reasonable for management to grant leave
from the job for certain duties of a trade-union nature'. The
Report stated that there should be some joint agreement on
what is considered 'reasonable'.

The Commission found that 'despite the efforts of various
kinds to provide for lost earnings, a significant proportion of
shop stewards do lose some pay as a result of their representative role'. It went on to recommend that there should
be no loss of earnings suffered by the shop steward as a
result of activities agreed to be 'industrial relations' business.

There appeared to be a general reluctance on the part of
both managements and the unions to issue *joint* credentials
to stewards. Only four of the forty firms studied issued such
credentials. Yet the CIR believes that '... the value of
joint credentials is that they afford an opportunity for both
management and the trade unions to acknowledge that each
have rights and obligations arising out of the procedures and
institutions of the industrial relations system.' The joint
signing of plant credentials by management, the union, and
the individual steward appointed gives credence to these
institutions and thus strengthens the status of the steward and
the process of collective bargaining. There is the additional
advantage that joint credentials indicate to lower-line
management the standing of the steward.'

The Report notes further that the provision of office
accommodation specifically for the use of shop stewards
appears to be extremely limited in practice. It points out
that the need for such accommodation varies, of course,

depending on such factors as the size of the establishment and the nature of the shop steward system. It recommends that, where the size of the establishment and the nature and volume of the stewards' work justifies it, management should make every effort to provide appropriate office accommodation. On the other hand, such facilities as locker spaces, filing sets and other items of office furniture are needed on a fairly general basis. 'These facilities do not appear to be at all well developed. The provision of filing cabinets and locker space was reported in only a minority of establishments. However, this facility was not limited to those cases where offices were also provided.' Typing and duplicating facilities may also be needed and the Report suggests that they should be provided 'where the need has been established'.

Finally, on the question of training, the Report notes that 'the main requirements, if stewards are to have access to training courses (which, given the increased complexity of the steward's job, the CIR strongly recommend) are time off from the job and payment to compensate for the loss of earnings incurred'. It notes further that there has been, in recent years, 'an increasing tendency for employers and unions at industry and company level to encourage the joint provision of training courses for the shop steward'. The Commission recommends that stewards should be given leave from the job, with compensation for loss of earnings, when attending acceptable training courses.

The CIR makes it quite clear that unions, too, need to improve facilities for shop stewards and also that facilities need to be determined in the light of their appropriateness to the circumstances of individual industries, companies and establishments. Nevertheless there is scope for managerial initiative here, which could help considerably to raise the quality of industrial relations.

Many of the CIR's recommendations would appear to be essential prerequisites for good industrial relationships and it is surprising that they found such deficiencies among their sample of companies and the trade unions they inquired about. The major, and very obvious, point in this field, as in others, is that management should set its objectives (which in most cases will include the improvement of industrial relationships) and act in a positive manner to try to achieve them.

Positive management

As previously stated, the need for management definition of objectives has to be accompanied by action to achieve them; nowhere is this more necessary than in labour utilization. Disguised unemployment has been pervasive in the British economy and excessive overtime is another manifestation of the misuse of labour. Thus Allan Flanders states,[9] 'No one denies that part of this sustained post-war overtime in Britain has been deliberately contrived for no other purpose than to produce an adequate weekly pay packet. Employers provide such "policy overtime", as it is called, to attract or to keep workers whose earnings cannot be supplemented sufficiently or at all through payments-by-result systems or plus rates and bonuses of various kinds.' Professor Clegg notes how this undermines attempts to increase efficiency, writing that,[10] 'Large sections of British workers are taught by their system of payments to waste time at work. Quite apart from the unfortunate results (of overtime) on their own lives of not being able to use their own leisure time as they might wish, this has unfortunate consequences within industry. What is the point of telling workers that machine time is valuable, that wastage of material must be avoided at all costs, that the aim of the firm is to make efficient use of its resources, if their own time is being wasted in this way.' These views on overtime are not universally accepted."

Whatever the specific situation, however, the need to utilize labour fully faces all managements, since it is, fundamentally, their responsibility to alter the situation. To quote Flanders again,[12] 'When managements blame trade unions for standing in the way of change what they are really objecting to in most cases is the challenging task that confronts all democratic governments of having to win the consent of the governed.' This is possible, despite those who accuse unions of obstructionism. The following case study shows how one management set out, and succeeded, to win consent for radical innovations.

Refining Ltd: A case study

It was decided at Refining Limited[13] in 1963 that overtime should be reduced, demarcation lines broken down, some workers absorbed into more productive work, and craft shiftwork introduced to secure higher productivity and 'to provide a framework for the future within which change will be more acceptable'.

Ideas of change originated in 1960, when consultants suggested changes involving reduction of both hourly rated and staff employees. Therefore, changes were made, managers and office staffs becoming redundant. Redundancy among the hourly paid staff did not materialize, the eleven trade unions refusing to discuss redundancies and threatening sanctions.

Further management changes were made in 1962, with the appointment of a new Refinery Manager and a new Employee Relations Manager. Changes on the lines of the Fawley Blue Book were suggested, and the two newcomers were instrumental in getting them accepted. Both, being tolerant and humane, quickly became popular among employees, which was important in improving relations with the stewards, suspicious after the actual and threatened redundancies of 1960.

In 1962, the company conceded a forty-hour week after a few sporadic stoppages. Union officials, both local full-time and lay, were then told that the company wished soon to negotiate a productivity plan for the refinery. This did not surprise the unions, management hints of change and the presence of consultants for about two years indicating coming changes.

Management did not, however, move until October 1963, and meanwhile an addition to the labour-relations staff had been made. A new officer was appointed to help in negotiation of the plan. Previously he had been a T & GWU branch secretary in South Wales. Together with the Employee Relations Manager, he undertook most of the detailed discussions with stewards and union officials, and he acted as a bridge between the two cultures.[14] Performing most day-to-day detailed consultation with the stewards, his personality helped win their trust.

The first official meeting was held in November 1963. The company presented the maintenance stewards and their full-time officials with outline proposals to provide a stable salary, a 'genuine' forty-hour week, to maintain working, and to improve refinery productivity. The unions allowed the stewards to discuss the details, calling in officials for negotiation. Management stressed that all the discussions assumed that the unions would be involved in negotiating the package. There were to be no redundancies under the plan, while the company was willing to add 25 per cent to the basic rate to compensate for overtime and condition money lost. This was to be a weekly salary, not hourly pay, being calculated from the average take-home pay, which was 25 per cent above basic rates.

For months, discussion took place between the stewards and management, and stewards and their constituents. Meetings with full-time union officials covered matters of union policy, as well as progress. The convenor and deputy convenor acted almost full-time as plant union representatives, and as matters affecting each trade group arose, the appropriate steward was called in.

The negotiations were difficult, certain groups opposing the plan at times. As agreement was voluntary, these groups could have compromised the whole plan. The civil trades group at first refused to grant 'flexibility', ie, to break down demarcation lines, but were eventually persuaded by management's increasing the compensation rate to 32·5 per cent of the basic rate. The CEU and the pipefitters, HDEU, opposed next, also being worried about dilution of their skills; again, they eventually accepted. Those reluctant, then, were members of unions where the skill gap was narrow. They felt more vulnerable to broken demarcation lines than other groups. In the latter case, the skill necessary for the job obviated the fear that the supply of labour could be quickly increased. Flanders notes that every craft-union member guards against any breach of demarcation lines because 'the fences (of demarcation) are not fixed and unalterable; they would be more secure if they were. As it is, much depends on the vigilance and militancy shown in their defence at the place of work. And almost every craftsman knows, with the instinctive knowledge that embodies the historical lessons of his social group, that it is his duty to the union and to his fellows to prevent trespass and, if possible, to gain more ground. Anything deliberately done to reduce even slightly the existing territory is suspect because it might eventually lead to destruction of the craft. One can never tell for sure where it will end; where one step on this slippery slope may lead.'[15]

The ETU were also worried over upgradings, a special agreement being made providing that the upgraded personnel should not do more hazardous skilled jobs for a period. Eventually, all groups accepted the proposals, only individuals with special reasons for not transferring being allowed to stay. For instance, those close to retirement remained as shop helpers but not as craftsmen's mates.

After fourteen months, both sides agreed to a documented plan which came into operation in January 1965. In certain respects, the plan surpassed the suggested outline. More flexibilities were obtained than had been bargained for, employees worked some overtime without pay in the six months, and overtime was reduced from an average of 20·5 per cent to 5 per cent within a month. On the other hand, the company increased its offer from 25 per cent to 32·5 per cent (addition to the basic rate), plus £50 per annum per man after six months. This £50 was partly to satisfy those unions asking more than 32·5 per cent before implementation of the plan and partly to encourage employees to cooperate during the vital first six months of the plan, when craftsmen's mates were upgraded to craftsmen and employees worked up to 16 extra hours per quarter without pay. Also, of course, these months were psychologically important in winning employees' acceptance of the plan.

The negotiation of this plan was extremely smooth and successful. Since such positive action by management is increasingly essential, it is appropriate to analyse its success.

The reasons for success at Refining Ltd

(1) *The success of the Esso Blue Book*
The success of the Blue Book experiment set a precedent, allowing the stewards to feel they were not first to intrude into the demarcation preserves of craft groups. There was greater readiness to accept the plan at the outset than at Fawley.[16] In addition, before discussions, the convenor had attended a course run by the Industrial Welfare Society which was centred on the Esso Blue Book, and the reasons for its success. He was, therefore, well informed about the case for 'productivity bargaining' and how far management had succeeded, and how much the unions had conceded, at Fawley.

Also, of course, management could use the Blue Book as a challenge. Both sides determined to do at least as well as Fawley. Being a smaller unit of 880 employees with only eighteen shop stewards, Refining Ltd was more compact in organization, and therefore had a better chance of success. The plan came into operation immediately, except for the time necessary to retrain staff, though at Esso it was phased over two years. Overtime dropped from an average of 20·5 per cent in the six months before the plan to a 5 per cent average in the two months after. Shortly after this, it was eliminated. The union obtained 32·5 per cent in real terms, representing a wage increase of, on average, 5·5 per cent per man per week. At Fawley, a supplementary settlement was necessary in 1962 to give some craftsmen an income gain in real terms at all.[17]

(2) *The voluntary nature of the agreement*
The fact that agreement was voluntary reassured the stewards that their wishes would be respected since, obviously, management wanted everyone to participate. Also, it enabled those stewards in favour of the plan, fourteen out of the total of eighteen, to pressurize those against. If groups remained outside, dissension among employees could compromise any acceptance. As the company introductory letter to the final agreement states: 'If the plan is finally accepted, the spirit in which it is implemented will determine its success or failure.'

(3) *The size of the wage agreement*
The real increase in wages for those employees in the plan was a sufficiently large inducement for cooperation. As from July 1965, the new weekly salary was 10·4 per cent higher than average earnings during January–November 1964. No steward wanted his constituents left outside, earning about 10 per cent less than other maintenance workers. Also, psychologically, it demonstrated management's determination that employees should not suffer from the change but that their interests were important.

(4) *The role of the stewards*
Success was facilitated by the willingness of management and unions to let the stewards help determine the final plan. Thus, those responsible for implementing the plan also participated in its construction. The stewards felt that it was their plan as well as management's, they were interested in it, as well as showing a general determination to see it through. The chief opponents were the two T & GWU stewards who felt that, since the craft unions supported it, they must oppose it. Representing such semi- and unskilled T &

GWU maintenance staff as drivers, labourers, and canteen workers, they resented the strong position of the craft unions. Yet their *constituents* were almost wholly in favour, forcing them to accept it!

If the stewards had not participated so fully, negotiations having taken place over their heads, they might have felt that the plan had been imposed upon them. Their resentfulness might have reduced their willingness to implement it.

Indeed, in some instances, this involvement has gone even further. At Petrochemicals Limited, stewards presented proposals for a flexible approach to the operation and maintenance of the chemical plant. Some skilled tasks were listed for trained craftsmen, but others were to be done by staff immediately available. Management invited the approach, allowing stewards to widen the proposals which were then put into practice.[18]

Certainly, the participation of stewards in productivity bargaining is necessary if those they represent are to have an opportunity to influence their working conditions within the changing pattern of circumstances. Lacking this opportunity, work groups may act unconstructively, opposing proposals put forward by management.

Indeed the procedure may need to be broken down further if consultation is to succeed. The breakdown of work groups within many stewards' constituencies may create informal leaders. Stewards may need to consult with them if their groups are to be fully involved. Otherwise, 'unofficial' opposition may arise with unhappy consequences for proposed productivity deals.

Indeed, the implementation of such bargains greatly affects the relationships between management and stewards. The crux of productivity bargaining is that management settles such problems, neglected over the years, as demarcation problems and inefficient use of labour, some points of dispute between management and unions being removed. Not all disappear; in a dynamic situation this is scarcely possible. Nevertheless, the scope for steward bargaining may well be restricted as a result, leaving the steward less powerful.

Members may apply pressure on him to justify his election by producing improvements. This could result, in time, in erosion of some of the control management regained through the productivity agreement. The full-time official is also important here. Though it is possible to use him to restrain stewards and defend the agreement, doubtless such action would alienate workers while undermining the position of the official.

It is said that those workers with no 'restrictive practices' to concede in a productivity agreement will invent them. Also, possibly, those involved in earlier productivity deals will create new rigidities to justify the improved conditions another one would bring. In fact, the work-group pressures expressed through stewards plus technological change lead to fluctuations in the pattern of plant agreements.

(5) *The role of the full-time officials*

That stewards played a large part in determining the final shape of the plan reflects the trust felt in management and stewards by the officials. The ex-T & G W U branch secretary insisted that his discussions with stewards were detailed and, where agreement seemed likely, that information was quickly passed to the union officials for ratification. He avoided reaching agreements with the stewards alone, seeing that this would reduce the full-time officials' support for the plan. They would have resented what appeared as agreements reached behind their backs. These threaten to undermine their status, and by introducing agreements locally with far-reaching implications for future bargaining elsewhere could cause problems for the unions. The opposition of the full-time officials could, of course, have killed the plan.

While stewards are vital in such radical agreements, they act as union officers. Agreements reached concern their superiors, who must be consulted if lasting progress is to be made.

(6) *Managerial skill*

This discussion has touched on the ability of the managers in these negotiations. A further illustration suggests the very high quality of management necessary to succeed in such ventures.

The Employee Relations Department in the refinery faced the prospect of discussing the plan with a craft convenor who, largely because of his own enthusiasm for it, could not persuade his fellow stewards. They thought him too pro-management to protect their interests adequately. Management, therefore, sent two stewards to an IWS course on the Esso Blue Book. One was probably the most intelligent unionist in the plant. He was in favour of the plan, but much more cautious than the convenor. On returning, he was most knowledgeable about productivity bargaining. Being more acceptable to the other stewards than the existing convenor, he was elected to this position in the annual craft-union elections. The ex-convenor resigned, being offered the position of supervisor. The new convenor was allowed, with his deputy who had accompanied him on the course and who was also extremely able, to spend fifteen months in full-time consultations about the plan with management. It was he who patiently ironed out points of difference between his fellow stewards and management. Without him, management admitted, the plan would probably not have gone through.

Managerial skill was also displayed in the decentralization of the administration of the plan, so that departmental managers and supervisors had to aid its implementation. A research group studying the behaviour of supervisors at Refining found they were disgruntled because, they claimed, the stewards knew more about the plan than they did. Management, realizing that by discussing with stewards they had indeed created this situation and seeing the dangers of alienating supervisors, arranged weekend courses. Here, their supervisors were fully briefed about the scheme and its progress. Having done this, the management could rely on supervisory cooperation as the plan was introduced. De-centralization of the responsibility for implementation is inevitable if managerial initiative is to be fully rewarded. It is pointless for major ventures by top management to fail departmentally because supervisors cannot or will not effectively implement them.

A leading industrial relations expert from Ford's in the USA has observed, '. . . of all the management specialities, the personnel function is perhaps the one least capable of being effectively carried out solely by a corps of specialists. Practically everyone in management, at all levels, is dealing with people in carrying out his responsibilities, and thus is involved in implementing personnel policies and affecting, in greater or lesser degree, the nature and extent of personnel problems. Quite aside from that aspect, major decisions in this area of management responsibility usually have an important effect in other areas, and the reverse is often equally true. The labour-relations activity functions most effectively as a built-in, continuous, fully integrated part of the total managerial effort.'[19] Positive labour policies need total managerial effort, not just a specialist one.

This study of the introduction of a productivity plan does, however, great credit to the management. British managements are often compared unfavourably with those abroad. A example of criticism of the traditional approach of British management to labour utilization was contained in the *Financial Times* editorial on December 21st, 1964. Analysing the results of Professor Dunning's article in the *Philip Hill Higginson Review*, the editorial points out that Professor Dunning proves, taking the years 1958–62, that the average US returns on overseas investment were 10·2 per cent, compared with the UK's 7·8 per cent. The difference was greatest in Western Europe, the Commonwealth, and Britain itself. The editorial concludes that American firms are more rigorous in their investment decisions. It summarizes these findings thus: 'The implications of this study, even though tentative, could be wide ranging. One of the arguments advanced to explain Britain's weak performance has been the poor quality of British labour and its lack of effort. If so, then British investment in foreign countries with less troublesome unions should show better returns. But these statistics

show that the rate of return on British capital is no better –
even if it is located in "industrious" countries such as Italy
and America – than in the UK. One cannot yet be sure, but
the implication could well follow that it is management, and
the quality of its decisions, which stands at the real centre of
Britain's sluggish rate of growth.'

The above case study is an example of managerial initiative and success in labour relations, showing the way to
better utilization of company resources through productivity bargaining.

(7) *The gradual nature of the change*
Planned change in detailed working arrangements affecting
routines of many employees is an exercise in management.
It also tests the quality of the worker's representatives. Too
much enthusiasm for and too little questioning of the scheme
can jeopardize its success. Thus, the attitude of the original
convenor at Refining threatened to alienate other stewards,
concerned that their constituents' interests should be carefully considered. The successful convenor consulted slowly
on the proposed change, taking all interests into account. If
such changes are to be introduced in British industry, the
lesson of this study is that bargaining must be gradual.

Conclusions
The implications of productivity bargaining for shop stewards are important although some stewards have not welcomed it favourably.[20] The NBPI has disclosed that
'productivity negotiations have had the effect of thrusting
greater authority and responsibility on trade-union representatives at plant level'.[21] More specifically, productivity
bargaining has probably increased the importance of stewards as negotiators, representatives and lay union officials.
Stewards have experienced an upward adjustment in their
bargaining roles as they negotiated with more senior levels
of management within the perimeters of productivity
bargaining. Having established such relationships, stewards may have continued to bargain at this level also.

Perhaps, in many cases, a ratchet effect took place.

In their representative roles stewards will have been important spokesmen for primary work groups. Such groups, aware of the importance of the changes which were proposed in many productivity-bargaining situations, will usually have wanted to influence the course and the result of these negotiations. In most cases they will have done this through their stewards.

Finally, as lay union officials, stewards are most important representatives of their union to the members, since they are the only point of contact which most workers have with the union. The behaviour of stewards can, and usually does, colour the attitudes of members to their unions and this, of course, greatly affects the degree of success which stewards have as recruiters of new members and retainers of existing ones. Where productivity bargaining has occurred, there will often have been a direct connexion between the intensity of interest of the trade-union members and the degree of change proposed. The performance of a steward in the productivity-bargaining situation will often have been very important to his success or otherwise as a lay union official.

This increase in importance of the role of the shop steward has not always been accompanied by positive recognition by management or positive action to grant the steward facilities. However, it is easy to point to deficiencies in management; it is necessary to gain balance by pointing out their difficulties. Certainly, collective bargaining presents many, the most intractable being to know when to submit to shop-floor pressure and when to resist it. Whichever management does is likely to bring criticism from some interested party, yet there are few guides to what is correct. Closely connected is how management functions are to be reconciled with the increasing number of topics claimed as negotiable by stewards. Often, stewards negotiate on topics connected with production management, such as safety measures and incentive schemes, intrusive on management's right to manage. In practice, reactions to this problem help set the tone of industrial relationships in a factory. Again, the problem of what facilities to afford stewards is not easily resolved. A liberal attitude may further their success, which may be unwelcome to management, while curtailment leads to difficulties in collective bargaining. To quote one manager, 'Before we act in relation to our stewards we have a very complicated balance sheet to construct and interpret.'

These problems are exacerbated by personalities which, even in a good atmosphere, can easily produce friction. This is especially true if turnover of stewards is so high as to prevent the development of steady relationships with managers. Management also finds itself dealing with more bargaining in the workplace as the dynamic of industrial relations shifts there. Several managers declined to comment on where they drew the line of demarcation between stewards and officials in negotiations.

Finally, the advent of the Industrial Relations Act may not have made management's task easier in this area. Thus a survey of personnel managers, carried out by the *Sunday Times*, into what such managers think about the Act was partially concerned with whether the members of the sample[22] thought that the Act would make their job easier or not. The following table presents the results.

Table 9.1

	Multi-national companies %	Managers from Domestic companies %	All companies %
Will the Act make your Job:			
Much easier	1	2	2
Easier	13	11	11
More difficult	61	60	60
Much more difficult	4	7	6
About the same	21	20	20
Don't know	1	1	2
No answer	0	0	0

References

1. *Op cit*, p 86, para 4.87.
2. *Op cit*, p 85, para 4.86.
3. *The Role of Shop Stewards in British Industrial Relations*, *op cit*, para 19.
4. Seear, Nancy, 'Relations at Factory Level', *Industrial Relations: Contemporary Problems and Perspectives*, ed B. C. Roberts, Methuen, 1962, p 164.
5. NBPI Report No 123, p 34, para 16.
6. See Towers, B. and Whittingham, T. G., 'Productivity Bargaining in the United Kingdom. An Overview', *Journal of Industrial Relations*, Vol 13, No 3, Sydney, September 1971.
7. *Ibid*.
8. HMSO, Cmnd 4668, May 1971. References are taken from Chapter 5 of this document.
9. Flanders, Allan, *The Fawley Productivity Agreements*, *op cit*, p 226.
10. Clegg, H. A., *Implications of the Shorter Working Week for Management*, BIM Paper No 1962, p 13.
11. See H. A. Turner in review of the Royal Commission's Research Papers, BJIR Vol VI No 3, p 355.
12. Flanders, *op cit*, p 237.
13. This section is based on discussions with management and shop stewards at an oil refinery. We are deeply grateful for their cooperation, but a guarantee of anonymity prevents mention of their names.
14. It is a commonplace that management is inclined towards efficiency and employees towards security, though this generalization is not equally applicable in all cases. Management here were recognizing what Jack Barbash states. 'The problem of industrial relations, then, arises out of the tensions between the employers' application of rational pressures and the worker's resistance to these pressures through his protective devices'. See *British Journal of Industrial Relations*, March 1964, p 72.
15. Flanders, *op cit*, p 217.
16. See Flanders, *op cit*, pp 107–37.
17. Flanders, *op cit*, p 164.
18. Royal Commission on Trade Unions and Employers' Associations. Research Paper No 4, 1967, p 6.

19. Denise, M. L., 'The Personnel Manager and his Educational Preparation', *Industrial and Labour Relations Review*, October 1962.
20. See, for example, NBPI Report No 36, Cmnd 3311, HMSO, London, 1967, p 27, para 123.
21. Report No 123, Cmnd 4136, HMSO, 1969, p 27, para 93.
22. The sample consisted of 516 managers who attended the Annual Conference of the Institute of Personnel Management at Harrogate in the week October 25th–30th, 1971. 345 managers completed and returned a 32-point coded questionnaire. Taken from 'What Managers Think About the Industrial Relations Act' by Vincent Hanna, *Sunday Times Review of Industry*, October 31st, 1971. (NB, the three columns do not total 100 because of rounding.)

Chapter Ten

Recent Developments and the Future Role of Shop Stewards

It is intended in this chapter to present an overview of the position and role of shop stewards, together with the issues and problems involved as they appear in the early 1970s and, secondly, to examine the nature and probable effects of various proposals for reform. The latter section will deal in particular with the Donovan Report, the Industrial Relations Act 1971 and its associated Code of Practice, the CIR report on shop stewards' facilities, and other post-Donovan developments.

Summary and present problems

The problems associated with the emergence of shop stewards are related to wider changes in the industrial relations system, and beyond that system to changes in both the economy and society at large. The latter include, for example, higher material standards of living and expectations of continually rising standards, increased worker interest in factors beyond the wage bargain which affect their working lives, the growing size and complexity of industrial organizations and approximately thirty years' experience of full employment. These and other broad changes may be identified as generating pressures to extend the area of employment issues which are subject to joint regulation, and to increase the intensity or detail in which the issues are regulated by agreement, but the role of shop stewards has also been influenced by the way the parties in industrial relations have responded to these changes. Indeed, the present power of shop stewards can, in large measure, be attributed to the post-war rigidity of our industrial relations institutions, which has ensured that stewards' roles developed pragmatically and informally. This is especially true of stewards' bargaining activities, since conditions favourable for workplace bargaining failed to provoke any *general* structural reforms to cater for its development. As we shall see, recent proposals to alter the system of industrial relations have almost without exception concentrated on the task of changing the nature, form and character of bargaining at the workplace. The unions have rarely solved the difficult problem of maintaining their authority without forgoing workplace-bargaining opportunities, while many managements have responded with *ad hoc* expedients rather than with forward-looking plans for the development of industrial relations at the place of employment. The atmosphere has been permissive; many would claim excessively so. The functions of old procedures and institutions have been widely eroded to the point where fundamental changes in the machinery of industrial relations are necessary.

However, pragmatism and flexibility have brought advantages to both sides, sufficient at least to create substantial barriers to reform. What appears as a jungle of disorder which taxes the understanding of an outsider is often considered by those who operate within it to 'work' satisfactorily. Assessment of the need for reform and, beyond that, of the direction reform should take, raises a number of questions. Whether the existing arrangements should be 'rationalized' simply by codifying and formalizing current practice, whether new institutions should be developed, or whether further evolution along post-war lines is preferable, are questions of interest not only to unions and managements but also to the Government. In recent years successive governments have restated their support for the principle of collective bargaining but have expressed their concern over some of the results of its present organization. The major policy question in this area is perhaps that of whether work-place bargaining is to be promoted or to be checked. The answer rests ultimately on the structure thought most likely to reconcile union members' demands for higher standards of living, greater security and greater influence over the whole environment of their jobs, with company and government concern over competitiveness and prices.

The coincidence of a buoyant economic climate from 1945 to the late 1960s with both managements' and unions' preference for informality has often led to relationships based on opportunism. Managements often resent the effects of the increasingly internalized system, though their policies have in part helped foster it. It holds advantages for them, but when its disadvantages appear the tendency is to call on the old procedures. Similarly, stewards have preferred to regulate relationships domestically, but they have retained access to and rely on the external 'reserve' power of their unions. However, it is significant that, for many managers and stewards, external alliances have become supplementary rather than primary, as was the case earlier this century.

Although many managements have well-intentioned policies designed to improve labour relations internally, generally the level of labour management, at least until the late 1960s, appeared low. Despite the pressures from the shop floor, or perhaps because of them, only rarely have firms scrutinized industrial relations as closely as, for example, products, technical methods and markets. 'Research and development' has been non-existent, with a few exceptions. Too many senior managers have taken a contemporary absence of strife as indicating that all is well, whilst the anticipated difficulties of introducing changes in procedural and substantive agreements and understandings and in labour utilization dissuaded others from regarding this area as a profitable field for their attention. However, the successes of some well-publicized plant productivity agreements revealed simultaneously how far wasteful practices had developed even in companies thought to be well managed, and how they could be removed by imaginative management. Productivity bargaining indicated the indispensable role of employee representatives on the same wavelength as rank-and-file members. Thus stewards appeared to be an essential element in one of the most encouraging features of recent collective-bargaining practice.[1]

Clearly stewards seek the best they can achieve for their members from the shop-floor situation they face, and if they are not met by a purposive management, with a long-term design for workplace relations, then expedients proliferate and anomalies can multiply. Many aspects of the employment relationship which are important to union members cannot be regulated effectively by multi-employer agreements. Topics such as manning, internal labour mobility, discipline, overtime allocation, work organization and job demarcation cannot be regulated in detail in agreements which cover a wide variety of companies. In the absence of comprehensive company or plant agreements, most have been left to informality. The issues at stake here are, in microcosm, those of management prerogatives and of worker control. They indicate that work groups and their representatives want to influence not only the price of their labour, but also to regulate its utilization. Often it is this encroachment by stewards on to new topics, rather than greater pressure on money matters, which managers find most galling. These issues provide sufficient scope for active workplace representatives, even in the absence of bargaining over financial matters. Moreover, the importance of issues concerned with status, degrees of influence over work organization, styles of treatment, etc, may well increase as attitudes continue to change. The effect on short-run earnings may not be great, but their influence on labour costs is important.

For managements, the enhanced importance of shop stewards has brought both advantages and disadvantages. Some have openly welcomed the development, have afforded stewards good facilities in the plant, and have sought to develop good relations with them. Some have utilized the opportunity afforded by the presence of stewards to introduce innovations, such as major changes in payment systems and productivity agreements, and to add a new dimension to the concept of 'management by consent', but others have emphasized what they see as the negative aspects and have ignored its possibilities.

Some managements deeply resent stewards' scrutiny of their decisions, with their attempts to circumscribe traditional management freedoms, regarding the process as an endless stream of impossible demands. Typically, management strategy has been the defensive one of containment, rather than of seeking to advance their own interests positively or jointly. Many managers still regard facilities for stewards and agreements reached with them as privileges and concessions. Consequently, the facilities enjoyed in practice often go far beyond the terms of any written agreement, maintaining the illusion that they could be withdrawn in changed circumstances. Thus, most agreements understate the role of stewards, and the lack of realistic formal agreements widens the gap between stewards and the rules of the industrial relations system. This is a topic to which we shall return later.

Stewards also present a challenge to the unions, although they remain indispensable in recruiting members, collecting dues, handling workplace problems, and as channels of communication. The challenge to the unions is essentially one of maintaining unity and control without alienating the membership or stifling local initiative. The internal structure of unions, particularly the division of authority within them, was fashioned to the needs of industry-wide bargaining. As this has declined in significance since 1945, this structure might well be called into question. Certainly the challenge from below is as much one to the unions as it is to employers' associations and the old collective-bargaining structure. The primacy of national union executives is more appropriate to unions in industries where bargaining is concentrated at that level, but it is less justified where industry-wide machinery has declined. However, practice differs; unions have been indulgent towards variations between rulebooks and reality, trusting loyalty and tradition rather than close definition. The unions have continued to stress the unity of their organizations, while allowing the acquisition of bargaining functions by stewards. Generally, until the late 1960s, this was accepted rather than promoted, but recent statements, particularly by the leaders of the T & GWU and AUEW, have emphasized the desirability of rank-and-file involvement in, or at least explicit approval of, negotiations which affect their terms and conditions of employment. Some unions still fear their stewards are insufficiently skilled and lack the resources to deal unaided with higher levels of management, but increasingly the solution is seen in terms of greater training and access to information rather than withholding authority to negotiate.

The nature of a union's authority over its members is an involved question. In practice few trade unions can insist, on pain of sanctions, on the acceptance of bald instructions from above. Such obedience may be necessary to the career of a manager, but it is not for most unionists. Discussion of a union's control over its members soon provokes questions about the purposes of union organization, and the methods appropriate to them. If it is primarily to advance the interests of its members, sectionally, unions clearly cannot do this only by industry-wide negotiations, which typically set only minima and are not comprehensive. Workplace representatives can negotiate with individual managements, and they have secured financial and other improvments of a kind and often at a pace not possible at higher, more remote, levels. Consequently, the workplace has become the major focus of attention for workers in many manufacturing industries, though the logic of the traditional formal system suggests it should be supplementary. The tardy acknowledgement of this change of emphasis, and lingering doubts about whether it should be perpetuated by formalization, has left unions and managements ill equipped to regulate it. Thus much workplace bargaining is somewhat secretive, opportunistic and piecemeal – its very status has affected its nature and results. Where managements have taken positive initiatives, as recently through productivity bargaining, the results have often been rather different.

The steward, as a negotiator representing constituents, draws strength from his ability to carry his members with him, yet he may on occasion find himself in an uncomfortable position created by a difference between the demands of his members and the advice, instructions or policy of his union. Union fears of creating alternative devices for the determination of policies outside the established internal machinery have often left their members without an 'official' workplace unit in which to express their views. Union democracy is typically based on branches, membership of which does not coincide with employment in a single establishment or company. Some unions have brought members closer to the union externally by encouraging shop or factory *organization* rather than relying simply on residentially based branches. This emphasis is found in the printing unions, and is also advocated in a NUFTO handbook. In both cases, workplace representatives attend periodic shop meetings, giving members an opportunity to hear reports from their representatives and to raise topics. However, formal provision for such meetings is rare, although they appear an obvious way of preventing representatives and constituents from losing touch. Some firms, however, give facilities for such *ad hoc* meetings in periods of crisis.

The closer association of stewards with unions *appears* to be a difficult problem, although the extent to which it is a real problem in practice is arguable. As we have shown, stewards tend to participate fully in branch organization and activities. Evidently stewards build up a close relationship with full-time officials if they find this useful functionally, rather than merely being a duty. If stewards respect their local official, and are satisfied with his interest and assistance, they are less likely to take action before consultation or to ignore his advice. If union committees and officials yield helpful information and advice, problems are more likely to be referred to them than if the only reason for doing so is a clause in the rulebook. The survey evidence suggests that generally the relationship between shop steward and full-time official is mutually regarded as being complementary and supportive, rather than competitive, as has sometimes been alleged and is no doubt true in a small minority of cases. Nevertheless, there are strong reasons to avoid complacency on this subject, since the relationship between the union outside the factory and the rank-and-file members within it is crucial. A number of suggestions have been made to improve the contact between the many stewards and the few full-time officials. Some, including the Donovan Commission, have recommended that more full-time officials be appointed, so they would be more easily available to stewards and perhaps better able to specialize. Another idea is to build up the research staff of trade unions, perhaps on an industry basis, so that stewards could be provided with much more detailed and sophisticated data for use in bargaining. Certainly stewards appear to want more information about the affairs of their companies, and they have in the past found it difficult to obtain information or to accept that proffered by managements. The provisions of the Industrial Relations Act may help here, although the precise information which unions and stewards will be entitled to receive is not yet clear, and union registration is a condition of entitlement. Without objective and factual information stewards' actions may seem, and may be, misguided if not selfish. If the local union office could be built up as a source of information on company, district and industry matters it would strengthen the link between stewards and their unions. Another suggestion for improving this link through structural changes in the form of workplace bargaining is examined in the section on the Donovan Report below.

Much depends on whether the unions want to stimulate or to restrain the development of the bargaining activities of workplace representatives. The two largest unions, at least, appear to favour the former, but it is evident that the Industrial Relations Act is intended to increase the responsibilities and bolster the authority of the unions centrally. If the development of the steward's bargaining role becomes an explicit and general union policy, it raises the question of training. Few training officers operate without detailed job descriptions, yet that of the steward is particularly difficult to define. They are important communicators, but they are also decision-makers, and are now much more than simply custodians of constituents' established rights. Their quality is crucial to both unions and managements, but over the post-war period both have been hesitant about providing training on a large scale. Its effects and implications are not well established. Whilst some courses may draw stewards closer to their unions and increase their understanding of the wider context in which both union and management operate, there remains the fear that constituents will misunderstand or suspect the motives of management in assisting in shop-steward training courses. Although training, if geared to meet agreed objectives, may improve the steward's capacity to do his job effectively and thus will be of benefit to his constituents, there is a danger that it will perhaps make him somewhat more remote from his members. In the last analysis it is his continued acceptance by the work groups he represents that makes the steward important to both management and union.

The most intractable problem in relations between shop stewards and their union is that of union structure and the existence of multi-unionism at plant, company and other levels. Bargaining at company or plant levels emphasizes the need for inter-union cooperation, which joint steward organizations amply demonstrate. The potential independence of joint shop-steward committees remains a problem in the absence of effective schemes of joint supervision or single unionism, and here again structural changes in workplace-bargaining institutions seem necessary.

The challenge from below, represented by the development of shop stewards, the enlarging of their functions and the broadening of their activities, has threatened the traditional industrial relations system in Britain in many ways. The increased internalization of dealings between management and employees enhances the roles of stewards and labour relations and other managers at the expense of employers' associations and trade-union officials. The unplanned de- centralization of bargaining has emphasized workplace rather than union loyalties among union members. In acute situations both unions and managements have been unable to coerce or persuade members and employees to follow their advice, and unofficial strikes have increased. The piece- meal and fragmented nature of much workplace bargaining has added to the difficulties of developing an effective nat- ional policy for incomes. The gap between wage rates and earnings has reduced the significance of many industry- wide agreements, and has called into question the adequacy and suitability of negotiations at this level on all but a re- stricted range of topics; whilst the dispute and grievance procedures which they usually incorporate are widely re- garded as inappropriate for all but a small minority of issues. Thus a major problem facing the industrial relations system is that of reconciling plant bargaining with industry-wide bargaining machinery, and reconciling both with the 'national interest'. An associated problem of equal prominence is the change in the pattern and level of expression of industrial conflict which has coincided with the rise of workplace bar- gaining. These two issues, which directly involve the role of shop stewards, have dominated the debate over the need to reform the British industrial relations system, to which we now turn.

The reform of the system

The late 1960s and early 1970s was a period of intense debate about the direction and methods of reform in industrial relations. The major proposals are examined in chrono- logical sequence, particular attention being paid to their implications for shop stewards.

(a) *The Report of the Royal Commission on Trade Unions and Employers' Associations, June 1968*

Although many of its recommendations about the role of the law in industrial relations have been superseded, the

Donovan Commission's analysis and recommendations for the reform of industrial relations remain influential, and indicate the probable direction of reform in many cases. The central theme of the report was that there were two systems of industrial relations, the formal, ie, the traditional, with its externally based institutions regulating relationships through industry-wide agreements, and the informal, ie, the workplace regulation of work and pay by managers and shop stewards. The former was considered, somewhat sweepingly, to be a façade, and the latter to be the reality. The Commission concluded that the central defect in British industrial relations was the disorder in factory and workshop relations and pay structures. Its major recommendations were aimed not at coercing shop stewards but rather at changing the *conditions* which in the Commission's view promoted disorder. The preferred instrument of reform was the plant or company agreement. This would facilitate changes in the character and conduct of workplace bargaining, which was criticized as being 'autonomous, fragmented and informal'. In recommending the conclusion of comprehensive factory or company agreements the Donovan Commission pointed to a number of advantages. In contrast with industry-wide agreements an agreement at this level could regulate *actual* pay and settle an effective and coherent pay structure. Issues such as overtime, payment-by-results schemes, etc, could be agreed in detail. The rights and obligations of shop stewards and convenors could be defined, it could establish a grievance procedure to suit the firm's organization and management structure, and include agreements on redundancy, discipline, etc.

At first sight the support given in the report to decentralization appears to favour the extension of shop stewards' bargaining activities. However, the Commission's principal objective was to change the character and form of workplace bargaining, particularly in large firms in private manufacturing industry, through the development of factory or company negotiating committees on which it was hoped all unions with members would participate. The Commission suggested that 'the constitution of the company and factory negotiating committees will require the presence of full-time officers, at least for certain decisions and the ratification of proceedings by unions'.[2] Thus the Commission wanted to draw full-time officers into the negotiations, to reduce or eliminate sectional or fractional bargaining outside the new negotiating committees, and detailed written agreements which codified and consolidated existing agreements and understandings. If re-negotiation of such issues was reserved to the committee and written agreements were as comprehensive both in the subjects covered and in their detail as the Commission hoped, then the nature of bargaining by ordinary stewards would be changed and its frequency probably reduced. If 'Donovan-style' plant agreements were negotiated then stewards' day-to-day activities would be largely those of applying and interpreting the agreement between periodic re-negotiation by the full committee. The more orderly arrangements that would stem from such comprehensive agreements would reduce uncertainty both for stewards and managers, and depending on the decisions made about the relationship between such committees and any industry-wide procedure agreements, could lead to quicker handling of factory issues.

One problem, apart from those of the inter-union co-operation needed to establish them and of defining the appropriate coverage of such bargaining units, is the part to be played in such negotiating committees by shop stewards. The interests of union supervision of the agreements reached may demand the participation of full-time officials, and the arguments for limiting the size of the committee in the interests of easier negotiation might limit the number of stewards who could participate. However, if formal factory or company negotiating committees were widely adopted, they would increase the demands on the time of already busy full-time officials, a factor which could materially affect the nature and quality of the agreements. If stewards were excluded then the agreements reached might be resisted, and stewards might resent the officials taking over functions

which are currently theirs. Whilst the unions might have
reservations about leaving the negotiations entirely to the
stewards, for example on the grounds of their bargaining
experience or competence, there is no doubt they are closer
to rank-and-file members than the full-time officials. They
are also more easily available, and are better aware of existing practices and understandings and the implications in
their plant of any agreements which might be reached. They
would, in any event, have to interpret and operate the agreements, and involvement in their negotiation might assist
implementation subsequently and increase their commitment to the agreements.

The problem is thus to find an adequate framework which
would utilize the experience and broader view, but limited
availability, of full-time officials and the advantages which
shop stewards derive from their position. As we have seen,
latent union factory negotiating committees already exist in
the form of joint shop-steward committees or 'works committees' of senior stewards. Also many companies found *ad
hoc* committees of shop stewards and full-time officials useful
in negotiating productivity agreements. A two-tier system of
committees might provide the means of resolving some of the
problems raised by the Donovan proposals. On the lower
tier a joint shop stewards/management committee would
help ensure acceptable representation of stewards. It could
meet more frequently and if necessary more quickly than one
which required the simultaneous attendance of a number of
full-time officials, who would be released from initial
negotiations, and would allow negotiations to be conducted
by those best informed on the detail of factory practices and
requirements. Such a committee could be supplemented by a
committee consisting of full-time officials and management
at factory or company level which might resolve failures to
agree, set guidelines for negotiations in the lower-level
committee and ratify agreements reached at that level. This
committee would probably be more effective if a few senior
stewards were members of both this and the lower-level
committee.

This arrangement for factory-wide bargaining would have a number of advantages, particularly in medium or large plants. It would provide direct supervision of the bargaining activities of shop stewards by a multi-union committee of local officials, thus bringing a clarity and functional responsibility into a relationship which is often obscure. It would formally give stewards a bargaining role which many currently exercise, but which is rarely formally acknowledged. It would also economize the demands made on the time of full-time officials, but would enable them to keep in touch on a regular basis. Developing the responsibilities of stewards through formal factory agreements would perhaps obviate the need for a large increase in the number of full-time officials which would otherwise be required, but which the unions find it difficult to finance. Whilst such a framework would tend to maintain the present hierarchy in the unions, it would also fit in with current trends in several unions by emphasizing the role of the union externally in advising, guiding and assisting the bargaining activities of their stewards. Clearly the exact nature and functions of Donovan-style negotiating arrangements would need to be devised by managements and unions to meet the particular situation of each company and to take account of its size, the desired relationship between different plants in multi-plant firms, etc.

Thus the Donovan Commission concentrated on the need for reform at workplace level. As we have seen in earlier chapters, its research surveys did much to rehabilitate the image of shop stewards, and it stressed particularly the need to achieve greater clarity, certainty and coordination into the conduct of industrial relations at plant and company levels. It strongly suggested that 'comprehensive, orderly and systematic' agreements on a wide range of topics were necessary at this level as a means of reducing the prevailing disorder which it saw as the root of industrial relations problems in many sectors of British industry. The Commission gave a higher priority to reform than to the application of legal sanctions, which it suggested would hamper rather than assist reform, and consequently it advocated that the traditional voluntary methods should be relied on although some members of the Commission doubted the efficiency of this in galvanizing employers and unions. One area which the Report singled out as appropriate for formal written agreements at plant or company level was that of shop stewards' rights, responsibilities and facilities, and its suggestions on this topic have been amplified by a CIR Report.

(b) *The Commission on Industrial Relations*

In the period between its establishment in 1969 and late 1971, when it operated as a voluntary body, the CIR cautiously applied many of the Donovan recommendations for the reform of workplace procedures and institutions to a number of companies. In its 'company procedural' reports the CIR often recommended more formalized arrangements for handling workplace issues, the creation of new plant and company-wide negotiating committees, the merging of consultative and bargaining bodies, greater involvement of full-time officials and closer liaison between them and with shop stewards, the introduction of differentiated procedures for different types of issue or involving different groups of workers, more training, etc. One aspect of reform which the CIR has repeatedly recommended in its reports has been the conclusion of formal agreements covering the role of shop stewards, and in 1971 a separate report was published on shop steward facilities.[3]

Currently the facilities given to shop stewards to perform their duties in the workplace rest largely on custom and practice developed over the years as a result of periodic pressure by stewards. The comparative rarity of written agreements on facilities itself reflects the general failure of the parties to incorporate the enlarged functions of shop stewards – which give rise to the need for facilities – in written agreements. Agreement about stewards' functions is a prerequisite of any realistic statement of what facilities are necessary to allow them to be fulfilled effectively. Indeed the widespread, though not universal, absence of formal agreements reflects the lingering resistance of managements to workplace representation and organization, and seems to owe more to a continuing conflict than to a shared preference for informality. Many managers consider allowing a steward relatively free access to talk to his constituents, or to meet other stewards prior to discussions with management, to be *privileges* – for which the steward should be demonstrably grateful. However, stewards tend to see such facilities as *rights*, either because they are essential to the performance of their job, or because they have become customary. Formal agreement would change their status, transforming them unequivocally into rights. Many managers feel that written agreements would represent some loss of flexibility, that the written provisions would merely set a new minimum platform which would be further supplemented, that the facilities might be more easily abused, and that revealing the facilities that had been conceded might prove embarrassing. These beliefs may be countered by the argument that if jointly agreed facilities were expressed in a formal agreement then this might foster a more stable and secure relationship. Also, the argument that unwritten understandings may be open to subsequent 're-interpretation' can work both ways, and unilateral changes by management might well provoke retaliatory action. Indeed, it is not self-evident that such understandings are easier to change than formal agreements.

The CIR Report in May 1971 strongly recommended that action should be taken, following reviews of their functions, to formalize the facilities available to shop stewards in written agreements. Whilst industry-wide agreements could go much further than most do by outlining general principles and providing guidelines, the CIR felt that detailed agreements should be reached at company and establishment level. It was argued that the absence of such agreements reflected either a strategy of resistance to commitment on the issue or a reluctance to think deeply about and face the issues involved. In favouring formal agreements on stewards' facilities the CIR felt that their negotiation would stimulate joint discussion between unions and managements about the functions and activities of stewards, that formalization would increase clarity and the degree of understanding, and would strengthen and stabilize relationships within the establishment. There is little doubt that the inclusion in a formal agreement of at least the current *de facto* facilities given to stewards would be regarded as a major gain by most stewards and thus might be a useful bargaining counter for employers anxious to introduce procedural changes. Specifically, the Report recommended that managements should, with union agreement, give assistance in the conduct of shop steward elections, that joint credentials might be issued, that stewards should not lose pay as a result of their 'industrial relations activities', and indeed that assisting their trade-union functions (eg, collecting dues, recruiting new entrants) would often lead to improved industrial relations. Agreements should also be reached with the unions defining the number, size and composition of constituencies, the facilities stewards should have to consult and report back to members both individually and collectively, and for meeting other stewards. Release with pay for training should be agreed, and adequate physical and administrative facilities such as access to telephones, typing and duplicating, office furniture, etc, should also be agreed, if stewards' functions have developed to the point where these are justified. Many of the CIR's recommendations are included in the Code of Industrial Relations Practice, although this does not specifically mention workshop meetings of rank-and-file members or meetings of stewards within the establishment.

(c) *The Industrial Relations Act, 1971*

The Donovan Report can be said to have favoured pushing the conduct of industrial relations firmly in the direction in which it was already going, especially in some private manufacturing industries, subject to strong recommendations for the re-vamping of workplace industrial relations institutions. The early work of the CIR tended to support the Donovan proposals, and sought by its treatment of particular situations to disseminate 'good practice' on a voluntary basis. The Industrial Relations Act is *in part* designed to accelerate the process of collective bargaining reform by adding legal force to CIR recommendations in certain circumstances, but the Act embodies a philosophy alien to British traditions, and the opposition this has generated may prove counter-productive of reform in bargaining structure and practice in the short run.

The Act rarely mentions shop stewards. Schedule 4 makes it a condition of union registration that, 'if the organization has officials . . . (whether they are shop stewards, workplace representatives or other officials) the rules must make provision for their election or appointment and for the manner in which they can be removed from office'. Also, 'the rules must specify the powers and duties . . . of officials who are not officers of the organization'; and '. . . any official by whom instructions may be given . . . for any kind of industrial action, and the circumstances in which any such instructions may be given'. These provisions might have stimulated a long overdue revision of union rulebooks to specify the position and duties of shop stewards more closely, for which the TUC called on a voluntary basis in a circular to affiliate unions in December 1969, but the decision of most major unions not to register has given rules-revision conferences other priorities.

Although the Act seldom refers specifically to shop stewards, its provisions have substantial implications for them, particularly so given union opposition to registration. For example, the provision that pre-entry closed-shop agreements are void and that post-entry closed shops are contrary to the Act in all but the most exceptional circumstances will make recruitment and organization more difficult. The agency shop is available as a substitute only to registered trade unions, and collusive continuation of existing unwritten practices regarding 100-per-cent union membership will leave the parties, especially the employer, open to actions by individuals before the Industrial Tribunals. Another innovation introduced by the Act is the presumption that written agreements will be legally binding on the parties unless they contain a clause disclaiming this. It seems unlikely that many unions will enter into agreements without an exclusion clause, and they may indeed be reluctant to negotiate new, more detailed, precise and comprehensive agreements on procedural topics, fearing that such agreements will be more easily interpreted than present ones by the National Industrial Relations Court. Rather than encouraging the conclusion of more comprehensive and precise agreements, the immediate effect may thus be to drive workplace arrangements further into informality, or in some instances may result in the total absence of written procedure agreements, although the Act makes possible the imposition of CIR-recommended procedures in such situations.

However, perhaps the most significant changes are those concerning the inducement of breach of contracts, a situation common in many unofficial strikes. The key section for shop stewards covering strikes and irregular action short of a strike is the provision that it is 'an unfair industrial practice for any person in contemplation or furtherance of an industrial dispute, knowingly to induce or threaten to induce another person to break a contract to which that other person is a party, unless that person ... is a (registered) trade union ... or does so within the scope of his authority on behalf of a (registered) trade union ...' (Section 96). This suggests that any shop steward who is not duly authorized by a registered union to call industrial action which would involve a breach of the employment contracts of those participating, would be liable, on complaint to the NIRC, to a restraining order and/or to the award of unlimited damages against him, or against his (unregistered) union if the Lords' decision in the Heaton's case were applied. This provision is clearly aimed against one of the most frequently criticized aspects of contemporary industrial relations in Britain, that is, the unconstitutional strike – whatever its causes – which takes place without explicit union approval. This provision raises many questions which also apply to others in the Act. That is, how employers and unions will react to it, whether it will be pursued in practice and, if not, whether it will have more than a transitory influence on behaviour; and, not least, how it may be evaded. The simplest method of evasion, assuming all unions were registered, would be for them to authorize all their shop stewards to call such action, although such a response might carry the decentralization of authority much further than most unions seem prepared to contemplate, and it might – in the absence of amendment to their rules – expose their strike funds to rapid depletion. Moreover it may be that some union leaders at least will privately welcome the bolstering of their authority which is implicit in the clause. Secondly, this course of action would afford shop stewards protection only if the relevant procedure agreement remained not legally binding on the parties.

If the union is unregistered, as is probable, then the Act will expose stewards and others to legal actions if they are closely identified with the application of sanctions unless there is no breach of the employment contracts of those participating. To meet this condition, those calling or inducing, for example, a strike would have to ensure that such notice was given as would be required to terminate the employment contract (usually one week in the case of manual workers), and that the action was not in breach of any term of the employment contracts of those concerned which restricted their right to take part in a strike, eg full exhaustion of a disputes procedure if this was incorporated into the contract of employment as a pre-condition of strike action. Since it seems likely that most major unions will not register, the continuation of strikes of the type which have become most common in the post-war period will leave those who induce them open to legal actions and penalties.

Perhaps the major question surrounding the effectiveness of the Act in deterring this kind of industrial action is whether the employers affected by it will in fact initiate legal action. In the past few employers have been prepared to proceed against individual employees who have appeared to break their contracts of employment by taking part in such strikes. The Act gives new powers for complaints to be made by employers against those who *lead* action of this kind. The Donovan Commission felt that any legal sanctions which relied on the employer initiating and pursuing legal sanctions against his own employees would be ineffective, as most employers – for a variety of reasons – would be likely to take the view that legally imposed penalties would exacerbate relations and would not foster cooperative day-to-day attitudes. This may not apply so much to temporary restraining orders. It may be that the Act will induce more caution amongst those who play a leading part in workplace industrial action, and the new law may have an effect on attitudes in the longer term. It is equally possible that responsibility for such stoppages may be spread more widely, making it difficult for employers to identify and prove leadership and that tactics may change the use of sanctions towards those which are less easily attributable but no less effective. The temptation for managements to assume that a shop steward is responsible for any action which takes place in his shop and thus bring a complaint against him or his union seems unlikely to make the position of shop steward any more attractive or more keenly sought.

This question about responsibility for unofficial action, and in particular the responsibility of (unregistered) unions for the actions of their shop stewards, was at the centre of early cases under the Industrial Relations Act. These arose out of the 'containerization' dispute and involved certain road haulage firms, the T & GWU, and its shop stewards in the docks at Liverpool and Hull. The issues raised in the Heaton's case and the final decision of the House of Lords making the T & GWU responsible for the actions of its stewards have important implications for the future relationship between unregistered unions and their stewards.

From the outset the NIRC took the view that the union in question, the T & GWU, was responsible at law for the action of its docks shop stewards in 'blacking' the lorries of Heaton's and two other firms. The union's case, that the stewards' actions had not been authorized by the union and were 'beyond the scope of their authority', was not put at the NIRC, but succeeded in the Court of Appeal. Lord Denning held that in blacking the lorries concerned the shop stewards were acting not as representatives of the union, but as representatives of their work group, who had overwhelmingly endorsed the 'blacking' at mass meetings. It was further held that the stewards did not have express or implied authority 'from the top' of the union to take such action, and consequently that the union was not responsible.[4] This judgement was subsequently reversed by the House of Lords, the Law Lords arguing that the stewards' authority to take industrial action on behalf of the union could be implied from 'custom and practice', and from an *upward* delegation from the members rather than from a downward delegation from the union. Their Lordships further supported the initial view of the NIRC that such authority, and the responsibility of the union, continued until it was unequivocally withdrawn by the union, for example, by withdrawing the credentials of its shop stewards or, if necessary, taking disciplinary action.[5] It should be emphasized that this judgement referred to the particular case in question, and it should not be assumed that it would apply in other cases involving other unions or other industries and situations. However, the unanimous House of Lords judgement appeared to suggest that if shop stewards had authority to negotiate on matters affecting the employment of union members – whether this derived from union rules or handbooks, by reason of their office, by custom and practice, or otherwise – it extended to include implied authority to take industrial action ancillary to the process of negotiation on behalf of the union. If this view were applied generally there would be very few (unregistered) unions which could avoid legal responsibility for industrial action (which constituted an unfair industrial practice under the Act) led by shop stewards.

This clearly leaves the funds of any unregistered union vulnerable to depletion through legal actions for compensation brought by parties injured by 'unfair' industrial action led by shop stewards. To avoid this situation, it appears that unregistered unions must either register – and authorize stewards to take industrial action – or expressly limit the power of stewards to take such action, and consistently withdraw the credentials of those who do so. There is little doubt that the latter course of action, and the adoption of a 'policing' role over their members, would create considerable friction and disaffection between the union and the members concerned. The withdrawal of the credentials of shop stewards who led industrial action supported strongly by their constituents might simply lead to the election of others pledged to continue the action, and in cohesive and active groups such as the dockers, could easily lead to strikes, and a mass exodus from the established union, with its consequent loss of influence over the situation. The President of the NIRC, Sir John Donaldson, took the view that 'such dangers must be faced in order that in the longer term we may have an orderly system of industrial relations'.[6] Others take the view that such measures would push stewards further outside the rules of the system, increase their power as centres of dissension beyond the influence of union leadership, and put the union leadership in the position of appearing to take the side of management. This issue clearly needs careful consideration, and it seems unlikely that the leaders of unregistered unions will make hasty policy decisions, despite the House of Lords decision.

A further implication of the House of Lords decision, which was reached whilst five dockers' stewards were in prison for contempt of the NIRC's orders in a similar case, is that it reduces the possibility of individuals being imprisoned for contempt. If complaints arising out of the activities of stewards of unregistered unions are to be made against their unions, then fines and compensation can more easily be collected by means of sequestration orders. However, the early experience of the operation of the Industrial Relations Act showed a marked reluctance of employers to use its provisions. The cases in the docks involved employers taking actions against the employees of *other* employers, and it seems clear that most employers are conscious of the problems which would be provoked by taking legal action against unions with whom they will have to continue to deal.

(d) *The Code of Industrial Relations Practice*

Although the suggestions of 'good practice' embodied in the code are not legally obligatory, they express standards which will serve as guidelines for the CIR and which may be referred to in cases before the NIRC. It is perhaps this residual element of compulsion which has ensured a wide readership amongst managements. In contrast to the Act, the Code makes frequent reference to shop stewards and other workplace representatives.[7] The Code restates the Act's requirements quoted earlier concerning union rules covering election, removal from office and the specification of powers and duties within the union. Following the lines of the CIR Report the Code distinguishes between a steward's trade-union functions (eg, recruitment, maintaining membership and collecting contributions) and his industrial relations functions such as negotiation, consultation and grievance handling. It stresses that the latter functions should be jointly agreed between the parties. Trade unions and management should seek agreement on the number of stewards, including senior stewards and deputies, needed in an establishment, and the work groups for which each steward is responsible. The issuing of joint credentials is recommended, as is the appointment of a senior steward to coordinate activities of stewards belonging to one union, and of a convenor to perform a similar role in multi-union situations. The case for joint agreements on shop stewards' facilities is similarly pressed, and the Code sets as a minimum 'time off from the job to the extent reasonably required for their industrial relations functions . . . and maintenance of earnings while carrying out these functions'. It is suggested that management should also make available other facilities appropriate to the circumstances, such as lists of new employees; accommodation for meetings with constituents, other stewards, and full-time officials; access to a telephone and the provision of notice boards; and the use of office facilities where this is justified by the volume of the steward's work. Joint reviews of appropriate training for shop stewards, jointly conducted courses, and agreed arrangements for leave to attend training courses, including compensation for loss of earnings, are recommended. Management should ensure that the stewards are adequately informed about its objectives and employment policies. Each union should ensure that its own stewards are adequately informed about its policies and organization and about agreements to which it is a party. A shop steward should observe all such agreements and should take all reasonable steps to ensure that those whom he represents also observe them.

The Code avoids any reference to meetings with constituents during working time, though it suggests that employee representatives should 'ensure that they have the means to communicate effectively with those whom they represent'. More broadly, the Code makes many recommendations covering topics such as written procedure agreements, employment policies, payment systems, communications, etc, which, if widely achieved, would do much to remove many of the factors which the Donovan Report diagnosed as being at the root of many workplace industrial-relations problems. Whilst the Code may be criticized from a number of angles, eg, the danger of imposing uniformity on widely diverse situations, of exaggerating the role of consultation as opposed to negotiation, and of setting relatively unambitious standards, it may prove a suitable vehicle for accelerating the spread of improved industrial relations policies and procedures more than is possible on a case-by-case basis. The provision for its periodic revision is important, and it may claim some credit for having encouraged the TUC to issue its own guidelines for the achievement of 'good' industrial relations, which we examine overleaf. Finally, the Act (Section 56) has imposed obligations on employers to disclose certain information for negotiating purposes to representatives of (registered) trade unions, and the Code will elaborate on the nature of such information when this section becomes operative. Although the non-registration of their unions will prevent most stewards from benefiting from this as a legal right, the principle is an important one and, in fact, many may benefit from the reference to this in the Code. In the longer term the increased flow of information about the undertaking should give stewards a deeper understanding of the context in which they operate. It will, however, also increase the need for training stewards to handle the often complicated data, and whilst potentially this may increase their ability to influence their members, it may also expose them to rank-and-file accusations of having been 'blinded by science' or, at worst, 'brain-washed' by management. Individual stewards will need to take care that what appears to be a major advance does not rebound against them.

(e) *The TUC*

The TUC gave a cautious welcome to the Donovan Report and quickly organized a series of conferences to examine bargaining arrangements in a number of sectors. The Report stimulated a number of policy statements of a reforming type, and the TUC and its affiliated unions began to develop close relationships and cooperation with the CIR. However, some of the policy measures proposed and/or introduced by governments since late 1968 have found the TUC in a position of deep opposition. Much of this opposition has been focused on the *substance* of the changes introduced, but it has also been underpinned by a deep-seated objection to the extensive departure from voluntarism in industrial relations. Just as the introduction of a statutory incomes policy stimulated the TUC to develop its own voluntary policy, so the Industrial Relations Act and the Code have brought a statement from the TUC on what it regards as good industrial relations and the essential conditions for achieving this objective. This guide[8], which has been widely circulated to shop stewards, contains standards and policies which the TUC has stressed in a number of publications in recent years. It is important not only as a statement of trade-union policy towards shop stewards and wide areas of the subject matter of industrial relations, but also because it reveals the direction and nature of reforms for which unions may be expected to press more firmly in future years.

The TUC guide has some similarities with the Code, and indeed both documents, for example, specifically suggest that no disciplinary action should be taken against shop stewards until managements have discussed the circumstances of the case with a full-time official of the trade union concerned. Not surprisingly, the TUC pitches its standards for shop-steward facilities somewhat higher than those suggested in the Code, and it does not distinguish between a steward's union duties and his 'industrial relations' duties as the Code does. Facilities to meet new employees, to collect contributions, and the use of a suitable room for consulting and reporting to members when necessary during working hours are examples. The TUC guide stresses the role of collective bargaining as the only satisfactory and effective method of conducting industrial relations, and supports the Donovan diagnosis that many current difficulties in industrial relations stem from the inadequacy of collective-bargaining arrangements, including the procedures for settling disputes, and from poorly designed or managed payment systems which are inappropriate or inequitable. The desirability of written disputes procedures is emphasized, as is the need for special written agreements on redundancy, discipline and other issues, and – where appropriate – comprehensive and authoritative collective-bargaining machinery at company or factory level. However the TUC guide is noticeably stronger on the need for 'adequate *status quo* provisions' than is the Code on consultation and agreement prior to changes in current practice. It also commends the resolution of disputes at the level at which they arise, or at least *within* the establishment, thus emphasizing the role of internal trade-union representatives.

The guide consolidates a number of earlier TUC recommendations concerning relations between stewards and their unions, and in doing so again has similarities with both the Donovan Report and with the Code. It suggests that unions should ensure that their rulebooks, or shop-steward handbooks or other appropriate publications, state clearly the method of election or appointment of shop stewards and the body within the trade union to whom the steward is responsible; they should also give clear guidance on duties and responsibilities and the action which a shop steward may take on his own authority, so long as he observes the policy of the union and obligations arising out of agreements to which the trade union is a party. Union documents should also recognize that workplace meetings of members are a useful and authorized method of consultation but that they are not entitled to make decisions or to instruct shop stewards to take actions at variance with union policy or the obligations of agreements. Recognition of joint shop-steward committees should also be included explicitly, and guidance given about the reporting of views expressed at all workplace meetings to the appropriate union body. The TUC report on shop-steward training issued in 1968 is examined in Appendix B.

The period since the publication of the Donovan Report has witnessed a welter of events on the industrial relations scene. The so-called industrial relations system has been subject to a wide variety of proposals and suggestions for structural reform by governments of different political complexions, and others. Government industrial relations policy, for so long dominated by a non-partisan role of conciliation and a philosophy of minimum intervention, has been drawn fully into the arena of party politics. Most of the post-1968 events have occurred at the national political level and press coverage has been huge, almost certainly exaggerating the practical importance of these central developments. Certainly most of these events have been remote from single establishments and ordinary shop stewards, and their effect on industrial relations at this level is far from clear and may not have been great, especially as a state of uncertainty about the future will remain until the next election and perhaps beyond it. The plethora of activity at the centre appears, as yet, to have had less impact on the shop floor and on the activities of stewards, than, for example, the ending of the incomes policy and the decline of productivity bargaining, the 'wage explosion' of 1969–71, and the increase in unemployment to post-war record levels with its associated increase in redundancies, closures and the emergence of new types of worker protest in the form of 'work-ins' and 'sit-ins'.

Despite the somewhat sceptical and cautious reaction of managements to many of the policy prescriptions, and the deep opposition of the unions to the 1971 legislation, the controversies of the 1968–71 period have perhaps clarified the issues and objectives of reform in industrial relations. Most prominent is the search for more orderly relationships at workplace level, and the advocacy of a higher degree of formal agreements covering topics regulated at this level. The political hiatus has diverted energies and attention from reform, and the new legislation may continue to increase union suspicion of the motives behind management initiatives to introduce procedural changes and new frameworks for the regulation of workplace relations. Although progress has been slow and piecemeal the importance of shop stewards within the system is now widely acknowledged, their continued presence is accepted, and both management and unions are belatedly coming to terms with this and attempting to utilize the positive opportunities which it presents. Consequently the steward seems likely to be drawn within the rules of a reformed and more orderly industrial relations system, enabling him to make a more constructive contribution to the settlement of the inevitable and continuing problems of industrial relations in a society in which expectations are constantly changing and in which the critical appraisal of the decisions of those in authority and the demand for participation in rule-making have increased most perceptibly.

References

1. See National Board for Prices and Incomes, Report No 123, *Productivity Agreements*, Cmnd 4136, HMSO, 1969, paras 90–93.
2. Report of the Royal Commission on Trade Unions and Employers' Associations, June 1968, Cmnd 3623, HMSO, para 171.
3. Commission on Industrial Relations, *Facilities afforded to Shop Stewards*, Report No 17, Cmnd 4668, HMSO, 1971.
4. See Heaton's Transport (St. Helens) Ltd *v* Transport and General Workers' Union, *The Times* Law Report, June 13th, 1972.
5. See *The Times* Law Report, July 28th, 1972.
6. See *The Times* Law Report, May 12th, 1972.
7. *Industrial Relations, Code of Practice*. HMSO, 1972. See especially paras 99–119.
8. Trades Union Congress, *Good Industrial Relations – A Guide for Negotiators*, TUC, November 1971.

Appendix A

Statistics on Stoppages of Work

The source of statistics concerning stoppages of work is the Department of Employment, and unless otherwise stated the figures given have been derived from this source. There are a number of facts which must be taken into account in assessing these figures. The Department's published figures do not distinguish between strikes and lockouts, or between official, unofficial, constitutional, and unconstitutional stoppages. Stoppages involving less than ten workers and those which lasted for less than one day are excluded, except where the aggregate number of working days lost exceeds 100. Moreover, it is widely acknowledged that by no means all stoppages are reported to the Department, and other forms of industrial action, eg, overtime bans, go-slows, etc, are not included. The classification of single or principal causes is necessarily arbitrary. Finally, the days-lost figures do not include time lost at establishments other than that at which the stoppage took place.

Table A.1

Stoppages of work beginning in each year 1914–71

Year	Stop-pages in year	Workers involved	Aggre-gate working days lost	Year	Stop-pages in year	Workers involved	Aggre-gate working days lost
	(thousands)				(thousands)		
1914	972	447	9,360	1943	1,785	557	1,830
1915	672	448	2,970	1944	2,194	821	3,700
1916	532	276	2,370	1945	2,293	531	2,850
1917	730	872	5,870	1946	2,205	526	2,180
1918	1,165	1,161	5,890	1947	1,721	620	1,400
1919	1,352	2,591	36,030	1948	1,759	424	1,940
1920	1,607	1,932	28,860	1949	1,426	433	1,820
1921	763	1,801	82,270	1950	1,339	302	1,380
1922	576	552	19,650	1951	1,719	379	1,710
1923	628	405	10,950	1952	1,714	415	1,800
1924	710	613	8,360	1953	1,746	1,370	2,170
1925	603	441	8,910	1954	1,989	448	2,480
1926	323	2,734	161,300	1955	2,419	659	3,790
1927	308	108	870	1956	2,648	507	2,050
1928	302	124	1,390	1957	2,859	1,356	8,400
1929	431	533	8,290	1958	2,629	523	3,470
1930	422	307	4,450	1959	2,093	645	5,280
1931	420	490	7,010	1960	2,832	814	3,050
1932	389	379	6,430	1961	2,686	771	3,040
1933	357	136	1,020	1962	2,449	4,420	5,780
1934	474	134	1,060	1963	2,068	590	2,000
1935	553	271	1,950	1964	2,524	873	2,030
1936	818	316	2,010	1965	2,354	868	2,932
1937	1,129	597	3,140	1966	1,937	530	2,395
1938	875	274	1,330	1967	2,116	732	2,783
1939	940	337	1,350	1968	2,378	2,256	4,672
1940	922	299	940	1969	3,116	1,656	6,789
1941	1,251	360	1,080	1970	3,906	1,793	10,854
1942	1,303	456	1,530	1971	2,228	1,171	13,589

Table A.2

Strikes in the coal industry, and elsewhere
(Stoppages beginning in each year)

Year	Number	Total %	Days lost %	Number of strikes outside the coal industry
1945	1,306	57	23	987
1946	1,329	60	20	876
1947	1,053	61	37	668
1948	1,116	63	24	643
1949	874	61	39	552
1950	860	64	31	479
1951	1,058	61	20	661
1952	1,221	71	38	493
1953	1,307	75	18	439
1954	1,464	74	19	525
1955	1,783	74	29	636
1956	2,076	78	24	572
1957	2,224	78	6	635
1958	1,963	77	13	666
1959	1,307	62	7	786
1960	1,666	59	16	1,166
1961	1,458	54	24	1,228
1962	1,205	49	27	1,244
1963	987	48	16	1,081
1964	1,058	42	13	1,466
1965	740	31	14	1,614
1966	553	29	5	1,384
1967	339	14	14	1,717
1968	225	10	1	2,125
1969	186	5	17	2,930
1970	160	4	10	3,746
1971	138	6	0·5	2,090

Table A.3

Number of stoppages of work outside the coal industry by cause 1960–70 (Stoppages beginning in each year)

Causes	1960 No.	%	1962 No.	%	1964 No.	%	1966 No.	%	1968 No.	%	1970 No.	%
(a) Claims for increases	420	36	343	28	531	36	429	31	921	43	2,154	58
(b) Other wage disputes	172	15	175	14	159	11	224	16	225	10	255	7
All wage disputes	592	51	518	42	690	47	653	47	1,146	53	2,409	65
(c) Hours of labour	37	3	8	1	23	2	26	2	28	1	27	1
(d) Demarcation disputes	48	4	58	5	58	4	55	4	83	4	69	2
(e) Disputes concerning the employment or discharge of workers (including redundancy questions)	186	16	276	22	249	17	275	20	319	15	425	11
(f) Other disputes mainly concerning personnel questions	51	4	102	8	47	3	44	3	63	3	49	1
(g) Other working arrangements, rules, and discipline	161	14	164	13	279	19	255	19	374	17	506	13
(h) Trade-union status	63	5	100	8	97	7	59	4	109	5	180	5
(i) Sympathetic action	25	2	24	2	16	1	14	1	29	1	76	2
All causes	1,163	100	1,242	100	1,461	100	1,381	100	2,151	100	3,741	100

Table A.4

Days lost due to industrial disputes per thousand persons employed in mining, manufacturing, construction and transport in various countries, 1960–69

Country	Average for 5 years	Average for 5 years	Average for 10 years
	1960–64	1965–9	1960–69
Switzerland	10	—	1
Sweden	6	28	17
West Germany	34	10	22
Netherlands	62	12	37
Norway	212	4	108
Belgium	164	156	160
New Zealand	154	242	198
Japan	302	198	250
United Kingdom	242	294	268
Finland	340	206	273
France	352	243	303
Australia	350	456	403
Denmark	708	110	409
India	498	976	737
USA	722	1,232	977
Canada	460	1,556	1,008
Ireland	686	1,350	1,018
Italy	1,220	1,574	1,397

(Source: International Labour Office, as published in the Department of Employment *Gazette*, February 1971. This should be seen for statistical notes.)

Table A.5

Number of stoppages per million employees in various countries

Country	Yearly average over 5 years 1959–63
1. Switzerland	0·14
2. Sweden	0·58
3. India	0·78
4. Norway	0·89
5. South Africa	0·98
6. Belgium	1·4
7. Netherlands	1·8
8. Denmark	1·8
9. Finland	2·4
10. Japan	2·5
11. Canada	4·7
12. United States	5·2
13. Ireland	6·4
14. New Zealand	8·1
15. United Kingdom	10·2
16. Italy	15·7
17. France	19·1
18. Australia	33·2

West Germany's figures not available. (Source: International Labour Office.)

The Education and Training of Shop Stewards

The attention given to this subject in recent years is a measure of the realization, by all parties in the industrial relations system, of its increasing significance. Perhaps the culminating part of this process has been the commissioning of a CIR Report on Industrial Relations Training[1], which, no doubt, will include detailed and influential suggestions on shop-steward training.

First, it is pertinent to ask why shop stewards are trained and we begin with an analysis of the reasons why various institutions are in this field.

Reasons for training shop stewards

(1) *Trade unions*

Developments since the Second World War have made stewards a powerful force in many unions. Consequently, the unions have a *prima facie* interest in developing not only the level of stewards' skills and information, but also their loyalty to the union and its policies. This reason seems to account for much of the subject matter of many courses given by the unions. They normally deal with the union's history, structure, and policies, the role of the steward and the contents of agreements. Most union-run courses emphasize the traditions and unity of the union, and the interdependence of its officers, attempting to win the allegiance of those attending. The enhanced importance of stewards as bargainers and the often wide gap between their education and that of managers puts them at a disadvantage unless they are natural bargainers. Thus, the unions have an obvious reason for ensuring that their representatives and members do not suffer as a result, and the courses often include bargaining exercises as well as outlines of the principles of negotiating.

Naturally unions, within the limits of scarce resources, want to train *all* their officers to improve their performance and effectiveness. Consequently, most do not regard the steward as a distinctive entity, but rather as a voluntary officer who may rise to such higher union office as branch secretary, chairman, or full-time official. Thus, his education and training are part of an overall scheme within the union, rather than specifically equipping him for his present role. The unions are often suspicious of external courses which may stress the steward's distinctive role rather than seeing it as part of the union machine. This point was emphasized in conversation with TUC officials. Organizers of such courses may include subject matter within the responsibilities and duties of a steward ranging wider than a union wishes. Unions want to train stewards, but not to stimulate a widening of their powers and responsibilities. However, not all unions train their stewards – to our knowledge about sixteen do so.[2]

(2) *Management*

The reasons why many managements prefer to deal with stewards have been given in the text. Undoubtedly, many feel more confident when dealing with representatives they employ than with a union official. In-company steward training may foster this situation, for information given to stewards about company piece rates, bonus schemes, work-study practices, and other issues peculiar to the company makes stewards better placed as bargainers and improves their position as against officials unlikely to be briefed in such detail. Managements often find themselves dealing with stewards whether they positively sought it or not, because of frequent non-availability among full-time officials at short notice. Given that managements do negotiate with stewards, they obviously prefer representatives who understand their language and who can be moved by facts. Education in the background to management policies and the techniques they employ is one way of achieving this, in removing resistance arising from ignorance rather than from fact. This is probably the main reason for managements providing training courses for stewards. Managements may also hope that they will create a rapport between stewards and management, and a wider knowledge, showing itself in an enhanced respect for constitutional methods.

(3) *Academic bodies*

Many bodies have become involved in steward education and training through their more general activities in adult education. Partly through cooperation with the WEA, university extra-mural departments have expanded considerably since 1945, and many are active in union education. Some, such as London and Nottingham, devote themselves mostly to broader educational work, while others such as Oxford run training courses in topics specific to stewards' vocational needs.

Many technical colleges and colleges of further education are also engaged in this work. Contacts with local industry have led through management courses to an interest in union education, and naturally to those most likely to benefit from further education, the shop stewards.

One major problem for academic bodies is lack of sufficient staff with knowledgeable experience to teach the subjects. This is an obstacle to rapid expansion.

Present coverage and an evaluation of training

Certainly stewards can benefit from education and training – especially given the complex nature of their roles. Recent research into this area has shown that a small number of stewards (29) on two courses were satisfied that their objectives for attending the courses were being met.[3] The same research findings reported that managers (who sent stewards on courses) 'were confident that stewards were obtaining a greater understanding of management prob lems'.[4] Similarly, course tutors 'felt that a well-designed course can go some way towards harnessing conflicting objectives.'[5] In spite of this agreement, however, the objectives of the various parties involved in training shop stewards may be different. Certainly, the research found different objectives in sending stewards on courses. 'The managers in the case study hope that an educational process will have the effect of broadening the stewards' understanding of management's position in order that they will be more "rational" in their demands; the TUC view is that educational courses will assist stewards to carry out their tasks as union representatives efficiently. The stewards stated they were seeking background information into their roles and responsibilities, the more experienced groups especially into the implications of their role within the trade-union movement; but stewards additionally see their responsibilities as extending to their members' immediate needs – judging by the range of duties which they considered important and the topics which they felt were of particular value.'[6] As the researcher points out, 'These findings seem to substantiate the idea that each member of the steward's role set will have a different notion of the steward's role and responsibilities and the steward himself looks to the expectations of his members and his union to interpret his position.'[7] Given these different objectives, there will often be conflicts over the expected outcome of courses and this situation will affect the various views of the parties as to syllabus, staffing, and venue. Thus, the TUC has strictly defined views on the subject, for it states 'The selection or endorsement of students will automatically involve unions in judging the suitability of courses. It is still worth stating separately, however, that all courses of training for union workplace representatives ought to be considered by the union, the TUC Regional Advisory Committee and the TUC itself in order to get the endorsement of the movement of which workplace representatives are a part. Unless courses are endorsed in this manner, unions should not provide students for them.'[8] Yet the TUC and some trade unions are not the only institutions involved in this area – there are others such as university extra-mural departments, polytechnics, the WEA, etc. All have interests and experience in this field. Since such factors as syllabus determination and the selection of students are just as significant to lecturers as to students and since such lecturers might be better equipped to assess the needs of potential students, it may be that, in practice, the statement of the TUC cannot be translated into reality. Indeed, in many cases shop stewards and managers may wish to attend joint courses – as may shop stewards and full-time officials – or, indeed, all of the actors involved in the industrial relations system of a particular organization. In such situations, as in others, the students may demand to be the arbiters of courses. What appears to be needed is a more rationalized approach in this field with cooperation between the various institutions involved and a division of labour, with each institution offering those courses which it is best suited to provide.

Whichever institutions provide courses in this field, however, there is plenty of scope for expansion and the question of financial resources is obviously a key one. The TUC General Council has already suggested to the Russell Committee of Inquiry into Adult Education that trade-union education must be officially recognized and receive increased public funds which could then be used to improve teaching resources and the general facilities of educational bodies identified by the trade-union movement as appropriate to assist in providing courses for trade unionists.[9] The Donovan Report had earlier commented in this vein also when discussing the training of shop stewards, although warning against indiscriminate expansion. The Commission noted that 'additional resources are undoubtedly required.

They should be used to develop competent teachers and adequate syllabuses with a view to using training of stewards as part of a planned move to more orderly industrial relations based on comprehensive and formal factory or company agreements. This is where shop steward training will be able to make its biggest contribution.'[10]

If it is accepted that more funds are needed, then the Government might now be seen as the most likely source of finance. Many of the industrial training boards are cutting back on the levy-and-grant system and adopting more of an advisory role and, for some firms, an important source of finance is being cut off. This may well act as a disincentive to some managements to engage in shop steward training or to help to finance courses put on by outside bodies (by, for example, paying course fees or students' wages whilst they are away from their jobs). Some courses would, therefore, have to be terminated.

Whatever happens in the future, however, we are dealing with a complex area about which not a great deal is known. For example, we know little about the educational and training requirements of stewards themselves. Which problems cause them the most trouble? What kind of balance would they like between specific training and broader education? More research and analysis is needed to balance whatever expansion takes place in this field – that is, if the work is to be effective.

Of course, there are uncertainties about the results of training of any kind. But it is surely unrealistic to suggest that it has no beneficial effects on relationships in the workplace.

References

1. This Report was not yet available at the time of going to press.
2. These include the three largest unions: the NUGMW, the T&GWU, and the AUEW. Altogether the sixteen unions

account for approximately 6,800,000 trade unionists. The quality of the training provided for shop stewards varies greatly from union to union and sometimes, within a union, from district to district. The calculations are based on 'Study on Unions and Productivity Bargaining', *Incomes Data*, Incomes Data Services Ltd, London, January 1970.

3. See Alexandra Warren, 'The Aims and Methods of the Education and Training of Shop Stewards', *Industrial Relations Journal*, Vol 2, No 1, Spring 1971, pp 48–9.

4. *Ibid*, p 49.

5. *Ibid*.

6. *Ibid*, pp 48–9.

7. *Ibid*.

8. *Training Shop Stewards*, TUC, 1968, p 13.

9. See *The Technical Journal*, July 1970, p 24.

10. Report of the Royal Commission on Trade Unions and Employers' Associations, *op cit*, p 191, para 712.

Index

Rosemary Stewart

HOW COMPUTERS AFFECT
MANAGEMENT   75p

Through a series of case studies Rosemary
Stewart traces the development and implementation of three groups of computer
application – clerical procedures, production
control, and long-term planning – and examines
their effect upon management policy and
understanding.

'As with all her books, she has produced a
concise, lucid and highly readable book on
a difficult subject' – FINANCIAL TIMES

Avison Wormald

INTERNATIONAL BUSINESS   75p

Avison Wormald brings the distillation of twenty-five years experience to this wide-ranging analysis of the factors involved in the decision-making process of international management.

A book which will help every manager meet the challenge of 'an exceptionally exciting and increasing activity' . . .